ETRUSCAN TREASURES FROM THE CINI-ALLIATA COLLECTION

Francesco Buranelli - Maurizio Sannibale
Editors

Etruscan Treasures from the Cini-Alliata Collection
Published in conjunction with the exhibition held at the Mabee-Gerrer Museum of Art, Shawnee, Oklahoma,
June 1 – October 31, 2004

EXHIBIT

Curators
Francesco Buranelli
Maurizio Sannibale
Debby Williams

Mabee-Gerrer Museum of Art
Staff
Debby Williams, Director and Chief Curator
Sharla Hall, Director of Development
Jamee Telford, Curator of Education, Volunteer Coordinator
Delaynna Trim, Registrar
Chris Owens, Collections Manager, Preparator
Kathy McMillan, Director of Guest Services
Anne Barajas Harp, Director of Public Relations
Jennifer Eve, Marketing Director
Hank Land, Director of Security
Aaron Jones, Education Consultant
Sha Buchanan, Gift Shop Assistant

National Exhibits Foundation
Father Malcolm Neyland, M.C.L., J.C.L.
Executive Director

Italian Organization
Crisalide s.r.l.

Restoration & handling
Fabiana Francescangeli
Luciano Ermo
Angelica Mazzucato

Transportation
Montenovi s.r.l.

Insurance
INA Assitalia

Development and Special Events Committee
Megan Clement
Linda Peterson
Nancy Powell
Kathy Rick

Associate Volunteer Coordinators
Mary Atwood
Megan Clement
Ann Jones
Linda Peterson
Nancy Powell
Kathy Rick

Mabee-Gerrer Museum of Art
Volunteer Society
Gloria Vandaveer, President

St. Gregory's Abbey
Abbot Martin Lugo, O.S.B.
Fr. Nicholas Ast, O.S.B.
Fr. Philip Berning, O.S.B.
Fr. Matthew Brown, O.S.B.
Fr. Charles Buckley, O.S.B.
Br. Benet Exton, O.S.B.
Br. Boniface Copelin, O.S.B.
Br. Isidore Harden, O.S.B.
Fr. Brendan Helbing, O.S.B.
Br. George Hubl, O.S.B.
Fr. Maurus Jaeb, O.S.B.
Br. Basil Keenan, O.S.B.
Fr. Manuel Magallanes, O.S.B.

Fr. Timothy Maloney, O.S.B.
Fr. Eugene Marshall, O.S.B.
Fr. Charles Massoth, O.S.B.
Fr. Patrick McCool, O.S.B.
Br. Kevin McGuire, O.S.B.
Br. Joseph Niichel, O.S.B.
Br. Dominic Ramirez, O.S.B.
Br. Andrew Raple, O.S.B.
Fr. Theodore Seneschal, O.S.B.
Br. Ambrose Sontag, O.S.B.
Fr. Joachim Spexarth, O.S.B.
Fr. Lawrence Stasyszen, O.S.B.
Fr. Daniel Suellentrop, O.S.B.
Fr. Louis VanderLey, O.S.B.
Fr. Adrian Vonderlandwehr, O.S.B.
Br. Damian Whalen, O.S.B.
Fr. Paul Zahler, O.S.B.

CATALOGUE

Editors
Francesco Buranelli
Maurizio Sannibale

Entries and Essays
Maurizio Sannibale

Contributors
Francesco Buranelli
Mario Cappozzo
Fabiana Francescangeli

Translations
Sara Levi

Photo Credits
Biblioteca Apostolica Vaticana, Città del Vaticano
Kunsthistorisches Museum, Wien
Metropolitan Museum of Art, New York
Musei Vaticani, Città del Vaticano
Soprintendenza per i Beni Archeologici dell' Etruria Meridionale, Roma
Soprintendenza per i Beni Archeologici del Lazio, Roma
Soprintendenza per i Beni Archeologici della Toscana, Firenze
Soprintendenza per i Beni Archeologici dell'Umbria, Perugia

Photographers
Alberto Bertini
Alessandro Bracchetti

Layout & graphics
Plan Out s.r.l. Roma

Designer
Leonardo Di Blasi (maps)

LOANING INSTITUTIONS AND PRIVATE COLLECTIONS

Fabrizio Alliata di Montereale, Roma; Musei Vaticani, Città del Vaticano; Soprintendenza per i Beni Archeologici del Lazio, Roma; Soprintendenza per i Beni Archeologici della Toscana, Firenze; Soprintendenza per i Beni Archeologici dell'Umbria, Perugia; Soprintendenza per i Beni Archeologici dell'Etruria Meridionale, Roma; Alessandro Cinelli, Chianciano Terme.

SPECIAL THANKS

Fabrizio Alliata di Montereale
Patrizia Aureli
Francesca Boitani
Angelo Bottini
Paolo Bruschetti
Daniela Candilio
Andrea Carignani
Alessandro Cinelli
Francesca Festa
Mario Iozzo
Adriano La Regina
Paolo Liverani
Anna Maria Moretti Sgubini
Franca Motta
Giulio Paolucci
Antonia Pasqua Recchia
Anna Reggiani
Mariarosaria Salvatore
Giandomenico Spinola
Fabiana Vinella

CATALOGUE

Crisalide s.r.l.

Editorial coordination
Andrea Fontecedro
Sara Levi

Via di Ripetta, 70
00186 Roma

printed and bound in Italy
ISBN: 88-88540-01-6

CONTENTS

MESSAGE OF APPRECIATION

It is a special honor for Shawnee's Mabee-Gerrer Museum of Art to be the only venue for Etruscan Treasures. *We are grateful for this once-in-a-lifetime opportunity to explore the fascinating Etruscan world that thrived so long ago and contributed much to our modern society.*

Seeing Etruscan Treasures from the Cini-Alliata Collection is also an excellent occasion for those who are not familiar with our own treasure, the Mabee-Gerrer Museum of Art.

This museum is one of the many outstanding cultural centers in Oklahoma that enhances our quality of life and expands educational opportunities for all of our citizens. There is so much to discover in this remarkable facility. Art transcends the barriers of language or geographical borders. Art can unite, further understanding, promote meaningful partnerships and create long-lasting friendships.

This is an exciting opportunity for Oklahoma and we are proud to host this unique collection of ancient Etruscan and Roman jewelry and artifacts, none of which have ever been seen by the public until today. We extend our appreciation to everyone who made this exhibition possible.

The Honorable Brad Henry
Governor of the State of Oklahoma

Since 1915, the collections of the Mabee-Gerrer Museum of Art have served to celebrate the innate creativity of humankind regardless of time or geography. So we are particularly delighted to be the only venue for the Etruscan Treasures *exhibit. This extraordinary collection of 225 pieces of goldwork, mainly Etruscan and Roman, marvellously illustrates the level of artistic skill of the Etruscans and other peoples of ancient Italy. This exhibit includes not only jewels, which are the main focus, but also marble sculptures, terracotta statues and various objects that allow us to better understand how these jewels were really used in the Etruscan and Roman tradition. This significant selection of artifacts helps us to appreciate this fascinating culture from north-central Italy, known as Etruria in ancient times. These rare, beautiful pieces emphatically reaffirm our founder Fr. Gregory Gerrer's vision, the mission of the museum, and the celebration of spirit and art.*

We hope that visitors to this exhibition will not only enjoy and learn from their "Etruscan experience" but will also notice that, despite the thousands of years that have passed, we still benefit from many of the Etruscans' significant contributions. Fortunately, thanks to the dedication of countless scholars and archaeologists who have solved some of the Etruscan "mysteries," we better understand how the Etruscan culture has had an impact on our lives.

It is an honor to host Etruscan Treasures *and participate in promoting the increasing knowledge about these fascinating people. There are many people who have made this exhibition possible, all of whom we thank. We wish to thank Fr. Malcolm Neyland and the staff of the National Exhibits Foundation for their assistance in bringing this exhibition to the Mabee-Gerrer Museum of Art. We offer a very special thank you to Prince Fabrizio Alliata for loaning his remarkable collection of Etruscan jewelry, and the Director of the Vatican Museums, Dr. Francesco Buranelli, for the loan of artifacts from the Etrusco-Italic and Classical Antiquities Departments. We wish also to thank the Lazio Archaeological office, the Tuscany Archaeological Monuments office, the Umbria Achaeological Monuments office, the Southern Etruria Archaeological Monuments office and Alessandro Cinelli for the loan of their artifacts. Thank you also to Ellen Censky, Director, and Jason Baird Jackson, Assistant Curator of Ethnology, Sam Noble Oklahoma Museum of Natural History, Norman, Oklahoma for the loan of exquisite Etruscan bucchero ware and pottery and for his cooperation and assistance.*

The Mabee-Gerrer Museum of Art was able to host the exhibition because of the generosity of many supporters who we thank for believing in the museum and this project. Thank you to Cox Communications, Lamar Outdoor Production, Dorie Barrett, and Oklahoma Arts Council for being our partners in this exhibition.

There have been many other people and organizations that have assisted in various ways to make this exhibition possible; the Archdiocese of Oklahoma City, Oklahoma

Centennial Commission, Oklahoma Tourism and Recreation Department, Oklahoma Department of Transportation and the City of Shawnee.

We want to thank our honorary co-chairmen for their help and support; The Honorable Governor Brad Henry, Archbishop Eusebius J. Beltran, D.D., former Governor George Nigh, and former Governor Frank Keating. In addition, a special thanks to the Board of Trustees of the Mabee-Gerrer Museum of Art, the members of St. Gregory's Abbey and our dedicated volunteers.

Debby Williams
Director and Chief Curator
Mabee-Gerrer Museum of Art

The National Exhibits Foundation is proud to have assisted in bringing this exhibit to the Mabee-Gerrer Museum of Art, Shawnee and the state of Oklahoma. The Foundation's mission is to bring about an appreciation and educational awareness of historical art and artifacts to the people of the United States, especially to those who might not otherwise have an opportunity to view such magnificent art and artifacts. It has been our privilege to work with Debby Williams, Director of the Museum, her staff and volunteers in presenting this exhibit.

The National Exhibits Foundation thanks Prince Fabrizio Alliata for the loan of his Etruscan Gold jewelry collection as well as the Director of the Vatican Museums, Dr. Francesco Buranelli, for his contribution of the pieces from the Etrusco-Italic and Classical Antiquities Departments, and Edmund Casimir Cardinal Szoka, President of the Governatorato, Vatican City, who helped make this exhibition possible, as well as Dr. Maurizio Sannibale, author of the catalogue. We also wish to extend our thanks to the Lazio Archaeological office, the Tuscany Archaeological Monuments office, the Umbria Archaeological Monuments office, the Southern Etruria Archaeological Monuments office and Alessandro Cinelli for loaning their artifacts. We thank Archbishop Eusebius J. Beltran, D.D., Oklahoma City, and Bishop Edward J. Slattery, Tulsa, for their support.

We thank Sara Levi, Art Director, Crisalide Srl, and Montenovi Srl, for their efforts in coordinating this exhibit in Rome on our behalf. We recognize and thank Fabiana Francescangeli for the restoration of the jewelry collection.

On behalf of the Foundation's Board of Directors (The Honorable Giles McCrary, Dr. David Hentges, and Dr. Lou Diekemper) and our Advisor Board (Patty D'Alise, Marjorie Kastman, John Malouf, Kay Sanford, Debbie Scioli, David Seim, Gwen Stafford and Idris Traylor), we wish to say we are all proud to be a part of this exhibit.

Sincerely in His Service,
Rev. Malcolm Neyland, M.C.L., J.C.L.
President and Executive Director, National Exhibits Foundation

In the spring of 2002 I was so pleased to bring Father Richard Bourgeois, O.S.B., to Shawnee to visit the Mabee-Gerrer Museum of Art. Father Richard lived in Dallas and was the director of the North American Patrons for the Arts in the Vatican Museums. Mabee-Gerrer Museum Director/Curator Debby Williams and members of the Board of Directors told Father Richard about the plans for renovating and expanding the museum and showed him the museum's collection. Father Richard said that the museum would be a wonderful place to showcase some pieces from the Vatican Museums. This was the beginning of a dream for all of us.

Unfortunately, Father Richard suffered an untimely death and is not able to see what he helped start. Following Father Richard's death we began to work with John Grimes, Chairman of the Executive Committee of the North American Patrons of the Arts. Mr. Grimes told us about a Vatican Museums exhibition that would be in Houston and suggested that it might be a good opportunity to meet with representatives from the museums.

We then wrote a letter to Dr. Francesco Buranelli, Director of the Vatican Museums, about the Mabee-Gerrer Museum of Art and Father Richard's visit. In March of 2003 we received a gracious letter from Dr. Buranelli expressing his interest in the museum and in discussing a project that could also involve the Vatican Museums.

We had also been working on contacting Father Malcolm Neyland in Lubbock, Texas, since he was instrumental in bringing an exhibit of Italian frescoes to Lubbock. In the meantime, Father Malcolm's mother told him about the museum after she read about it in an article in Southern Living. When Father Malcolm saw the article he knew that the museum could be his answer for finding the perfect place in the United States for an exhibition of Etruscan artifacts. We're so glad that Father Malcolm picked up the ball where Father Richard left off.

Clearly, this dream was meant to come true. Hosting Etruscan Treasures *is a once-in-a-lifetime opportunity and a wonderful way to celebrate Oklahoma's Centennial. We are pleased to be able to serve as a sponsor for the exhibition. We know that Oklahomans and visitors to our state will delight in learning about this ancient civilization.*

J. Blake Wade
Executive Director
Oklahoma Centennial Commission

Welcome, Visitors to the wonderful exhibit of Etruscan Treasures here at the Mabee-Gerrer Museum of Art, Shawnee, Oklahoma. This exhibit was possible thanks to the collaboration and assistance of Prince Fabrizio Alliata, who agreed to present his precious collection for the first time, as well as the Vatican Museums and other prestigious National Institutions of Italy that loaned several of their important artifacts. We are appreciative also for the time and effort in the preparation for this fine exhibit by Debby Williams, the Mabee-Gerrer Museum Director, the staff, Board members and the many volunteers. We are all happy to have you on our beautiful campus which is the site of the Benedictine Abbey of St. Gregory's, the University and the Museum itself.

Fr. Gregory Gerrer, O.S.B., a member of St. Gregory's Abbey, was the monk founder of the museum. It was primarily through his artistic endeavors that it was possible to realize the Museum's most valuable collection of art and artifacts; however, because of the size of the present Etruscan exhibit, you will only see a fraction of the permanent collection. We hope that you will return again in order to enjoy the extensive exhibition of our permanent collection. The Mabee-Gerrer Museum is indeed, as someone described it, a "hidden jewel" of Oklahoma. We invite you to come again.

Abbot Martin Lugo, O.S.B.
Saint Gregory's Abbey
Shawnee, Oklahoma

INTRODUCTION

I met Prince Fabrizio Alliata di Montereale about ten years ago, in his magnificent home in the countryside surrounded by the Roman ruins that line the Via Appia Antica in Rome. In the house, famous paintings and antique family furnishings mingled effortlessly with ultra-modern technology, reflecting the multifaceted personality of don Fabrizio, a man of our time with deep, ancient roots.

Our meeting was a result of Prince Alliata's wish for this unique and outstanding collection, inherited from his father-in-law, Count Vittorio Cini, to be properly promoted and studied.

I realized immediately that this was a very rich collection indeed, worthy – both in terms of the number of objects and their quality – of the most famous collections of ancient jewelry exhibited in the most prestigious museums in the world. The two hundred and twenty-five artifacts of various typologies and various provenances document from the eighth century BC to late-Empire examples (third-fourth centuries AD), showing a history of the taste and techniques of the ancient Etruscan and Roman goldsmiths. With the collaboration of Rome's Superintendent of Archaeological Monuments, Professor Adriano La Regina, and Dr. Daniela Candilio we instrumented the certification that recognized this collection as a "monument of national interest" in order to better protect its integrity and to avoid its possible dispersion in the future.

The collection – compiled in the turbulent period between the two World Wars and during the second post-war reconstruction – was put together by one of the major protagonists of Italy's industrial and cultural world in that period, Count Vittorio Cini, whose adventurous life and audacious entrepreneurial activities spanned the entire twentieth century.

Vittorio Cini, the great entrepreneur and collector, with his daughter, Yana Alliata di Montereale, in his Venetian home in San Vio that displayed many important artworks. Some were donated by Yana, along with the portion of the building that house them, to the Giorgio Cini Foundation.

Cini was born in Ferrara on February 20, 1885, to Giorgio and Eugenia Berti. After having brilliantly completed his studies in Italy and abroad, he immediately set off for the world of Italian industry, proving himself with ability and intelligence in the field of large-scale infrastructure construction (roads, railroads, sea and river port facilities) and becoming one of Europe's most important ship owner, rapidly acquiring fame and economic wealth. After World War I, in which he voluntarily enrolled as a cavalry officer, he married the young but already well-known theatre and cinema actress, Lyda Borelli, who bore him four children: Giorgio, born in 1918, Mynna, in 1920, and the twins Yana and Ylda, in 1924.

The World War II years was for Vittorio Cini a period of contradictions and decisive turnarounds. After being awarded, in 1940, the title of Count of Monselice he accepted a nomination to the Ministry of Communication in 1943, although he was already developing a growing detachment from the fascist regime. He soon convinced himself of the need to take his distance from Nazi Germany and to draw closer to the democracies of the United States and England. He made a public statement of his beliefs and subsequently resigned from the Government one month before the *Gran Consiglio* of July 1943. Deemed a traitor of the regime, he was sentenced to the Dachau concentration camp, from which he escaped only thanks to an airplane rescue organized by his son, Giorgio.

In August 1949, an airplane accident killed Giorgio, Vittorio Cini's firstborn son and only male heir, to whom Cini dedicated in April 1951 a cultural Foundation based in the ancient Benedictine convent on the island of San Giorgio Maggiore in Venice. He generously dedicated the remaining years of his long life to this Foundation; with his typical spirit and energy he was able to transform the painful loss of his son into an enterprise that left its mark on Italy's cultural history.

Vittorio Cini dedicated a large part of his estate to this cultural institution and donated the greatest masterpieces from the splendid collection that he had passionately gathered in the course of his life to the Foundation. The most important group is composed of a hundred or so paintings, mostly housed at the San Vio home, bequeathed to the Foundation by Yana in 1984, that range from Medieval pieces to Contemporary art. Of equal interest is the fascinating collection of Renaissance majolica ceramics that once belonged to the Castello di Moselice, as well as the three hundred-plus illuminated pages from ancient manuscripts, the two thousand incunabulae and illustrated books from the fifteenth century, along with the tapestries, furniture, sculptures, drawings and prints.

Following his death on September 18, 1977, part of Vittorio's substantial estate was also divided among his three daughters, and the collection of ancient jewels in particular was given to Yana, who wed Prince Fabrizio Alliata.

Although not all the details are known regarding the provenance of every item in this collection, the main nucleus, composed of Etruscan and Roman specimens, appears to derive from the Tuscan family Contini Bonacossi purchase, while for the Magno-Graecian part there exist no certain documents.

That meeting ten years ago and Prince Alliata's desire to continue in the optimization process of the Cini collection resulted in this event, which has now given us the possibility to publish the complete catalogue of the jewelry collection, thanks to our publisher, Andrea Fontecedro, and to the accurate and brilliant work of my colleague and friend, Maurizio Sannibale.

This extraordinary material will be exhibited for the first time to the public in the rooms of the Mabee-Gerrer Museum of Art in Shawnee, Oklahoma, directed with skill and dedication by Debby Williams; the event was organized and promoted in close collaboration with the National Exhibits Foundation, thanks to the professional and friendly support of Father Malcolm Neyland.

Francesco Buranelli

THE CINI - ALLIATA COLLECTION

This catalogue illustrates a notable collection of jewels of various typologies, relating to different historical and cultural settings, but all of which are traceable to the realm of Classical civilization: Greece, Etruria, and Rome. The considerable analogies between this collection and similar ones found in museums in Europe and North America, with regards to style and materials, may be noted at a glance.

When dealing with objects that circulated widely throughout antiquity, there is often a lack of information as to the context in which these pieces were found (a particularly common characteristic among items that come from the antique market). This has made it impossible to rigorously define the catalogue by cultural area. It was therefore decided to follow the only practical method, namely that of ordering by typology and chronology.

The jewelry presented here begins with head ornaments and proceeds downward through the various parts of an imaginary human body that, anachronistically, wears objects that span at least twelve centuries.

Among the most ancient pieces in the collection are the distinctive disc pendants, which date back to the second half of the eighth century BC, in the Iron Age, and are peculiar not only to Etruria but also to ancient Latium and Campania (**78-82**). Etruria's Orientalizing period produced the necklace with anchor-shaped pendants and the bead decorated with granulation (**68-69**), as well as the scarab pendants of Near-Eastern origin (**83-88**) and the spiral hair decorations (**2-4**), which may comprehensively be placed around the seventh - first half of the sixth century BC. Some types of fibulae are dated between the end of the eighth century and the beginning of the seventh century BC. Aside from Etruria (**125-126**), these fibulae were also known in Latium (**124**) and Campania (**121-123**). One of the most remarkable pieces in this collection, and a characteristic product of Etruria's Orientalizing period, is the silver openwork bracelet (**130**). Its style was popular in Vetulonia and other maritime areas of Etruria, but was equally documented in southern Etruria. Meanwhile, a number of necklaces reassembled from various elements, on the whole dating between the second half of the seventh and the fifth centuries BC (**70-71**), were found both in Etruria and in southern Italy.

Representative of Archaic jewelry are the pervasive *bauletto* or rounded trunk-shaped earrings (**8-9**). The second half of the sixth through at least all of the fifth century BC is the period to which are attributed the finger rings with engraved oval bezels (**135-136**). Originally Greek designs but typical to Etruria, these finger rings were also widespread throughout southern Italy. Rings with smooth oval bezels (**137-138**) were common in Etruria, Spina and southern Italy in the fifth-fourth centuries BC.

The same may be said for the plain smooth bands, in both gold and silver (**131-132**); this type endured considerably. Probably originating between the late Archaic and the Classical periods is an embossed plaque (**189**).

Another type that became popular in the second half of the sixth century BC was the ring with a revolving scarab on a swivel bezel (**134**). Other examples of this kind are known from later in the fourth century BC (**141**), also documented in southern Italy during the same period. Probably dated to the late sixth century BC is an element from a diadem that appears to be closely related to, or perhaps belonging to the only known comparable piece, housed in New York's Metropolitan Museum of Art (**6**).

Jewelry that was characteristic of Etruria, and particularly of Vulci, throughout the fourth century BC, is well-represented in this collection by two magnificent examples of illustrated *bullae* or circular pendants (**74, 96**). Related to these pieces are other types of Etruscan jewelry, such as the *a grappolo* or cluster earrings, documented here with various examples of uncertain authenticity (given that they are comparable only to collection material) (**12**), of difficult classification (**11, 15-16**), or that are manifestly false (**13-14**). The Fortnum Group is a distinctive production of Etruscan rings with die-formed bezels that originate between the second half of the fifth century and the first half of the fourth century BC (**139**).

Generally dated between the Classical and early Hellenistic periods (fourth-third centuries BC) are certain *olla-* and pomegranate-shaped pendants (**104-106**). Another piece attributed to this period is a wreath which is typologically akin to Etruscan examples (**5**).

Relating to Magna Graecia is an enigmatic ensemble of embossed and cut-out decorative plaques (**190-196**) whose stylistic elements are Archaic in taste; a probable date for these, supported by other findings, is between the fifth and the fourth centuries BC. Dating between the fourth and third centuries BC are several earrings, which, upon comparison, are clearly related to the Tarantine gold works (**18, 20, 22**). Another earring type, with an inverted pyramid pendant, was documented in southern Italy starting from the second half of the fourth century BC but enjoyed a lasting popularity in Etruria throughout the second century BC (**28**). Next are finger rings, dated between the fourth and third centuries BC (**142-143**). Distinctive of the Hellenistic period is a silver fibula, an item characteristic of Campanian necropoles from the third century BC (**127**).

Other designs, such as the earrings with Nike pendants (**21**), Erotes pendants (**23-27**), and earrings with animal heads (**30-31**), were widely diffused and thus difficult to ascribe to single areas (for an exception, cf. no. **22**). Etruria, as has been shown, was not immune to this extensive circulation of luxury goods, exemplified by the bird-shaped earrings, typical of the Apulia region (**32**). Other styles, such as the earrings with vase-shaped pendants (**29**), ultimately conditioned the production of the Roman era.

The Roman period is characterized by a considerably large and typologically varied number of items. The characteristic necklaces from the first and second centuries AD (**72-73, 75**) are associated with a variety of pendants: *olla*-shaped (**111**), bust-shaped (**114**), and illustrated (**115**), as well as amulets such as the lunar crescent (**109**), the recurring Harpokrates (**110**), and the sun (**112**). Here again the *bulla* (**108**) is represented, a neck ornament of Etruscan origin which re-emerges in the early empire. Particularly worth noting is an intaglio medallion with a portrait from the early Augustan age (**107**). A hairpin (**1**) and a diadem (**7**), the latter possibly funerary, are the only hair ornaments attributable to the Roman era. A more problematic issue is the placement of the scaraboid elements (**199-222**), comparable only to collection material.

The selection of rings is fairly well articulated, ranging from Hellenistic tradition (**144-146**), to early empire specimens (**147-156**) to styles from the middle and late empires, through to fourth-century AD (**157-159, 161-167, 170**) and possibly Byzantine pieces (**171**). Two particularly noteworthy rings feature incised portraits on the bezel, inspired by the middle- and late-Severian typologies (**168**) and those of Constantine II or Costans (**169**).

The assortment of earrings is also remarkable as it illustrates the principal styles prevalent in the Roman sphere between the first century BC and the third century AD (**33-43, 45-51, 53-59**), reaching probably as far as proto-Byzantine specimens (**52**). Among these is a group of pieces that stand out for their probable provenance in the Eastern Mediterranean, particularly Egypt, Palestine, Lebanon, and Syria (**45-46, 49, 53, 57-59**). Similarly ascribable to the same area are the amulet against the evil eye (**113**) and the engraved gem depicting Abrasax (**160**), both pieces associated with the realm of magic, which circulated mainly in the second and third centuries AD.

Finally, reaching as far as Byzantine art, the collection includes a belt element attributed to the sixth-seventh centuries AD (**224**), while a fourteenth-century ring constitutes the most recent chronological reference of the entire collection (**172**).

As is the case with all collections, items of dubious authenticity (earrings **17**, series of mask pendants **97-102**, pendant **103**) or uncertain classification (necklace **77**, pendants **117-119**, bracteates **173-188**, earrings **60-65**, various **223, 225**) have been included alongside objects whose attribution is given. Finally, as a result of mainly style-based comparisons, it was reasonably possible to identify certain fakes (earrings **66-67**, hathoric head pendants **89-95**, acorn pendant **120**, fibulae **128-129**) or *pastiches* (necklace **76**). These too have been illustrated together with material that is uncertain or which has not been classified due to a lack of cross-reference material, in order to supply a means of comparison that may prove enlightening for future studies of analogous cases.

Maurizio Sannibale

NOTE TO READERS

- Measurements are expressed in centimeters.
- The single asterisk (*) next to the catalogue number denotes items of uncertain authenticity.
- The double asterisk (**) next to the catalogue number denotes false items.

BY MAURIZIO SANNIBALE

HAIRPINS

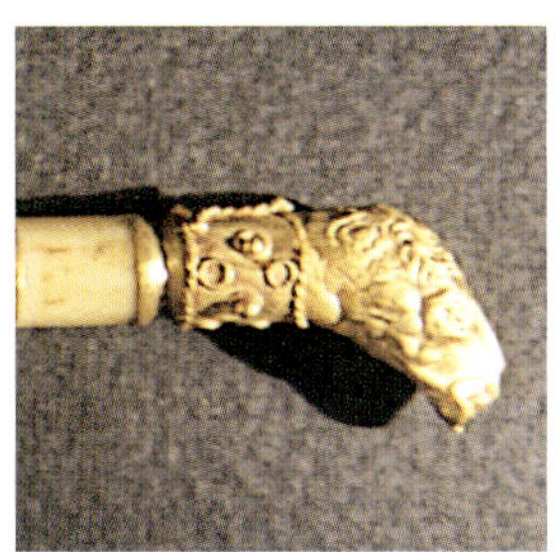

1. Hairpin

Bone and gold. Length 20.7; head 2.4 x 0.8

This large bone pin's upper extremity is encased with a gold ram's head. The head, made from two die-formed sheet gold halves soldered together, is decorated at the collar with three staggered tiers of plain wire circles, each surmounted by a small gold sphere and set within a band bordered by a row of double twisted wire.

Large bone pins, used to separate locks of hair while combing, arranging hairstyles and applying ointments, were widespread in the Roman Imperial era and were particularly concentrated in the first to third centuries AD, although they persisted at least until the fourth-fifth centuries AD.[1] The distinctive gold ram's head, in the absence of a specific comparison, may be paralleled to a large bone pin with a pine cone-shaped terminal in die-formed gold, from the second or third century AD, formerly in the Burton Y. Berry Collection.[2]

Probably Roman Imperial era.

1. Bianchi 1995.
2. Rudolph, Rudolph 1973, pp. 116-117, no. 93f.

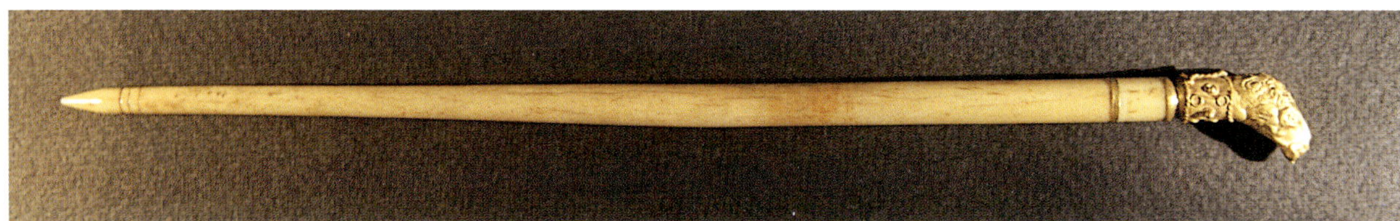

SPIRAL HAIR ORNAMENTS

2. Pair of small 5-turn hair spirals

Silver. Height 1.8; diameter 1.8; wire diameter 0.13

Each spiral is made from a circular-section wire, which increases in thickness at one extremity.

This type, made in both gold and in silver, is particularly recurrent among grave goods from northern Etruria's Orientalizing period, found in the necropoles of Vetulonia[1] and Populonia,[2] all of whose diameters, however, range from 3 to 3.8

cm. Originating from the Avori Tomb at Marsiliana D'Albegna are three gold spirals with a smaller diameter (1.3-1.7 cm), comparable to this specimen.[3] A particularly persuasive comparison may be made with the previously mentioned pair of spirals from the Littore Tomb in Vetulonia, in Florence's Museo Archeologico.[4] Another documented variety is identified by its spool-shaped terminal[5].

Second half seventh century BC.

1. Karo 1902, pp. 115-116, Figs 78-80: Three Navicelle Tomb, purchased by Guidi in Vetulonia, Littore Tomb.
2. Minto 1943, p. 140, pl. XXX/8, 12: Poggio della Porcareccia, Flabelli di Bronzo Tomb.
3. *Civiltà degli Etruschi* 1985, pp. 95-96, no. 3.14.3.
4. Cristofani, Martelli 1983, pp. 270-271, no. 59, with previous bibliography.
5. Scarpignato 1985, p.56, no 54; Caliò 2000, pp. 45-46, no. 41.

3. Pair of small 3-turn hair spirals

Gold. Height 0.8; diameter 0.9; width of strip 0.2

Each spiral is composed of a slender ribbon decorated on the outer face with four spiral-beaded wires. Each extremity bears a small sphere surrounded by a ring of twisted wire, flanked by an oval fashioned from the same wire.

There is a similar example at the British Museum, in the former Castellani Collection.[1] Also from the Castellani Collection, now in the Museum of Villa

Giulia, is a spiral made using the same technique, but equipped with a drop-shaped terminal with an engraved lion rampant.[2] Also relating to the spiral's ribbon technique, with knurled wires on the outer face, are two comparable specimens from Vulci, from the Campanari excavations, now in Berlin.[3]

Second half seventh – first half sixth century BC.

1. Marshall 1969, pl. XVI, no. 1329.
2. Caruso 1988, pp. 23, 26, no. 32. For the terminal sphere at the extremities of the spiral: L. Berge, K. Alexander, *Ancient Gold from Chicago Collections,* in *AncWorld* 11, 1985, p. 13, no. 50.
3. Greifenhagen 1970, nos 12-13, pl. 71. Cf. also Cristofani, Martelli 1983, p. 276, nos 80-82; Scarpignato 1985, pp. 57-58, nos 58-62.

4. Pair of small 3- turn hair spirals

Gold. Diameter 2.1; height 2.1; width of strip 0.4

Each spiral is composed of a ribbon bordered by spiral-beaded wires. At each extremity, seven spiral-beaded wire circles form a flower. The ribbon is decorated with wire circles alternating with

flowers made up of seven granules.
For the floral decorations at their extremities, our specimens are comparable to three pairs of spirals at the Gregorian Etruscan Museum.[1] More generally, parallels may be made with specimens at the British Museum and others from the antique market[2].

Late seventh - first half sixth century BC.

1. Scarpignato 1985, pp. 56-57, nos 55-57.
2. For typology, cf.: Marshall 1969, no. 1325; *Werke* 1970, p. 22, no. 57. For notes on the production technique in general: *Art of Ancient Italy. Etruscans, Greeks and Romans,* André Emmerich Gallery, New York, April 1970, no. 23e.

WREATHS AND DIADEMS

5. Wreath

Gold sheet. Length 29.5; height 9.9; thickness 0.06

Composed of a smooth plate to which have been attached cut-out, die-formed lanceolated leaves (laurel, olive) with imprinted central midribs, thickly arranged on four partially overlapping tiers. In the center is a flower (rosette) flanked by two smaller ones of the same design, formed by two tiers of triangular and lobed petals, each made from a single sheet. The pistil is a hollow semisphere of sheet gold. The extremities are semicircular.

The use of wreaths is documented in Greece in historic times as the result of an influx of older Oriental customs, and is closely tied to religious and funerary contexts. The symbolic value of the floral wreath derives from sacred characteristics-

given to certain plant species, dedicated to particular divinities - laurel to Apollo, olive to Athena, myrtle to Aphrodite, ivy and vine to Dionysus, oak to Zeus. Reproduced in precious materials and used in rituals, the wreath acquired further meaning: it was adopted for military decorations, merit certificates, competition prizes, and was paraded for occasions such as symposia and weddings.

The use of the gold wreath in Etruria, while culturally derived from the Greek world, developed into its own peculiar typology. Aside from a few sporadic appearances in the Orientalizing and Archaic periods, archaeological and iconographic documentation in Etruria appears only beginning in the fifth century BC. Evidence of its use becomes particularly frequent between the second half of the fourth century and the beginning of the third century BC, only to reduce considerably and all but disappear by the beginning of the second century BC.

Technical and constructive characteristics indicate that this type of jewel would not have been intended for practical, daily use, but rather was reserved for symbolic and ritual purposes, for the most part funerary. The lack of an integral, documented context results in only partial facts, which do not indicate an exclusive use for this wreath. Evidence suggests that it was more common for women to wear wreaths and diadems, while their association with men concerns mostly warriors. Reports of nineteenth-century excavations support, in the case of men, a predilection for wreaths with oak leaves, but they do not, however, exclude other types. This ambivalence also applies to divinities, both male and female, who, in their iconographic appearance, were indiscriminately wreathed.

Gold wreaths were included among grave goods of a certain wealth, along with bronzes for symposia, weapons and jewelry (respectively for men and women), toilet accessories, and equipment for athletic exercises and games. A common ritual use was that of the burial, which in certain cases was a requisite even in areas that almost exclusively adopted cremation, especially Chiusi and to a lesser degree Volterra. In funerary use, the wreath was intimately tied to the concept of the heroization of the deceased (victory in the battle of life), but created a parallel affirmation of status by also evoking the honors acquired in life, which then took on a doubly symbolic value:

Fig. 1. Head of male divinity (part of haut-relief decorating the pediment) wearing a double wreath of laurel leaves. From Orvieto, temple of Via S. Leonardo. Late fifth century BC. Orvieto, Museo Archeologico. Polychrome terracotta. Height 17.5 cm.

worldly and otherworldly. It was, in fact, from Etruria that the theme of triumph was later transmitted to Rome.

Related to this aspect was the custom, documented in Etruria throughout the fourth century BC, and in Vulci in particular, of crowning helmets with gold wreaths. The helmet, represented in this way, became a triumphal weapon that at once symbolized victory, heroization, and identification with the divinity of the deceased, possibly triumphant in life and, in any case, becoming so in the moment of death.[1] The ritual helmet-wreath association was centered with particular success in Epirus and Macedonia, from which it was most likely transmitted to southern Italy. Aside from the finds at Ruvo,[2] its use was documented in Canosa and in an undefined southern location.[3]

In the context of the ritual use of the gold wreath, a possible connection has been identified with the Dionysiac cult, given its association with the themes of symposia and triumph, or with another mystery cult known as Orphism, which prescribed that the deceased should be decorated with a wreath in the vision of a beatitude, conceived as an eternal participation in a sacred feast.[4]

The diffusion in southern Italy of the wreath in precious metals took place, as a result of the relationship between Magna Graecia and Thraco-Macedonia, particularly throughout the fourth century BC. It is heavily documented in Taranto, along with other locations like Canosa, Ascoli Satriano, Metaponto, from the fourth to the second centuries BC,[5] the prevalent use being funerary. Isolated leaves from a diadem have also been found in a votive context, as in the case of the Cirò sanctuary of Apollo Aleus.[6] Notwithstanding the case of the above-mentioned helmets surmounted by gold wreaths, even in southern Italy this item does not appear to have belonged exclusively to the male sphere.

While Vulci has been recognized as a leader in the production and diffusion of gold wreaths,[7] other centers of production have been identified with certainty in Chiusi, Populonia and Volterra, and still others hypothesized in Perugia and Spina.[8] Type I, with laurel/olive leaves, was made in Vulci, Chiusi and Populonia/Volterra, while rosaceous specimens found in Populonia/Volterra are comparable to the wreath in this catalogue, which may be paralleled to type IIB crowns, with a wide band, of which three examples are known: from Tuscania, in the British Museum, former Castellani Collection; the second, of unknown provenance, from the former Max von Heyl Collection, Darmstadt; and the third, from the former A. De Sanctis Mangelli Collection.[9] This

Fig. 2. Detail from head of Velia from the Tomba dell'Orco I in Tarquinia, wearing a gold wreath of laurel leaves, *a grappolo* earrings, necklaces with spheroid and lenticular beads. Circa 350-325 BC.

last example, stylistically datable to the second half of the fourth century BC, is closest to the wreath in question for its three rosaceous flowers with central *bulla* and double tier of petals.

A chronological reference for this type is the wreath found in tomb 30 of Populonia-S. Cerbone, variety IIA, with a narrow band, datable toward the end of the fourth century BC:[10] the artifact, found in association with a female grave, documents the use of this type in the feminine sphere, a contrast to the only other iconographic documentation, consisting of the bronze figurine of the male divinity, Veioves/Vertumnus, found in Monterazzano.[11] The wreath of Populonia-S. Cerbone is in turn comparable to a specimen from Volterra in the Museo Guarnacci, having the same type of leaves and central rosette, ascribed however to the I.C5 variety.[12] Other wreaths found in Populonia also share this type of central rosette.[13] For its typology and arrangement of leaves, the wreath in question recalls the specimen from the former Campana Collection, in Paris' Louvre Museum, with a die-formed central stud;[14] this is an elaborate typology which iconographic evidence would trace to the feminine sphere, although Felsina/Bologna documents its association with the tomb of a warrior, thought to belong to a Celtic leader.[15] Iconographically, wreaths with laurel/olive leaves prove to be particularly preferred by males, despite the ostentatious exception of the Velia in the Orco I Tomb in Tarquinia.[16]

Other more generic comparisons, for the high band, type of leaves and central rosette, may be made with specimens of unknown provenance and from the art market, probably from Etruria.[17]

Second half fourth century – early third century BC.

1. Coen 1997.
2. Coen 1997, p. 95.
3. Guzzo 1993, pp. 276-277, A.II, 14-15.
4. On the use of the crown in general: F. Coarelli, *L'oreficeria nell'arte classica,* Milano 1966, pp. 84-90; L. Masiello, in *Ori di Taranto* 1985, pp. 71-87; Coen 1999, in particular pp. 93-227.
5. Guzzo 1993, pp. 111-114, 273-289.
6. Guzzo 1983, p. 280, no. 1.
7. Scarpignato 1981.
8. Cianferoni 1992, pp. 25-27, note 83, with bibliography; Coen 1999, pp. 158-170.
9. Coen 1999, pp. 258-259, nos 44-46, p. 25.
10. L.A. Milani, *Populonia. Relazione preliminare sulla prima campagna degli scavi governativi di Populonia nel comune di Piombino,* in *NotSc* 1908, pp. 201 ff., Fig. 3; Coen 1999, pp. 94 and 164, p. 257, no. 42, Fig. 41.
11. Coen 1999, pp. 132, 139, Fig. 96.
12. Cristofani, Martelli 1983, p. 218, 310, no. 233; Coen 1999, pp. 25, 251-252, no. 23, Fig. 22.
13. A. De Agostino, *Populonia (Livorno) Scoperte archeologiche nella necropoli negli anni 1957-1960,* in *NotSc* 1961, pp. 97- 98, Figs 34, 36; Cianferoni 1992, pp. 25-26, Figs 36-38; Coen 1999, p. 254, nos 29-31, Figs 28-30.
14. Coen 1999, p. 253, no. 26, Fig. 25a-b, type I.D1 var. B.
15. Coen 1999, p. 132.
16. Coen 1999, pp. 135-136.
17. *Kunstwerke der Antike,* Auktion XVIII, 29.11.1958, Münzen und Medaillen A.G., Basel, p. 54, nos 158-159, pl. 50 = Coen 1999, pp. 255-256, nos 33 and 38; *Sotheby & Co. Catalogue,* 3rd Dec. 1973, p. 46, no. 65, pl. XVIII; *Ancient Art of the Mediterranean World & Ancient Coins, NAAG, Numismatic & Ancient Gallery AG,* 7 April 1991, Zürich 1991, no. 173; cf. also Coen 1999, pp. 255-256, nos 34-37, Figs 33-36.

6. Diadem element

Sheet gold. Length 3.2; width 2.4; height 1.9

Composed of a sheet gold plate with slender cylindrical hollows at the upper and lower edges, which would have been strung with a fastening wire. Centrally, the plate is decorated with a three-tiered, gold sheet flower surmounted by a hollow bird crafted from two symmetrical valves

Fig. 3. Diadem composed of 12 plaques. Fifth – fourth centuries BC.. New York, The Metropolitan Museum of Art, Rogers Fund, 1947. (47. 11. 10 a-l) Gold. Length 27.3 cm. Length of plaques 2.38 cm.

soldered together at the seams. Applied to each outer edge is a crouching animal flanked by a palmette, each made from bivalve gold sheet.

This plaque is comparable to elements that make up a reconstructed gold crown from Corchiano, now in the Gregorian Etruscan Museum, of arguable chronology - between the sixth and fourth centuries BC - but which stylistic comparison with *bauletto* earrings and fibulae with floral decorations and animal figurines from Vulci would place in the second half of the sixth century BC.[1]
A further comparison for these kinds of objects, lacking until today the benefits of an archaeological context and real documentation, may be made with the diadem at New York's Metropolitan Museum of Art, reconstructed from twelve plaques that are very similar to this one and hypothetically referable to the same workshop.[2] (Fig.3)
Also known are isolated rosettes with six petals, analogous to those on the plaque in question.[3] For the rosette with cut-out petals on multiple rows, a comparable *bauletto* earring is known from Cerveteri.[4]
It is possible that a hetaera may be pictured wearing a diadem with plaques in the symposium scene painted on an Attic red-figured kylix fragment by the painter Douris.[5]

Second half or late sixth century BC.

1. A. Cozza, A. Pasqui, *Carta archeologica d'Italia (1881-1897). Materiali per l'agro falisco,* Firenze 1981, pp. 290-292, pl. B1, L. Ambrosini, S. Maurizi, L.M. Michetti, *Corchiano ed il suo territorio nell'antichità,* Viterbo 1996, p. 39, Fig. 21; Caliò 2000, pp. 22-23, no. 12; for the chronology: Coen 1999, pp. 156-157, pl. A9.
2. Oliver 1965-66, pp. 280-281, Figs 23-24.
3. Davidson, Oliver 1984, pp. 22-23, no. 20.
4. Becatti 1955, p. 182, no. 288, pl. LXXIV.
5. Beazley 1963, p. 432, no. 53.

7. Diadem or hair band with mounted stone

Gold. Length 12.5; width 1.0

The jewel is composed of a gold band, tapered and perforated at each end for fastening. The band widens centrally to accommodate an elliptical setting that holds a cabochon-cut garnet.

Elongated lozenge-shaped gold sheets that are functionally close to this specimen, with perforations at the terminals, and both with embossed decorations along the length of the band as well as with a die-formed central stud, were found in Toro, at Campo Laurelli, province of Campobasso,[1] and in the Vesuvian area, in Pompeii[2] and Herculaneum.[3]
For a generic formal analogy, comparisons may be made with a Roman-era diadem with a cameo, dated to 20-10 BC.[4] Sheet gold diadems with perforated extremities, made for funerary use, are documented in Cyprus.[5]
A close parallel may be made with a specimen visible in an archive photograph from Rome's Germanic Archeological Institute concerning material on the antique market,[6] which is in turn very similar to a specimen from the P. Canellopolous

Collection.[7]
A circular garnet may also be seen on a funerary Byzantine diadem from Kertch in Crimea, composed of a trapezoidal sheet, from the last quarter of the fourth century or first half of the fifth century AD.[8]

First century BC – first century AD (?).

1. Siviero 1954, no. 309, pl. 197b; Cantilena 1989, pp. 212-213, no. 47.
2. Siviero 1954, no. 308, pl. 197a.
3. *Ibid,* no. 310, pl. 197c.
4. Greifenhagen 1975, p. 13, no. 6, pl. 3.
5. Cesnola 1903, pl. XII, 1-8; cf. also: De Ridder 1924, pl. II.
6. Greifenhagen 1975, Fig. 3, no. 20
7. Laffineur 1980, pp. 410-411, Fig. 107, no. 98; cf. also *ibid,* p. 429, no. 126, Fig. 140.
8. Baldini Lippolis 1999, p. 65, no. 5.

EARRINGS

8. *Bauletto* earring

Gold. Width 0.9; diameter 1.0

The earring's frontal face is decorated with a flower with lanceolated petals, formed by oblong grains arranged in a cross, alternating with small spheres surrounded by rows of granules. The edges are outlined in funnel-beaded wire. The smooth rear face has four applied ridges of funnel-beaded wire. The original closing mechanism is integral.

This class of *bauletto* earrings was widespread in southern Etruria (Vulci, Cerveteri, Bisenzio) as well as in northern-central and Po Valley Etruria (Orvieto, Chiusi, S. Gimignano, Monteriggioni, Arezzo, Vetulonia, Populonia, Volterra, Bientina, Bologna), in addition to Faliscan territory, in the period between 570-560 BC and around 470 BC.[1] The typology of this earring brings us back to the most ancient examples of the *bauletto* class, dated to the first half of the sixth century BC, and may

be compared to earrings from the Flabelli tomb in Populonia, which feature the filigree version of the lanceolated petal motif, datable to 570-560 BC.[2] In Vetulonia the motif persists in earrings dated to the second half of the sixth century BC, as recalled by a specimen found in the city's territory, now in Naples' Museo Nazionale,[3] and probably a second one from the necropolis, distinctive for its ridges in beaded wire on the rear.[4] The decoration with lanceolated petals may also be found in Orvieto in tomb 26 at the Crocifisso del Tufo necropolis, in the filigree version but with petal gemination and ornamental edged spheres,[5] a specimen associated with Attic pottery dated to 540-515 BC. It has a parallel recurrence, but with the addition of cut-out flowers and a rich decoration of filigree and granules, in a pair from Vulci dated to the third quarter of the sixth century BC.[6] Two pairs, respectively from Chiusi[7] and Cerveteri,[8] feature side closure and an extensive use of granulation.[9]

Fig.4. Anthropomorphic cinerary Canopic vase with spiral gold earring inserted in the earlobe. Provenance unknown. Early sixth century BC. Chianciano Terme, Alessandro Cinelli Collection. Ceramic. Height 60.4 cm. Maximum diameter 32.8 cm.

The simple, open cylinder form is also shared by the series with iconic decoration such as the specimen from Vetulonia-Poggio alla Guardia, with masks that still rely on the Orientalizing tradition,[10] or the pair in Berlin with Pótnia thērōn (Mistress of wild animals) between two lions.[11]
A close parallel may be made with material from the antique market[12].

Third quarter sixth century BC.

1. For a general classification on the type, Cristofani, Martelli 1983, pp. 53-54.
2. Minto 1943, pl. XXX, 9 = *Magie des Goldes* 1996, pp. 44-45, no. 35; for chronology: M. Cristofani Martelli, *Documenti di arte orientalizzante da Chiusi*, in *StEtr* 41, 1973, p. 105, note 27.
3. Breglia 1941, p. 24, no. 18, pl. VII, 5= Cristofani, Martelli 1983, no. 145.
4. Minto 1943, pl. XXVIII, 3-4 = *Ori e argenti* 1961, p. 34, no. 56.
5. M. Bizzarri, *La necropoli di Crocifisso del Tufo in Orvieto,* in *StEtr* 30, 1962, pp. 107-108, Fig. 34; A.E. Feruglio, in *I Trucchi e le essenze* 2002, p. 37, no. 4.
6. Hoffmann, von Claer 1968, pp. 12-14, no. 10 = Cristofani,

Martelli 1983, pp. 155, 288, no. 123.
7. Cristofani, Martelli 1983, no. 143.
8. *Ibid*, no. 144 = *Magie des Goldes* 1996, p. 49, no. 45.
9. Cf. also: Zahn 1929, p. 32, no. 41a-b, pl. 43; Johnstone 1932, p. 445, no. 10325, pl. XX; Marshall 1969, nos 1291-1292, 1296-1297, pl. XVI, Castellani Collection; *Werke* 1970, p. 18, no. 38; *Frank Sternberg*, Auct. XXVII, 1994, no. 869, pl. XLIV; *Sotheby's, New York. Antiquities and Islamic Art*, 17 December 1997, pp. 207-208, no. 210.
10. Karo 1902, p. 124, Fig. 103 = Higgins 1980, p. 139, Fig. 20.
11. Greifenhagen 1970, pl. 71, 4; Cristofani, Martelli 1983, no. 142.
12. *Werke* 1970, p. 18, no. 39; *Art of Ancient Italy* 1970, p. 15, no. 23. Cf. also: De Ridder 1924, p. 22, nos 244-245, Campana Collection; Becatti 1955, p. 182, no. 286, pl. LXXIV, of unknown provenance, associated with the lanceolated-petal flower motif in the rear section; Bordenache Battaglia 1980, nos 29, 33, from Praeneste.

9. *Bauletto* earring

Gold. Width 1.4; diameter 1.2; height 1.8
Decoration: granulation, *pulviscolo*, filigree

The earring is composed of a semicylindrical plate. The frontal face is decorated with five flow-

ers arranged centrally and in each corner, alternating with semispheres decorated with granulation. The flowers are rendered with wires disposed radially around a granule and encircled by a spiral-beaded wire and a plain wire. The larger central flower has a double border of spiral-beaded wire and a pistil decorated with granulation. The edges of the earring are outlined in beaded wire. The rear face has a triple ridge of paired spiral-beaded wires. The closing mechanism, consisting of a double hinge, is integral; it is decorated on the front with a pine cone-shaped bud with beaded volutes and covered in granulation, and flanked by two spheres with apical granules.[1]

This earring, with its design of four corner radial flowers and a central one, represents one of the most popular types, articulated into different varieties according to the disposition of associated decorative elements: rosettes in cut-out sheet gold, *bullae* or granulated semispheres, theriomorphic elements, and so on.

Fig. 5. Urn with recumbent figure wearing *bauletto* earrings. From Cerveteri. Last quarter sixth century BC. Rome, Museo Nazionale di Villa Giulia. Terracotta. Dimensions of the lid: Height 33 cm. Length 55 cm. Width 29 cm.

For the type in question, in the variant form with open sides that generally indicate an element of relative antiquity, existing contexts in Orvieto[2] and Castel D'Asso[3] would date it to the last quarter of the sixth century BC.
Particularly significant comparisons may be made with specimens from Vulci[4] or from the Castellani Collection, most likely from southern Etruria.[5] A similar syntax may be found on a pair of earrings from Volterra.[6] Among recent acquisitions, one might recall a pair from Pescia Romana in the Chianciano Museum.[7]
In some specimens from Caere (Cerveteri) the radial central disc is associated with semispheres decorated with *pulviscolo*[8] or discs with lion protomes.[9]
The earring in question also corresponds to numerous materials of unknown provenance or only generically associated with Italy or Etruria.[10]
The frame on this earring may be compared to a specimen with a "checkerboard" decoration in the Dallas Museum of Fine Arts.[11] Granulated semispheres appear both in the "checkerboard" types[12] and in those with the central square.[13]

Last quarter sixth century BC.

1. For the class in general, cf. no. **8**.
2. Crocifisso del Tufo, tomb 6a, 530-510 BC: M. Bizzarri, *La necropoli di Crocifisso del Tufo – II*, in *StEtr* 34, 1966, pp. 9-10, Fig. 3; A.E. Feruglio, in *I trucchi e le essenze* 2002, p. 36, no. 3.
3. Associated with an amphora by the Antimenes Painter dated to 510 BC: E. Colonna Di Paolo, G. Colonna, *Castel D'Asso*, Firenze 1970, pp. 26-27, pl. CCCCLII, 1.
4. Scarpignato 1985, pp. 41-43, nos 34-35.
5. *Nuove scoperte e acquisizioni nell'Etruria meridionale*, exhibition catalogue, Roma 1975, pl. 87 on upper right = Caruso 1988, p. 27, no. 38.
6. E. Fiumi, *Materiali volterrani nel Museo Archeologico di Firenze*, in *StEtr* 25, 1957, p. 474, no. 8, p. 476, Fig. 1, former Cinci Collection = *Ori e argenti* 1961, p. 37, no. 71, pl. X.
7. Paolucci 1991, p. 104, no. 137.
8. Becatti 1955, p. 182, no. 287, pl. LXXIV.
9. Bordenache Battaglia 1980, no. 32.
10. C.H. Smith, C.A. Hutton, *Catalogue of the Antiquities in the Collection of the Late Wyndham Francis Cook, Esqre*, London 1908, p. 92, pl. XXI, 27; Marshall 1969, p. 116, pl. XVI, 1299-1300 (Campanari Collection); Breglia 1941, pp. 23-24, nos 15-16, pl. VII, 6-7; *Antike Kunstwerke*, Auktion II, Ars Antiqua AG Luzern (14.05.1960), Luzern 1960, p. 63, pl. 70, nos 179-180; *Antike Kunstwerke*, Auktion V, Ars Antiqua AG (7/11/1964), Luzern 1964, p. 37, pl. XXXIX, 139; Oliver 1965-66, p. 280, Fig. 22 = Higgins 1980, pl. 32, C; D. Ohly, *Die Antikensammlungen am Königsplatz in München*, Stiftland (1967), Fig. 62 on lower left; *Werke* 1970, p. 16, nos 36-37; Greifenhagen 1970, p. 93, pl. 71, 6-7; Hackens 1976, pp. 35-36, Fig. 3, a-b; *Christie's*, 6 July 1994, p. 103, 106, no. 319; Williams 1998, p. 39 and pl. 20 (London, Victoria and Albert Museum).
11. Hoffmann 1970, pp. 464-465, no. 214.
12. M.A. Johnstone, *Etruscan Collections in the Royal Scottish Museum Edinburgh, and the National Museum of Antiquities of Scotland, Edinburgh*, in *StEtr* 11, 1937, p. 402, pl. 54,1-6; P. Bocci Pacini, *Postilla su Arezzo arcaica*, in *StEtr* 47, 1979, p. 59 ff., pls VIIIb, XII, Poggio del Sole necropolis; *Kunst der Etrusker*, exhibition catalogue, (Interversa 13/08 – 2/10/1981), Hamburg 1981, p. 126, no. 159.
13. R.A. Higgins, *Jewellery from Classical Lands*, London 1965, p. 26, pl. 13B = Marshall 1969, p. 115, pl. XVI, 1294.

10. *Pair of earrings

Gold. Height 2.2; width 1.4

Composed of a semi-annular hollow element of moulded gold sheet whose widened extremities are sealed off by a semisphere edged with plain wire at the joint. Soldered onto one semisphere is the arched suspension loop, whose unfixed end locates into an opening in the second semisphere. A cluster on the underside is composed of four hollow spheres surmounted by a smaller apical sphere.

There is no exact parallel for this form, which only distantly recalls a Greco-Archaic typology, in which the suspension loop is of one piece with the body of the earring, datable to the sixth-fifth centuries BC,[1] or to more ancient Cypriot examples.[2] Further comparisons may be made with specimens from tomb 13 in Tharros, which in turn are similar to the long-lasting Cypriot (1050-600 BC) and Greco-Archaic versions from the sixth-fifth centuries BC.[3]

Probably sixth to fifth centuries BC.

1. Cf. Marshall 1969, pl. XXVI, no. 1593, from Smyrna.
2. Pierides 1971, p. 25, no. 10, pl. XIII, from Lapithos – tomb 403, 850-700 BC.
3. *Tharros* 1987, p. 175, no. 13/8, pls 38e, 44g, p. 80, type IIa.

11. Pair of *a grappolo* earrings

Gold. Height 3.9; width 1.5

The upper section is composed of a plate with parallel edges and rounded top, edged and subdivided into longitudinal tiers by a twisted double wire and rows of embossed dots. The suspen-

Fig. 6. Female head wearing *a grappolo* earrings and wreath. From Cerveteri. Second half fourth century BC. Vatican City, Vatican Museums, inv. 21620. Terracotta. Height 16.5 cm.

sion hook is a gold tongue moulded from the same sheet as the shield. The cluster below consists of a pyramid formed by four hollow lenticular spheres, each made from two die-formed valves soldered together at the seams. These alternate with three groups of smaller spheres, similar in shape and arrangement and separated from one another by rows of granules and a pair of hemispherical flowers.

These earrings are very similar to a pair conserved in the Rhode Island School of Design's Museum of Art.[1] A further comparison may be made with a specimen from the Berlin Museums, characterized by a rectangular, arched body terminating in a suspension hook.[2]

Fourth century BC.

1. Hackens 1976, pp. 40-41, no. 6.
2. Greifenhagen 1970, p. 96, pl. 73, 9.

12. *Pair of *a grappolo* earrings

Gold. Height 3.2; width 1.4

The upper section is composed of a plate with parallel edges and rounded top, edged and subdivided into three sections by double braided wire. The two outer sections are decorated with

plain wire circles, while the middle section has circles of double braided wire surmounted by granules. The cluster below consists of a pyramid formed by four hollow spheres, each made from two die-formed valves soldered together at the seams. These alternate with smaller spheres, similar in shape and disposition, as well as a pair of hemispherical flowers with central studs for pistils.

Fig. 7. Antefix with head of maenad wearing a diadem with rosettes and a pair of *a grappolo* earrings. From Cerveteri, Jacobini excavations, 1870. Fourth century BC. Vatican City, Vatican Museums, inv. 13978. Polychrome terracotta. Height 49 cm.

The only admissible parallel for these specimens is a pair from the Baurat Schiller Collection.[1]
In the absence of specific comparisons with material of known background, these earrings, while related to typologies documented in Etruria throughout the fourth century BC, nevertheless remain of uncertain authenticity.[2]

1. Zahn 1929, p. 32, no. 43a-b, pl. 46.
2. For a general classification, cf. no. **11**.

13. **Pair of *a grappolo* earrings

Gold. Height 3.4/3.5; width 1.3

The shield's outer edge is decorated with a strip of cut-out and hatched sheet gold. The inside

Fig. 8. Die for the manufacture of an *a grappolo* earring, either in terracotta as an appliqué for a votive statue, or in gold sheet for funerary use. From the Rome market; gift of Arvid Andrén. Fourth century BC. Vatican City, Vatican Museums, inv. 20628. Terracotta. Height 10.4 cm. Width 7 cm.

bears a longitudinal row of rings surmounted by granules, set in between two rows of smaller granules. The cluster below consists of a pyramid formed by four hollow lenticular spheres, each made from two die-formed valves soldered together at the seams. These alternate with three groups of smaller spheres, similar in shape and disposition, and separated from one another by granules and hemispherical flowers with central grains.

Cf. no. **14**.

14. **Pair of *a grappolo* earrings

Gold. Height 3.4/3.5; width 1.3
Spheres are dented in one example.

The upper section is composed of a plate with parallel edges and rounded top, bordered by a smooth, hollow tube, and decorated centrally with a snake alternating with granules. The suspension hook consists of a single piece and is

slightly curved in cross-section. The underlying cluster consists of a pyramid formed by four hollow lenticular spheres, each made from two die-formed valves soldered together at the seams. These alternate with three groups of smaller spheres, similar in shape and disposition and separated from one another by rows of granules.

These earrings, rather unusual in the shape of their upper section for the absence of a wedge-shaped body, are comparable only to a specimen from the Castellani Collection, from Civitella San Paolo, conserved in the Museo di Villa Giulia,[1] which is in turn comparable to an earring from

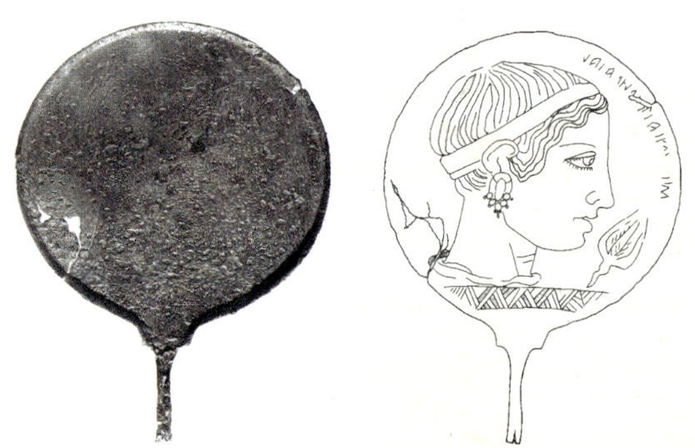

Fig. 9. Engraved mirror known as *Avia*'s *Mirror*. Pictures a female head in profile wearing an *a grappolo* earring. From Vulci, 1835-1837 excavations. 325-300 BC. Vatican City, Vatican Museums, inv. 12251. Bronze. Height 18.3 cm.

the Museum of Art at the Rhode Island School of Design.[2]
Technological details and a number of stylistic incongruences indicate that the specimens in question are fakes, made to imitate or inspired by the class of *a grappolo* earrings, widespread in Etruria throughout the fourth century BC.[3] Further comparisons may be made for the class in general, including specimens of funerary use.[4]

1. M.A. Rizzo, in Cristofani, Martelli 1983, pp. 223, 311, no. 240 = Caruso 1988, p. 32, no. 50, pl. VIII.
2. Hackens 1976, pp. 40-41, no. 6.
3. M.A. Rizzo, in Cristofani, Martelli 1983, p. 311, no. 239; Cristofani, Martelli 1983, pp. 62-63; for the fakes, *ibid.*, pp. 222, 311, no. 238.
4. Hadaczeck 1903, pp. 61-62, Fig. 118 (Museo di Tarquinia), 119-120 (Vatican, Gregorian Etruscan Museum); Marshall 1969, nos 2252-2259, pl. XLIV; De Ridder 1924, nos 315-350, pl. VII; Becatti 1955, nos 412, 415, 417; A. Andrén, *Una matrice fittile etrusca*, in *StEtr* 24, 1955-56, pp. 207-219; Coche de la Ferté 1956, p. 85, pl. XL, 3; *Kultura i Iskusstvo Etrurii*, Leningrad 1972, no. 113; Jehasse 1973, p. 428, no. 1684, pl. I; Hackens 1976, p. 37 ff.; Bordenache Battaglia 1980, no. 61; Scarpignato 1981, pp. 14-19; Platz-Horster 2001, pp. 41-42, no. 24, from Capena.

15. *Pair of *a grappolo* earrings

Gold. Height 3.4/3.5; width 1.3

The upper section is composed of an arched plate with a raised border and engraved ovolo decoration. Applied to the center is a repoussé plate picturing an owl. The suspension hook consists of a flat plate. The underlying cluster is composed of hollow bivalve spheres, made from two dieformed valves soldered together at the seams. These alternate with three groups of four grains arranged in a pyramid, pairs of grains, and hemispherical flowers with small studs for pistils.

16. *Pair of *a grappolo* earrings

Gold. Height 7.9/8.1; width 4.9

The upper section consists of an elliptical plate, decorated on top with a lion protome and on either side with two owls made from applied repoussé plates; a large roped ridge runs down the center. The edges and internal spaces are outlined with rows of embossed studs. The suspension hook is made from a U-shaped plate. The underlying cluster is composed of hollow spheres

alternating with hemispherical flowers with grains for pistils, and crowned with small pyramids of four grains, some of which are missing or damaged.

Fig. 10. Female votive statue from Pratica di Mare wearing *chiton* and cloak, also covering her head, and adorned with a wreath, *a grappolo* earrings, a series of necklaces and a large embossed breastplate with pendants. Circa 330-300 BC. Rome, Soprintendenza Archeologica per il Lazio, inv. P77.37. Terracotta. Height 77 cm.

17. *Pair of *a grappolo* earrings

Gold. Height 7.4/6.4; width 1.6/1.8

Each earring is composed of a double metal plate, die-formed in front and smooth in the back, in the form of an elongated triangle, and decorated with a row of studs between roped ridges. The underlying element is a cluster of six die-formed hemispheres. One specimen retains a segment of twisted wire on the summit.

18. Pair of leech-shaped earrings

Gold. Height 2.5/2.4; width 1.5/1.4

The body is made out of two valves soldered together at the seams. The central vertical band is marked by filigree decoration consisting of two braided wires separated by a spooled wire and bordered by plain wires. Attached to the underside is a graduated stack of four grains of decreasing diameter. A beaded wire collar decorates each terminal, where the arched suspension loop is inserted with one unfixed, pointed end.

The type is of ancient Oriental origin, as it appears in Ur in 2500 BC.[1] Similar typologies have been known in Syria beginning in the eighth to seventh centuries BC, such as a pair of earrings from Amrit in the de Clercq Collection,[2] from which they reached Greece, and where they proceeded to develop for about four centuries.

One of the most ancient specimens is from the Athens Acropolis, dated to the seventh century BC,[3] followed by findings from Ephesus[4] and Archaic examples dated to the sixth-fifth centuries BC,[5] found also in Cyprus,[6] ending with common types from Classical and Hellenistic Greece.[7]

Starting out in Greece, these typologies eventually reached the western colonies. It is, in fact, with specimens found in Taranto (which then spread to other cities of southern Italy, such as Lucania) datable to the second half of the fourth century BC, that a close comparison may be made for the earrings in question.[8]

Second half fourth century BC.

1. Higgins 1980, p. 119.
2. Coche de la Ferté 1954, p. 36, pl. II, 3.
3. A.B. Edwards, in *JHS* 2, 1881, pp. 324-325, Fig. n.no.; Hadaczek 1903, p. 24, Fig. 45.
4. D.G. Hogarth, *Excavations at Ephesus*, London 1908, pp. 104-105, pl. VI, 53, 69; Marshall 1969, pl. IX, 946; Higgins 1980, p. 119, pl. 21, E
5. Becatti 1955, pl. LXXV, no. 294, a-b, Athens, Benaki Museum.
6. Marshall 1969, pl. XXVI, no. 1593, from Poli-tis-Chrysokhou; Pierides 1971, pl. XX, nos 5-6, 475-400 BC.
7. Higgins 1980, pl. 25, C = Marshall 1969, no. 1660, from Kalymnos, fourth century BC; cf. Becatti 1955, no. 382; Marshall 1969, pl. XXX, no. 1659, fifth-third centuries BC; *Christie's London*, 21 April 1999, pp. 56-57, no. 132.
8. Guzzo 1993, pp. 90-92, 249-250, type IVB, nos 1 (= Becatti 1955, no. 381, a-b, pl. C), 2-5; cf. *Ori di Taranto* 1984, pp. 152-154, nos 63-67; Lippolis 1994, pl. XX, 1; Guzzo 1998, p. 57, Fig. 7.4, from Policoro; Moratello 1999, pp. 272-274, no. 11, pl. XCIX, 11; *Magna Graecia* 2002, pp. 154-155, no. 14. Cf also: *Werke* 1970, p. 10, no. 11; *Art of Ancient Italy* 1970, p. 41, no. 60; *Schmuck der Antike, Münzen und Medaillen AG*, Okt. -Nov. 1981, pp. 8-9, no. 20; *Christie's*, 14-15 May 2002, no. 292; *Christie's*, 11 December 2003, no. 364.

19. Pair of leech-shaped earrings

Gold. Height 3.5; width 1.3

The body of each earring consists of two die-formed valves soldered together and decorated longitudinally with spooled wire. Suspended from below is a hollow spherical pendant that terminates in a granule and is decorated with a double row of spooled wire. Attached to each terminal, where the denticulated suspension loop locates with one unfixed and pointed end, is a small hollow sphere decorated with three rows of spooled wire. The fixed extremity of the suspension loop is partially wrapped in a wound wire.

There is no known specific parallel for this pair, whose shape follows an ancient Mediterranean tradition. A similar type, in the shape of a "goatskin," Phoenician in style and dated between the seventh and fifth centuries BC, is documented at Tharros in Sardinia.[1] Analogous shapes were adopted for the contemporary *boat-earrings* from the Greco-Archaic jewelry tradition.[2]
Characteristics such as the longitudinal decora-

tion and the central pendant are shared at the same time with a late-Byzantine silver earring in the Istanbul Museum. This makes placement for the examples in question a more problematic issue.[3]

1. Coche de la Ferté 1956, pl. II, 2; G. Pisano, in *Tharros* 1987, pp. 78-79, type Ia, no. 8/11.
2. Bromberg 1990, p. 34, no. 11; Reiblich 1996, pp. 134-135, no. 22, pl. 12,1-2, from Assos, first half of the sixth century BC.
3. Ergil 1983, p. 59, no. 154.

20. Disc earring

Silver. Diameter 1.45; height 2.1

The earring element consists of a disc, equipped with a long pin on the rear, and picturing a frontal portrait in relief of the young head of Dionysus adorned with an ivy wreath and corymbs. The edge of the disc is hatched.

This may be paralleled with an example from Taranto, dated to the fourth century BC, decorated on its smaller disc with a frontal male head.[1] An earring from Kyme of the same type but with a phytomorphic motif is in the British Museum.[2]

Fourth - third centuries BC.

1. *Art of Ancient Italy* 1970, p. 41, no. 62. For the motif of the head of Dionysus: C. Gasparri, in *LIMC* III, s.v. *Dionysos*, Zürich-München 1986, p. 444, no. 192.
2. Marshall 1969, no. 2059, pl. XXXIX.

21. Pair of earrings with Nike pendant

Gold. Height 6.5/6.4; width 3.9; diameter 1.5
The wing on one pendant is damaged.

Fig. 11. Victory statuette with wreath and military spoils. Roman copy of original from late fourth century BC, 80-100 AD. Vatican City, Vatican Museums, inv. 2721. Marble. Height 91.5 cm.

The disc, decorated with filigree, is contained within a circular frame whose border is in relief and decorated with beaded wire. The pendant is in the form of a nude Nike wearing a shoulder strap and carrying a *patera* and military spoils (a cuirass on a staff); the figures are specular, so as to show their attributes symmetrically when the earrings are worn as a pair.

A common parallel for this type of earring, with pendants in the shape of female figures with spread wings, is an example from northern Greece, dated to the second half of the fourth century BC, at the Virginia Museum of Fine Arts in Richmond.[1]
Concerning Magna Graecia, worth noting is a pair from Taranto, with a disc set with a garnet and a female winged figure pendant.[2] For the motif of Victory bearing a trophy, a parallel may be made with a specimen in the British Museum[3].

Second half fourth – third century BC.

1 Hoffmann, Davidson 1965, p. 85, no. 13.
2 Guzzo 1993, p. 252, type V.B, no. 2, with previous bibliography; for classification, *ibid.*, pp. 92-96.
3. Marshall 1969, pl. XXXII, no. 1851.

22. Pair of earrings with Eros pendant

Gold. Height 6.2/6.0; width 2.5/2.4

The body is configured as a flower with three layers of petals. Each petal is edged with beaded wire, and a granule forms the pistil. Suspended from the center is an Eros figurine bearing a *patera* and a scroll. Suspended from either side are two acorn-shaped pendants, connected to the rosette by long, single loop-in-loop chains and decorated with beaded wire tongues and an underlying pyramid of four grains.

The type of flower or rosette that makes up the body of these earrings was widely adopted in late Classical and early Hellenistic Greek tradition,

starting from the fourth century BC.[1]
This decorative element was also adopted in southern Italian manufacture, particularly Tarantine; it recurs in the fifteen grains of a necklace from tomb 33 on Via Alto Adige in Taranto, dated to the end of the fourth – first decades of the third century BC.[2] Also said to come from Taranto is a similar necklace from the Castellani Collection, dated to the first half of the fourth century BC.[3] As far as the earrings are concerned, a triple rosette appears on an elaborate earring from Taranto, dated to the second half of the fourth century BC,[4] and, as a double rosette, at the extremities of a pair of leech-shaped earrings from Metaponto.[5]
A similar flower, but with a double layer of petals, recurs on two earrings from the Castellani Collection;[6] anonymous rosette elements are also known from the antique market.[7]

For the Eros pendant, see *infra,* nos **23-24, 26.**

Second half fourth century BC.

1. Marshall 1969, nos 1666-1667, pl. XXX, from Cyprus; S.G. Miller, *Two groups of Thessalian Gold*, Berkeley-Los Angeles-London 1979, pp. 17-18, pl. 3, d, leech-shaped earring from Eretria; *ibid.*, pp. 10-11, pl. 4, b, pendant; *ibid.*, pl. 5, a, from Temir Gora, pl. 5, c from Panticapaeum; cf. Greifenhagen 1970, p. 45, no. 13, pl. 22.
2. Guzzo 1993, p. 201, V.C.2; *Ori di Taranto* 1984, no. 143.
3. Marshall 1969, p. 214, no. 1952; Guzzo 1993, p. 201, V.C.1.
4. *Ori di Taranto* 1984, pp. 154-157, no. 68.
5. F.G. Lo Porto, *Metaponto (Matera). Nuovi scavi nella città e nella sua necropoli*, in *NotSc* 1981, p. 372, Fig. 95, late fourth - early third century BC.
6. Caruso 1988, p. 32, no. 49, pl. VII.
7. Frank Sternberg, *Aukt.* XXVII, 1994, no. 911, pl. XLIX; *Christie's*, 8 December 1999, pp. 26-27, no. 45.

23. Earring with Eros pendant

Gold and glass paste. Height 2.6; width 1.0

Composed of a round shield with a smooth, upturned border edged in spiral-beaded wire, bearing a central glass paste bead held in a dog-toothed setting. The pendant is in the shape of a naked Eros carrying a *patera* in his lowered right hand and a cylinder in his raised left hand. The suspension loop is made from a chain or a double pair of braided wires.

This was a very popular type throughout the Hellenistic period, which by definition starts at the end of the fourth century BC. For Eros's attributes, a parallel may be made with a specimen in the British Museum,[1] while for the disc type with upturned borders and central setting, an example known from the art market may be compared[2].

Cf. nos **24-26.**

Late fourth - third century BC.

1. Marshall 1969, no. 1876, pl. XXXII
2. *Werke* 1970, p. 15, no. 28.

24. Pair of earrings with Eros pendant

Gold. Height 3.8/3.6; width 1.3

Each earring consists of a disc decorated centrally with a flower bearing a central grain, and along the edges with two spiral-beaded wires. The pendant is an Eros figurine suspended from a ring, wearing a strap that interlaces in front, and holding a scroll and *patera*. The loop is made of a twisted plate forming a circular-section wire.

This typology of earring, with a pendant in the shape of Eros, established itself beginning in early Hellenism, a period in which it was highly recurrent, with specimens dating from the end of the fourth to the third centuries BC.[1]
This type, less elaborate in design and decoration, may be paralleled with the so-called Phase C of the "Palmette Group," dated now precisely to the second half of the third century BC from the excavations at Tell Atrib (ancient Atribis) in lower Egypt.[2]
The genre persisted in the Roman Imperial era, when cherubs with the *patera* and cylinder (variously interpreted as a flute, quiver, alabastron, sceptre or stick) were still used as earring pendants[3] or as brooch heads.[4]

Cf. also nos **23, 25-26.**

Second half third century BC.

1. Arneth 1850, S IV, G97; Hadaczek 1903, pp. 41-44, Figs 78-79 (Wiener Hofmuseum), 80 (Museo Faina, Orvieto); Marshall 1969, pl. XXXII, no. 1876, Castellani Collection; Becatti 1955, pl. CVI, no. 402a-b, formerly at Taranto's National Museum = *Ori di Taranto* 1984, no. 95 and Guzzo 1993, p. 252, V.B.6; Becatti 1955, no. 403, from Taranto = *Ori di Taranto* 1984, no. 96 and Guzzo 1993, p. 252, V.B.5; Oliver 1965-66, pp. 277-278, Fig. 17, from Rhodovani, Crete; Hoffmann, von Claer 1968, p. 122, no. 80, from the Smyrna market; Hoffmann 1970, pp. 468-469, no. 216; Greifenhagen 1975, pp. 50-51, pl.

41, nos 1-3, 5, fourth - third centuries BC; Laffineur 1980, pp. 419-423, Figs 124-126, Canellopoulos Collection; Davidson, Oliver 1984, p. 68, no. 66, Chr. Bastis Collection, late fourth - third century BC; Rudolph 1995, p. 146, no. 30.B.1-2, Burton Y. Berry Collection.
2. Jackson 1999, pp. 67, 70-71, 75, Figs 4-5.
3. Siviero 1954, no. 151, pl. 131, b, first century BC.
4. Siviero 1954, no. 148, pl. 130, c, from Herculaneum, first century BC - first century AD; Ondrejová 1976, pp. 50-51, nos 18-19, pl. III, 2a-b, pl. XI, 1a-b, from Kertch (Crimea), Roman era.

25. Disc earring fragment

Gold. Diameter 0.9
Only the disc and hook are preserved.

At the center of the disc is an empty setting made to hold a stone, edged with a series of small arch-

es enclosed by concentric circles of plain wire, double spiral-beaded wires and a beaded wire. The simple loop is formed from a moulded pin.

May pertain to the Eros pendant, no. **26**.

26. Eros earring pendant

Gold. Height 1.6

In the form of a naked Eros, holding a *patera* and a cylinder. May be associated with the previous disc (no. **25**).

An accurate parallel, both for the disc and for the Eros pendant, may also be made with a specimen from the Museum of Fine Arts in Houston.[1]

For the disc type, with a similar Eros pendant, a parallel may be made with a specimen from the former Castellani Collection[2].

See *infra* nos **23-24**.

Third - second centuries BC.

1 Hoffmann 1970, pp. 468-469, no. 216.
2. Marshall 1969, pl. XXXII, no. 1876. Cf. also: *Werke* 1970, p. 15, no. 27 (isolated disc), nos 29-33 (isolated Eros pendants); Zouhdi 1971, p. 99, pl. XV, no. 15; Rudolph 1995, p. 186, no. 41.B.1-2, Burton Y. Berry Collection; *Christie's*, 3 July 1996, p. 9, no. 102; *Christie's*, 5 December 2001, no. 130.

27. Pair of earrings with Erotes

Gold. Height 2.9; width 1.9

Each earring is composed of a simple circular-section hook to which is attached a naked Eros, bearing a *patera* and *oinochoe* in the act of pouring.

This type of earring, featuring Eros with his various attributes and a simple hook, was first defined in early Hellenism.[1] Accurate parallels may be made with collection material, respectively from the B. Schiller Collection[2] and from the P. Canellopoulos Collection.[3] There also exists a chronological reference for this type, represented by a tomb in Taranto dated to the first half of the second century BC, that contained an earring comparable to those in question.[4]
Earrings with hooks, similarly to those with discs (Cf. nos **22-26**), were highly popular in the Roman Imperial period, with examples dating between the first century BC and the first century AD, and

became increasingly inferior, both from a material and from a formal perspective.[5]

Probably second century BC.

1. Hoffmann, von Claer 1968, p. 122, no. 79; Greifenhagen 1975, p. 53, pl. 42, no. 8, from the Athens market; *ibid.*, no. 13, from Kertsch.
2. Zahn 1929, p. 36, nos 62a-b, pl. 52.
3. Laffineur 1980, pp. 413-415, Fig. 114.
4. *Ori di Taranto* 1984, no. 120; Guzzo 1993, p. 258, VII.B.3
5. For the type with a naked Eros bearing *patera* and *oinochoe*: Siviero 1954, nos 157 (unknown provenance), 160 (Avigliano); Hoffmann, von Claer 1968, pp. 129-130, nos 83-84, from the Smyrna market; Marshall 1969, pl. XXXII, no. 1861, Hamilton Collection, first century AD. Cf. also: Arneth 1850, S IV, G94; Hackens 1976, p. 92, no. 35, with an Eros playing a *sirinx*; *Schmuck der Antike* 1981, p. 10, no. 30; *Christie's*, 3 July 1996, p. 9, no. 115; *Christie's*, 8 December 1999, pp. 20-21, nos 30, 32.

28. Earring with pyramidal pendant

Gold. Height 2.0; width 0.5

Disc-shaped earring decorated with a six-petalled flower of beaded wire and central granule, inscribed in concentric circles of twisted, plain and spooled wire. Suspended from the disc is a pendant in the form of an inverted three-sided pyramid with a grain on the tip, decorated at the edges with spiral-beaded wire.

The inverted pyramid pendant was seen as early as the Archaic and Classical periods, but became particularly popular in the course of the fourth century BC. Very rich versions of earrings of this type are known, with complex decorations, pendants, and winged genies, from Cyprus[1] and Asia Minor.[2] Other elaborate examples were found in the Scythian tombs of southern Russia.[3]
The earring in question is comparable to types from Magna Graecia, particularly Taranto, that were widespread beginning in the fourth century BC[4] and persisted until the early second century BC.[5] Specimens with plain pendants without granulation are known to have existed at the end of the second century BC.[6]
In the Etruscan world, the shape was particularly popular between the third and second centuries BC, with special favor in Volterra,[7] which offers a parallel iconographic documentation, the form appearing frequently in *parures* worn by female figures pictured on the lids of cinerary urns.[8] An example from Cerveteri, from the Castellani Collection, shows an inverted pyramid pendant associated with a lunar crescent.[9] A pair in the Liverpool Museum was found in a clay cinerary urn of the Chiusi type from the first half of the second century BC;[10] interestingly, the recumbent deceased pictured on the urn's lid wears the same type of earring.[11]
Similar examples, especially regarding the disc, are known from the antique market.[12]

End fourth - first half second century BC.

Fig.12. Tomb marker in the form of a female bust. The figure, wrapped in a cloak with her head partially covered, wears a pair of earrings with pyramidal pendants and a two-string necklace with a sunburst of fusiform pendants. From Palestrina. Late third – second centuries BC. Vatican City, Vatican Museums, inv. 16253. Limestone. Height 36.2 cm.

Fig.13. Female head wearing a pair of rosette-shaped earrings with truncated-pyramid pendants and a diadem of ivy leaves alternating with rosettes. From Vulci (?). Late fourth – third centuries BC. Vatican City, Vatican Museums, inv. 16245. Nenfro. Height 29.5 cm.

1. Marshall 1969, p. 181, nos 1666-1667, pl. XXX.
2. Marshall 1969, nos 1664-1665, 1670-1671, 1672-1673.
3. M.I. Artamonov, *Treasures from Scythian Tombs in the Hermitage Museum, Leningrad,* London 1969, p. 77, pl. 309, from Great Bliznitsa, fourth century BC.
4. *Ori di Taranto* 1985, p. 162, no. 74; a pair of earrings with a similar pendant adorn the female head of an antefix at the Taranto Museum, first half of the fourth century BC: *Magna Graecia* 2002, pp. 146-147, no. 10.
5. *Ori di Taranto* 1985, no. 77 = Guzzo 1993, V.D.1.
6. *Ori di Taranto* 1985, no. 78.
7. Hadaczeck 1903, p. 71, Figs 138-139.
8. G. Cateni, in Cristofani, Martelli 1983, pp. 231, no. 254.
9. Caruso 1988, pp. 33-34, no. 58.
10. Johnstone 1932, p. 447, no. 16464, pl. XIX.
11. *Ibid.,* pp. 450-451, no. 10463-10464, pl. XXI.
12. *Kunstwerke der Antike, Auktion XVIII,* 29.11.1958, *Münzen und Medaillen AG,* Basel 1958, p. 51, no. 150, pl. 48.

29. Earring with vase pendant

Gold and garnet. Height 2.7; width 0.75

The disc has a filigree decoration of a central eight-petalled flower inscribed in concentric circles of beaded wire. The pendant is in the form of a vase, the body of which is a globular garnet fastened to a filigree setting.

The type of disc-shaped earring with amphora-shaped pendant was known in the eastern Mediterranean probably already by early Hellenism.[1] In Italy, the amphora in filigree, with a body consisting of one or two gems, is documented with certainty throughout the second century BC both in Magna Graecia as well as in Etruria. It may be paralleled with a disc-shaped earring from Taranto, in the Bari Museum, which features a garnet surmounted by a Crown of Isis and equipped with chains and amphora pendants.[2] For Etruria, it may be compared with a specimen with the same disc, also featuring beads set in the body of an amphora made of filigree, from Vulci in the Berlin Museum.[3] Also from Vulci is a Castellani Collection piece in the British Museum.[4]

A specific comparison for the specimen in this catalogue may be made with one of unknown provenance at Toronto's Royal Ontario Museum,[5] which in turn is comparable to an earring formerly in the Hermitage, from Selino on the island of Crete, later lost on the market.[6]
A style which probably preserved typologies derived from Hellenistic examples may be found in the earrings currently dated to the Roman era, distinguished by a disc inlaid with a cabochon-cut gem in place of the filigree decoration.[7]

Second century BC.

1. Hoffmann, von Claer 1968, pp. 102-103, no. 66, from the Smyrna market, fourth-third centuries BC.
2. *Ori di Taranto* 1985, no. 79a, but with Fig. no. 80 on p. 166 = Guzzo 1993, p. 252, V.B.var.a3.
3. Greifenhagen 1975, p. 48, pl. 39, no. 12.
4. Marshall 1969, pp. 274-275, no. 2335, pl. LI.
5. Denis 1996, pp. 208-209, Fig. 4.
6. *Sotheby's,* 9th November 1931, p. 13, no. 62, pl. VI. Compare also: Zahn 1929, pp. 59-60, no. 116a-b, pl. 52; Marshall 1969, pl. LI, no. 2334, Towneley Collection.
7. Marshall 1969, pp. 274-275, no. 2331, pl. LI, first century AD; Greifenhagen 1975, p. 48, no. 11, pl. 39, first century BC.

30. Antelope or gazelle head earring

Gold. Diameter 1.7

Composed of a hoop of wound gold wires terminating in the head of an antelope or gazelle, whose mouth grips the ring end of the clasp. The protome is made from two die-formed valves of sheet gold soldered together at the seams; the horns are made of spiral-beaded wire.

This earring belongs to a widely diffused class documented between the end of the fourth and the first half of the second century BC, and well defined in early Hellenism under the influence of Persian art.[1]
Many specimens come from Syria and southern Russia,[2] while various examples of Greek provenance are also known.[3] The class is also documented in

Egypt from collection material.[4]
In southern Italy, a similar earring was found in a tomb at Oppidio Mamertina dated to the third century BC.[5] This specimen may be added to the one previously known from Reggio Calabria,[6] where documentation also exists on the twisted wire variant form with a bezel on the clasp.[7] That the latter may have been directly imported from Alexandria, perhaps as a result of the mercenary practices of the Brezi, cannot be ruled out; this occurred with other types of materials at least

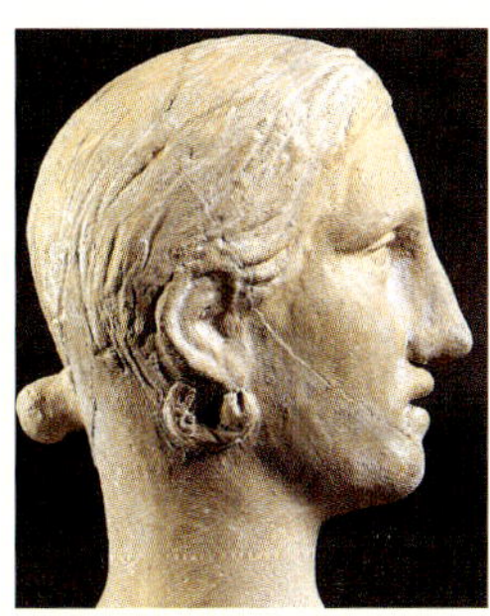

Fig. 14. Female head wearing twisted-wire earrings. From Cerveteri. Late fourth – third centuries BC. Vatican City, Vatican Museums, inv. 13960. Terracotta. Height 24 cm.

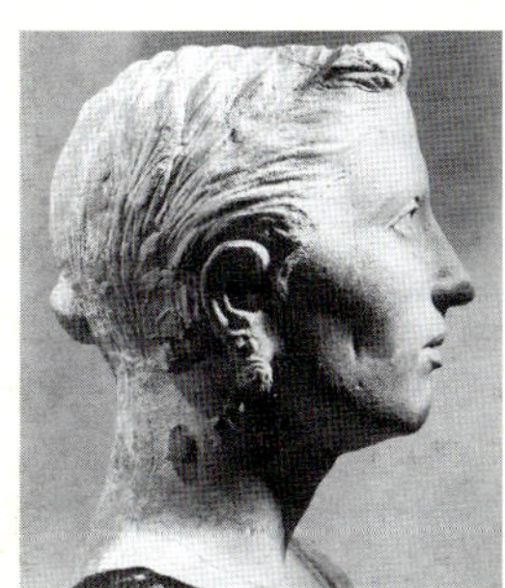

Fig 15. Bust with female head wearing coiled-wire earrings terminating in lion heads. From Cerveteri, at Vignali. 300-250 BC. Vatican City, Vatican Museums, inv. 14107. Terracotta. Height 34.7 cm.

through the end of the third century BC.[8]
The same protomes are also used in other classes of jewelry, as in the clasp of a necklace from Altamura[9] or the terminals of a bracelet from Mottola.[10]

End fourth – third century BC.

1. Pfrommer 1990, pp. 168-172, pl. 30. Cf. also: *Collection d'antiquités Grecques & Romaines, Vente du 11 au 14 mai 1903, Hotel Drouot, Salle n 7,* Paris 1903, no. 254, pl. IX, 15, from Crete; Parkhurst 1961, p. 131, no. 55e, Gutman Collection; *Werke* 1970, p. 10, nos 12-16; Pierides 1971, p. 33, nos 10-12, pl. XXI; Hackens 1976, p. 80, no. 27; Greifenhagen 1975, p. 55, pl. 44, no. 8; *Schmuck der Antike*, 1981, p. 9, no. 23; *Galerie Koller*, 15 November 1982, p. 21, nos 16-17; Ergil 1983, no. 34; *Christie's,* 6 December 2000, no. 59 ; *Christie's,* 11 December 2003, pp. 30-31, no. 368.
2 Hoffmann, Davidson 1965, p. 107; Greifenhagen 1970, p. 44, pl. 22, no. 2, from Kertsch, Merle de Massoneau Collection.
3. *Sammlung Naue* 1908, no. 411 (from a tomb in Athens); Hoffmann, von Claer 1968, p. 115, no. 73, p. 116, no. 74; Laffineur 1980, pp. 398-399, Figs 88-89; *Gold of Greece* 1990, p. 50, pl. 26; Pfrommer 1998, p. 80, Fig. 10, 3.
4. Williams 1924, pp. 135-138, pl. XVII, nos 70-71 (Thebes), 72-74 (Egypt), re-published by: Hoffmann, Davidson 1965, p. 107, nos 27-28 (Brooklyn Museum) and Davidson, Oliver 1984, pp. 48-52, nos 42-47 (Abbot Collection); Vernier 1927, nos 52522-52523, pl. XXXV, in the Cairo Museum, Huber Collection.
5. *Bellezza e lusso* 1992, p. 61, no. 1; Guzzo 1993, p. 258, VII.B.var.a1.
6. Guzzo 1993, p. 258, VII.B.var.a2.
7. *Ibid.*, p. 258, VII.C.var.b1.
8. Guzzo 1993, p. 101.
9. Guzzo 1993, p. 210, type VI.F, no. 4 = *Ori di Taranto* 1984, no. 157.
10. Guzzo 1993, pp. 78-79, Fig. 37, pp. 238, 314-315; *Magna Graecia* 2002, pp. 164-165, no.19.

31. Earring fragment

Gold. Diameter 1.2

Consists of a hoop with unattached terminals, formed from a pair of spiral-beaded wires and a plain wire braided together.

This is an incomplete earring, most likely pertaining to the animal protome typologies - lion, gazelle, bull, griffon - particularly widespread in the Hellenistic period between the last quarter of the fourth century and the third century BC.[1] A specimen from the antique market is known that features a stirrup-shaped terminal.[2]

1. Cf.: Davidson, Oliver 1984, pp. 47-63, nos 41-60; A.E. Feruglio, in *I trucchi e le essenze* 2002, p. 39, no. 2, Orvieto-Castellonchio tomb 2; *Magna Graecia* 2002, pp. 160-161, no. 17, Taranto, Via Molise tomb 1/1966.
2. *Schmuck der Antike* 1981, p. 10, no. 31.

32. Pair of earrings with bird pendant

Gold. Width 1.3

Each earring consists of a circular-section wire shaped into a hoop with both ends curved into hooks; suspended from one of these is a hollow bird-shaped pendant, made from two soldered die-formed valves.

This class was particularly attested in the Apulian area, especially in Canosa, Scocchera Tomb B[1] and

Taranto,[2] from which also derives a specimen with a mesh hoop decorated with fine plumage, stones and blue enamel.[3] There is a close parallel for the specimen in question in a finding from Ruvo[4].

Specimens of undocumented provenance are known from Greece and Asia Minor.[5]

For Etruria, examples are known both from contexts, as in the case of those with a double twisted wire hoop, from the tomb of the *Calisna śepu* of Monteriggioni[6], and from materials of undocumented provenance[7]. Further parallels are known

from materials of unknown provenance[8].

End third - first half second century BC.

1. Greifenhagen 1975, p. 57, pl. 46, 1; Ori di Taranto 1984, no. 124; Guzzo 1993, p. 258, VII.B.4.
2. *Ori di Taranto* 1984, no. 126; Guzzo 1993, p. 258, VII.B.5, variant form with setting on head; Platz - Horster 2001, pp. 77-79, no. 46.
3. *Ori di Taranto* 1984, no. 125; Guzzo 1993, VII.A.1.
4. Marshall 1969, pl. XXXIII, no. 1923.
5. Pollak 1903, pl. X, nos 173-174 (from Athens), 176 (from Smyrna); Greifenhagen 1975, pp. 57-58, no. 9 (purchased in Athens).
6. Hadaczeck 1903, p. 50, Fig. 92 = Greifenhagen 1970, p. 95, no. 8, pl. 72.
7. Caruso 1988, p. 33, no. 57, Castellani Collection; A. Romualdi (ed.), *Il patrimonio disperso. Reperti archeologici sequestrati dalla Guardia di Finanza,* Piombino, Roma 1989, p. 97, no. 118.
8. Amandry 1953, p. 142, pl. LII, 295-296, with a small, round setting on the hoop; Parkhurst 1961, p. 133, no. 56, Gutman Collection; Marshall 1969, no. 1840, pl. XXXII, with small setting; Greifenhagen 1970, p. 95, no. 6, pl. 72; Greifenhagen 1975, p. 58, pl. 46, no. 6.

33. Pair of ring-shaped earrings

Gold. Diameter 1.3/1.4

Earrings formed from a ring of circular-section

wire, with flattened ends shaped into a hook and a perforated plate.

These may be assimilated with the simple gold hoop typology, widely attested throughout the Mediterranean area beginning in the Hellenistic period, and particularly recurrent in the Roman Imperial period,[1] reaching as far as the late Antique and high Middle Ages.[2]

The particular shape of the clasp with perforated plate, in place of the more common ring, also recurs in an earring from the former Falcioni Collection, in the Gregorian Etruscan Museum.[3]

1. Mihovilić 1979, pp. 223-242, pl. 3, no. 14, from Slovenia; Deppert Lippitz 1985, nos 56-57, pls 25-26, second century AD, no. 61, pl. 27, first century AD; Rudolph 1995, p. 273, no. 80, second - fifth century AD; *Trésors d'orfèvrerie Gallo-Romains,* Paris 1989, p. 252, nos 217-218, from Talmont-Saint Hilaire (Vendée). Cf. also: Marshall 1969, pp. 296-297, pl. LIII, nos 2559-2560; Zahn 1929, p. 38, no. 68a-b, pl. 47; Ruseva Slokoska 1991, p. 110, no. 15; R. Laffineur, in AA.VV., *La nécropole d'Amathonte. Tombes 113-367, VI. Bijoux, armes, verre, astragales et coquillages, squelettes,* Nicosie, 1992, pl. I, tomb 199/8.
2. V. Fiocchi Nicolai et al., *Scavi ad Albano Laziale,* in *RAC* 68, 1992, pp. 117-118, sixth century AD; Caliò 2000, pp. 55-57, nos 62-65; Giuntella 2000, p. 33, nos 26-27, pl. IV, from Cornus, fourth - seventh century AD.
3. Caliò 2000, p. 57, no. 65.

34. Earring

Gold. Height 2.6; width 1.15

The earring consists of a curved plain wire hoop in which a suspended amphora-shaped pendant is strung.

Similar pendants have been found on necklaces from the Hellenistic period.[1]

For the annular portion, the earring may be paralleled with types from the Roman era dated between the first century BC and the first century AD.[2]

1. Greifenhagen 1975, p. 21, nos 4-5, pl. 12, from Kertsch, second half fourth - third century BC; cf. also: Rudolph 1995, p. 191, no. 45, from the eastern Mediterranean, Burton Y. Berry Collection.
2. Siviero 1954, p. 108, no. 474.

35. Pair of ring-shaped earrings with pendant

Gold and glass paste (?). Diameter 1.8; height 3.2

Each earring is made from a simple hoop of circular-section wire with both ends curved into hooks. The pendant consists of a bead of green glass paste (?), fastened to a looped pin suspended from the ring.

These earrings represent a variant form of the simple circle type with knotted ends; they may be paralleled with examples from the Vesuvian area, with threaded pearls.[1] In this area the earrings usually recurred from the first century BC to the first century AD.[2] The type, which varied for the most part in the form of the pendants, was widespread in the Roman Imperial era until the second and third centuries AD,[3] with later developments that may have reached as far as the fourth century AD.[4]
Cf. no. **36**.

First - second centuries AD.

1. Scatozza Höricht 1989, pp. 38-40, nos 24-25.
2. Siviero 1954, no. 298; D'Ambrosio, De Carolis 1997, p. 31, no. 27, pl. II, Pompeii-Porta Marina.
3. Gramatopol, Craciunescu 1967, p. 143, no. 72, pl. X, 14; Marshall 1969, p. 285, nos 2421-2422, pl. LII, with club pendant; Pfeiler 1970, pp. 19, 62, pl. 27, 6; Deppert Lippitz 1985, pl. 27, nos 61, 63, first century AD, pl. 27, no. 62, second century AD.
4. Jovanovic 1978, p. 39, no. 12, Fig. 65, from Ul. Knezelska, Niš, *Moesia superior*.

36. Pair of ring-shaped earrings with pendant

Gold and pearl. Diameter 1.0; height 2.4

Each specimen is composed of a simple hoop of circular-section wire with both ends curved into hooks. Suspended from the hoop is the pendant, consisting of a perforated pearl fastened to a coiled wire.

This earring typology, both with and without a pendant,[1] was highly recurrent from the first century BC in the Vesuvian region.[2]
The preference given to pearls in the creation of jewelry appeared particularly marked after the Roman conquest of Egypt, after which time, small pearls were even seen included in jewelry of ordinary manufacture.[3]
In general, parallels for this type of earring may be made in the realm of Roman Egypt,[4] with a chronology that, for objects similar to this one, reaches as far as the second and third centuries AD.[5] Such a chronological context seems to be confirmed by the earrings in the Eauze treasure, in Aquitaine, in which two-thirds of the coins found are dated between 249-261/262 AD.[6] A finding in the Balkan region, however, testifies to a wider diffusion of the type in the provinces of the Roman Empire.[7] Other specimens are known

from the antique market.[8]

Cf. no. **35.**

First - second/third centuries AD.

1. Siviero 1954, p. 108, no. 474, from Pompeii.
2. Siviero 1954, no. 300, pl. 194, c-d, from Herculaneum, with coiled wire and pearl pendant; Scatozza Höricht 1989, pp. 38-40, nos 24-25, from Herculaneum - Suburban Baths, arcade 4, with pearl.
3. Scatozza Höricht 1989, loc. cit.
4. W.M. Flinders Petrie, E. Mackay, *Heliopolis, Kafr Ammar and Shurafa,* London 1915, p. 45, pl. LII, 6, from Shurafa; W.M Flinders Petrie, *Hyksos and Israelite Cities,* London 1906, pl. XL, no. 475, from Gheyta.
5. Williams 1924, pp. 128-129, pl. XVI, nos 59-60 = Davidson, Oliver 1984, p. 112, no. 114, A-B.
6. Guiraud 1996, p. 63, Fig. 4.1.
7. Jovanovic 1978, p. 40, no. 19, Fig. 68, from Scupi, dated to the fourth century AD.
8. *Ars Antiqua AG,* Lagerkatalog 3, Dezember 1967, Luzern 1967, pl. XIV, no. 99d, with small setting inserted in the hoop; *Charles Ede LTD,* Catalogue 149, London 1990-93, no. 62g; *ibid.,* no. 62k, with a double pendant.

37. Earring

Gold, pearls and coral (?). Height 1.7

Simple hoop of circular-section wire strung with a coral bead and two small pearls.

The type undoubtedly has late-Hellenistic precedents: a hoop earring strung with small gold rings alternating with two glass paste beads derives from a first-century BC tomb in Taranto.[1] Another example, from the Hellenistic or Roman period, was found in the Cyprus excavations.[2] Other materials of similar typology are generally dated to the Roman Imperial period.[3]
Probably first - second centuries AD.

1. *Ori di Taranto* 1985, p. 192, no. 133.
2. *SwCypEx* IV, 3, p. 116, Fig. 34, 9, p. 118, no. 2.
3. Williams 1924, pp. 131-132, pl. XVI, no. 66 and Davidson, Oliver 1984, p. 125, no. 147, from Sakkara, first - third century AD; Ergil 1983, p. 35, no. 65, pair, at the Istanbul Museum; Deppert, Lippitz 1985, no. 64, pl. 28, first - second century AD, with a single glass paste bead, in the Römisch-Germanisches Zentralmuseum in Mainz.

38. Pair of earrings

Gold and pearl. Diameter 1.4

Each earring is formed from a circular-section wire to which is attached a bezel in the shape of a section of a sphere, decorated with a pearl. The two ends are shaped into a hook-and-eye clasp.

Similar examples are known without the pearl and with a shield bordered by knurled wire.[1]
These earrings may be considered a more elaborate version of the simple hoop type (Cf. no. **33**) and comparable to those with a stud or shield on the clasp.[2]

Second century AD.

1. Deppert Lippitz 1985, pl. 26, no. 58, mid-second century AD.
2. Caliò 2000, pp. 57-58, nos 67-68. For the shape in general, with shield and small stud in the place of the pearl, compare: C. Preda, *Callatis, Necropola romano-bizantina,* Bucuresti 1980, pl. XVII.

39. Pair of earrings with pendant and gems

Gold and glass paste. Height 2.7; width 0.6

Composed of a wire hoop attached to a square frame containing a red gem. The pendant consists of a simple wire fastened to a green prismatic (emerald-cut) stone with a perforation for the passage of the wire.

These find an immediate parallel with specimens found in Lyon, in the Musée des Beaux Arts, dated between the end of the second and first decades of the third century AD.[1] Other similar examples, with pearls, are known from the antique market.[2]

End second - first decades third century AD.

1. A. Comarmond, *Description de l'écrin d'une dame romaine trouvé à Lyon en 1841,* Paris-Lyon 1844, nos 19-20; Barini 1958, Fig. on p. 20; Pfeiler 1970, p. 96, pl. 32, 2.
2. *Christie's,* 11 December 2003, p. 57, no. 430, on right.

40. Pair of earrings with pendant and gems

Gold, glass paste and amethyst. Height 2.9; width 1.1

Composed of a wire hoop attached to a lozenge-shaped frame containing a green glass paste setting with a convex surface. The pendant consists of a simple wire fastened to a spheroid amethyst bead with a perforation for the passage of the wire.

Similar examples, but with a square rather than rhomboid frame, and with coiled wire on the pendant, are dated to the second century AD.[1]
Various earrings of this typology were found in the Cyprus excavations.[2]

Second - third centuries AD.

1. Davidson, Oliver 1984, p. 90, no. 78. For further comparison: Rudolph, Rudolph 1973, p. 164, no. 132b; Davidson, Oliver 1984, p. 119, no. 134, second - third century AD.
2. *SwCypEx* IV, 3, p. 116, Fig. 34,23-24, p. 119, no. 11a-11b.

41. Pair of earrings

Gold and stone. Max. diameter 2.2

Each earring is composed of a large, twisted hoop with open ends in the form of a cornucopia, made from a twisted square-section wire. One extremity, terminating in a perforated disc, is encased by a red ovoid stone or glass paste bead, set between a plain wire ring and a ring of granules. The smooth opposite end is tapered.

Twisted-hoop earrings, terminating in dolphin heads preceded by a bead set between rings of granules, are typical of late Hellenism, second-first centuries BC.[1]
A similar earring, the body made of a knurled wire and a plain wire twisted together and with a small pearl inserted on the clasp, comes from the island of Anaphe (Cyclades) and is dated to the second-third centuries AD.[2]

1. *Sotheby's*, 10th July 1990, p. 9, no. 191; Platz-Horster 2001, pp. 77-78, no. 45, from Smyrna, 250-150 BC.
2. Greifenhagen 1975, no. 4, pl. 49.

42. Pair of twisted-wire earrings

Gold. Diameter 1.1/1.2

Earrings formed from a thick hoop of double twisted wire, tapered toward the ends, which are tied with a coiled wire.

Twisted earrings with tapered ends that are smooth or terminate in hooks are documented in Etruria in the Hellenistic period.[1]
The pair in question appears to be fairly close to a popular type from the Roman Imperial era, particularly in the eastern Mediterranean. An accurate parallel may be made with earrings found in

a Roman-era tomb in Kirmasti, ancient Miletopolis, in Asia Minor, dated to the second century AD.[2] Other specimens of a similar typology, from Cyprus, are conserved in the British Museum[3] and are known from the art market[4]. Similar shapes were also adopted in much later Ostrogothic goldwork from southern France, dated to the fifth-eighth centuries AD,[5] or even Viking, from the tenth-eleventh centuries.[6]

Second century AD.

1. Orvieto-Castellonchio, tomb 2, late fourth – third century BC: A.E. Feruglio, in *I trucchi e le essenze* 2002, p. 39, no. 1 with comparisons; Gioiella tomb 5, early second century BC: L. Bonomi, in *I trucchi e le essenze* 2002, p. 61, no. 5.
2. Williams, Tatton-Brown, Walker 1991, pp. 77-83, Fig. 6, no. 5.
3. Marshall 1969, nos 2473, 2508, pl. LIII.
4. *Christie's*, 10 December 1985, pp. 12-13, nos 34-35.
5. von Jenny, Volbach 1933, p. 44, nos 5, 9, pl. 26.
6. *Sotheby's*, 10th July 1990, pp. 12-13, no. 201, from Sandy Cove, Devon.

43. Pair of earrings

Gold and glass paste. Max.diameter 2.2/2.3

Each earring is formed from a flattened metal hoop, lunate in form and terminating in tapered wire ends shaped into a hook and eye. Next to the closure the earring is ornamented with a setting in the form of a spherical section with a twisted-wire border, containing a white glass paste bead decorated with spiral ridges and fastened with a hammered pin.

A similarly "crescent"-shaped earring, known from the market, is hypothetically dated to the second century BC.[1]
For the variant form with a wire suspension hoop, a parallel may be found in a specimen generically dated to the Roman period.[2]

1. *Christie's* 1995, pp. 22-23, no. 133.
2. Greifenhagen 1975, p. 62, no. 17, pl. 49.

44. Pair of earrings

Gold. Max. diameter 1.3

Each earring is formed from a ring of semicircular-section wire, decorated at both ends by three

rings of spiral-beaded wire, alternating with plain wire rings; one extremity terminates in a hollow spherical element.

Earrings of similar typology, in the opening mechanism, are attested in a tomb in Adria dated to the third century BC.[1]

1. Fogolari 1958, p. 32, Fig. 7 in the center, with comparisons.

45. Earring with pyramidal-cluster pendant

Gold. Height 2.8; width 1.4

Composed of a simple hoop-shaped wire with hooked ends, equipped with an inverted triangular pyramid pendant composed of small spheres, to the tip of which is attached a second cluster of four spheres.

The circular earring type with a pyramid-of-spheres pendant is documented from the second century AD, in the Assos necropolis in Asia Minor,[1] and became subsequently widespread in late-Roman Egypt.[2] Other examples, formerly in the Merle de Massoneau Collection, come from southern Russia and are dated to the second-third

centuries AD.[3]
A similar or later chronological attribution is indicated for further analogous specimens[4].
This typology seems to have been the inspiration for high Medieval specimens in silver, found in the Sardinian necropolis of Cornu, dated to the sixth century AD.[5]

Third - fourth centuries AD.

1. Reiblich 1996, p. 134, no. 21, pl. 12, 4.
2. M.J. Clédat, *Fouilles à Qasr-Gheit,* in *Annales du Service des Antiquités de l'Egypte 12,* 1912, p. 160, pl. III, top center, from Qasr Gheit; Marshall 1969, no. 2601, from Cairo; Williams 1924, pp. 121-123, pl. XV, no. 51 = Davidson, Oliver 1984, pp. 93-94, no. 83, from Sakkara, third-fourth centuries AD; Greifenhagen 1975, p. 64, pl. 50, no. 12, from Egypt, fourth-fifth centuries AD; Vernier 1927, no. 52551, pl. XXXIV, with large grains, in the Cairo Museum, Huber Collection; *ibid.,* nos 52506-52507, pl. XXXVII, with a cluster of small grains and a final cluster of three larger grains, also in the Cairo Museum.
3. Greifenhagen 1970, pp. 45-47, pl. 23, no. 16 (similar, but with twisted wire hoop), nos 9-11, 14, 21.
4. Segall 1938, pp. 103-104, no. 138, pl. 35, with a cluster of three grains, fourth-fifth centuries AD; Marshall 1969, no. 2596-2597, pl. LIV, from Kouklia Paphos, circa second century AD; *ibid.,* no. 2600, pl. LIV; Hoffmann, von Claer 1968, pp. 133-134, no. 87, second-third centuries AD.
5. Giuntella 2000, pp. 33-34, no. 29.

46. Pair of hoop-shaped earrings with pyramidal-cluster pendant

Gold. Height 1.7; diameter 1.1

Each earring is composed of a ribbed hoop, decorated centrally with beaded wire. Suspended from the lower portion is a cluster of four hollow spheres arranged in a pyramid, alternating with grains, with a smaller underlying cluster of similarly disposed grains.

These present an affinity with late-Roman earrings, of Syro-Egyptian typology, that were widespread in the eastern Mediterranean, of controversial chronology due to the absence of definitive provenance contexts, but which are dated beginning in the second-third centuries AD, and which are generally characterized by a smooth or decorated shield inserted on the twisted wire hoop.[1]
The beaded decoration on the hoop associated with the cluster of spheres that characterizes the specimen in question, may also be found on later Byzantine earrings, dated to the sixth-seventh centuries AD based on monetary associations,[2] which evidently follow the tradition of typologies popular in the eastern Mediterranean during the late Roman Imperial period.
For the beading on the hoop, these may be compared to a specimen from the Cafiero Collection in the Barletta Museum, erroneously thought to be Etruscan,[3] and with a pair from the Gregorian Etruscan Museum, former Falcioni Collection.[4]
It is therefore possible to distinguish these earrings from those with analogous clusters but with plain, tubular bodies, referable instead to the Etruscans.[5]

Third century AD or later.

1. C.R. Clark, *Egyptian granular jewelry,* in *Bulletin of the Metropolitan Museum of Art* 23, 1928, pp. 252-253, Fig. 8, New York, Metropolitan Museum of Art; Zahn 1929, no. 70, a-b, pl. 52, former Schiller Collection; Amandry 1953, p. 143, nos 308-309, pl. LIII; *Antike Kunstwerke. Ars Antiqua,* AG Luzern, Auction II, (14/05/1960), Luzern 1960, p. 64, no. 186, pl. 72, from the antique market; A. Greifenhagen, *Antiker Goldschmuck in amerikanischen Privatbesitz,* in *Pantheon* 25, 1967, p. 88, Fig. 16, San Francisco, John Huston Collection; *Collection de Monsieur le Comte X... Bijoux d'or, orfèvrerie, vases phéniciens antiques,* Vente Hotel Drouot, Salle 8 (17/11/1972), Paris 1972, no. 35; Rudolph, Rudolph 1973, p. 208, no. 166, b, former Burton Y. Berry Collection; Davidson, Oliver 1984, p. 122, no. 138, A-B, Brooklyn Museum; *Christie's,* 16 July 1985, p. 14, nos 49-50.
2. Ross 1965, no. 85, pl. XLVIII, with comparisons.
3. van den Driessche 1975, pp. 9-10, no. 6, Fig. 6.
4. Caliò 2000, p. 63, no. 81; further comparisons from the market: *Christie's,* 16 July 1985, p. 14, no. 52; *Christie's,* 6 December 2000, no. 152, first row center.
5. Hadaczek 1903, p. 60, Fig. 117, in the Vatican's Gregorian Etruscan Museum; Marshall 1969, no. 2249, pl. XLIV, former Castellani Collection; Hoffmann, von Claer 1968, p. 189, no. 128.

47. Earring

Gold, stone and pearls. Max. height 2.8

Formed from a circular-section wire hoop, with the ends shaped into a wide hook and eye, on which are strung seven small pearls and a green stone or glass paste bead.

For classification, cf. no. **48**.

48. Earring

Gold, stone and pearls. Max. height 3.3

Formed from a circular-section wire hoop, with the ends shaped into a wide hook and eye, the latter reinforced by a coiled wire. Five small pearls and a gray stone or glass paste bead are strung onto the ring.

This finds parallels in Roman specimens from the early Imperial period, dated to the first-second centuries AD.[1] An earring from Taranto, out of context, is dated instead to the first half of the first century BC.[2]

First - second centuries AD.

1. London, British Museum, Castellani Collection (Marshall 1969, no. 2679, pl. LV); Mainz, Römische-Germanisches Zentralmuseum (Böhme 1974, pp. 8-10, 35, Fig. 9, lower left. Cf. also: Pollak 1903, p. 90, pl. XI, 254; *ibid.*, no. 255, from Costantinople; Amandry 1953, p. 143, nos 306-307, pl. LIII, Héléne Stathatos Collection; Greifenhagen 1975, pl. 49, 1-3; Laffineur 1980, p. 431, no. 129, Fig. 144; *Schmuck der Antike* 1981, p. 11, no. 33.
2. *Ori di Taranto* 1985, p. 192, no. 134.

49. Pair of earrings

Gold and stones. Max. height 3.2

Formed from an S-shaped circular-section wire terminating at one end in a small sphere, to which is fastened a wire thread that externally bears five

white semi-tooled stones with reddish striations.

These earrings may be paralleled with a pair in Hamburg's Museum für Kunst und Gewerbe, dated to the first-second centuries AD.[1]
This was a particularly widespread type in the Roman Imperial period, similar examples having been found in Cyprus.[2] It is iconographically documented in Roman Egypt in mummy portraits dated between the second half of the first and the first half of the second century AD.[3]

Second half first - second century AD.

1. Hoffmann, von Claer 1968, pp. 132-133, no. 86 = Higgins 1980, p. 178, pl. 54,G.
2. J.L. Myres, M. Ohnefalsch - Richter, *A Catalogue of the Cyprus Museum*, Oxford 1899, pl. VII, nos 4076-4077; Marshall 1969, nos 2677-2678, from Episkopi, with incised gems.
3. C.C. Edgar, *Graeco-Egyptian Coffins. Masks and Portraits*, Le Caire 1905, no. 33135, pl. XVI, from Meir, second half first century AD; *ibid.*, no. 33263, pl. XLII, from Fayoum, with Faustina Maggiore type portrait; cf. C.C. Edgar, *On the dating of the Fayoum portraits*, in *JHS* 25, 1905, pp. 229-230, Fig. 1,c.

50. Pair of earrings

Gold. Length 1.9; head 0.6

Each earring is formed from a moulded circular-section wire terminating in a hemispherical plain button.

These are most likely comparable to a type from the Roman period, datable based on second-third century AD contexts and particularly documented in Cypriot findings.[1] An accurate parallel for the version without a pendant may be made with an earring found in a Roman tomb in Karpathos, dated to the second-third centuries AD.[2] An analogous chronology is suggested by specimens from Slovenia.[3]
Similar examples are documented by collection material from the antique market.[4]

Second - third century AD.

1. A.S. Murray, A.H. Smith, H.B. Walters, *Excavations in Cyprus*, London 1900, p. 83, pl. XIII, no. 22 = Marshall 1969, no. 2376, pl. LII, from Curium, tomb 81, with pendant composed of a bead tied to a pin with coiled wire.
2. Marshall 1969, no. 2634, pl. LV.
3. Mihovilić 1979, p. 239, pl. 3, no. 16, third - fourth centuries AD.
4. Parkhurst 1961, p. 149, no. 72.

51. Earring with double garnet bezel

Gold and garnet. Height 2.4; Width 1.0

Earring with two adjacent bezels, one round and one drop-shaped, each composed of a plain wire bordered by spiral-beaded and beaded wires and flanked by tiny spirals surmounted by grains. Each bezel contains a red cabochon-cut garnet.
A similar drop-shaped bezel may be seen in an earring from Cyprus, dated to the second century AD,[1] and in later circular earrings from southern Russia, Merle de Massoneau Collection, dated to the third-fourth centuries AD.[2] The late chronology of these pieces with drop-shaped garnets was initially a cause for debate, which led to the proposition of a late-Hellenistic dating rather than late-Antique.[3] This uncertainty may now be adjusted by the study of contexts safely attributable to the Roman Imperial era. Analogous drop-shaped garnets may be observed in the beads of a Roman Imperial necklace from Mentana dated to the Claudian period,[4] as well as in the bezels of a necklace from Artena, from the second half of the second - first half of the third century AD.[5]

Further earrings worth noting are specimens from New York's Metropolitan Museum of Art[6] as well as very similar ones from the Zurich market.[7]

Second - third century AD.

1. Marshall 1969, no. 2595, pl. LIV.
2. Greifenhagen 1970, p. 45, pl. 22, nos 17-19.
3. Cf. review of Greifenhagen 1970 by B. Deppert Lippitz, in *Gnomon* 46, 1974, p. 390, whose observations were later acknowledged by Greifenhagen 1975, p. 66, pl. 52, no. 1.
4. Bordenache Battaglia 1983, pp. 40-45, no. 3.
5. Scarpignato 1978-79, p. 232, no. 1. pl. I.
6. Alexander 1928, pl. I below.
7. *Frank Sternberg*, Auct. XXVII, 1994, no. 891, pl. XLVII. Cf. also: Zahn 1929, p. 39, no. 72a-b, pl. 45; Rudolph, Rudolph 1973, pp. 217, 219, no. 171j; *Christie's*, 8 December 1999, p. 39, no. 75; *Christie's*, 13 December 2002, pp. 50-51, no. 615.

52. Earring

Gold and stone. Height 3.0; width 1.1

The earring, equipped with a simple hook, is composed of an elliptical fringed shield containing a smooth blue stone, from which are suspended two bar-like pendants with coiled extremities.

Similar examples are thought to be late-Roman or proto-Byzantine and are currently dated to the third-fourth centuries AD, without, however, ruling out a later placement.[1]

1. Hoffmann, von Claer 1968, p. 143, no. 92; Mihovilić 1979, p. 239, no. 33, pl. 3, no. 15, third century AD.

53. Pair of earrings

Gold and glass paste. Height 2.6/2.9; width 0.8

Each earring is formed from a hemispherical boss, open in back and equipped with a movable hook, from which is suspended a faceted blue glass paste pendant fastened to a thick wire terminating in a ring.

This appears to be an elaboration, with the enrichment of the pendant, of a type that was widespread in Italy,[1] Greece and the eastern Mediterranean between the first and second centuries AD.[2] In particular, it appears to be very similar to highly popular specimens in Syria and the eastern Mediterranean.[3]

Second - third centuries AD.

1. Higgins 1980, p. 178, pl. 54,H, from Pozzuoli, first - second centuries AD; D'Agostino, De Carolis 1997, p. 88, no. 261, pl. XXVI, from the ancient coast of Herculaneum, first century AD.
2. Atasoy 1974, p. 262, pl. 52, Fig. 4, from Turkey; Davidson, Oliver 1984, p. 89, no. 76.
3. For a close comparison: Davidson, Oliver 1984, p. 114, nos 119, A-B, 120, second century AD; *ibid.*, p. 115, no. 121, A-B, second - third centuries AD. Cf. also: Greifenhagen 1975, p. 62, pl. 49, 11; *Charles Ede LTD London*, Catalogue 149, London 1990-93, no. 62m; *Christie's*, 11 December 2003, p. 44, no. 394.

54. Pair of earrings

Gold and stone. Height 4.3/4.4; width 1.1

Consisting of a hollow boss in the form of a spherical section, to which are attached a simple wire hook and a pendant with a green semi-tooled stone (beryllium?), set between a double ring of grains and a small red bead that are joined by a pin terminating in a ring flanked by two grains.

For the typology in general, cf. no. **53**.

55. Earring bezel

Gold and glass paste. Diameter 1.0

Circular bezel with upturned borders containing a green glass paste button.

This is probably an unspecified element from an earring, traceable to typologies affirmed in the Roman world during the Imperial period.[1]

End second - third century AD.

1. Marshall 1969, nos 2668-2669, pl. LV; Zahn 1929, p. 39, no. 75a-b, pl. 45, with three pendants, Baurat Schiller Collection; Pfeiler 1970, p. 96, pl. 32, from Lyon, late second - first decades third century AD.

56. Pair of earrings with frontal face

Gold. Height 2.6; width 1.1

These earrings picture a frontal face in die-formed sheet gold, bordered by plain wire circles set between twisted wire filigree. Suspended from below are three tubular pendants of wound wire with a grain on each tip. A small boss is attached to the bottom of the suspension loop.

These are typologically akin to specimens from southern Russia, from the Merle de Massoneau Collection, dated to the second-third centuries AD, that differ only in the absence of the wire circle border and the boss.[1] Also comparable are two earrings from the area of Niš, dated between the second half of the

third and the fourth centuries AD.[2] Worth noting also are two similar specimens, with the head of Medusa in onyx and three pendants with pearls and amethysts.[3]

Third - fourth century AD.

1. Greifenhagen 1970, p. 44, pl. 21, no. 5.
2. Jovanovic 1978, p. 39, nos 4-5, p. 111, Figs 61-62.
3. Sotheby's, December 9, 2003, p. 34, no. 23.

57. *Pair of earrings with human mask

Gold. Height 3.0; width 1.2

Each earring is composed of an oval sheet gold apotropaic human mask, from which is suspended a bivalve die-formed pendant in the form of an owl. The suspension hook consists of a simple moulded wire.

For human mask typologies, known only from materials of undocumented provenance, cf. no. **58**.

58. Pair of earrings with human mask

Gold and glass paste. Height 3.9/4.0; width 1.1

Each earring is composed of a die-formed human mask bordered by a double braided wire. The plain, circular-section wire suspension hook is fixed to the rear. The pendant consists of a globular blue glass paste bead set between two sheet gold semispheres and suspended on a twisted and spirally wound wire.

The human mask type of earring, rendered in spiral-beaded or twisted wire, is documented by a specimen from the antique market in the region of Baalbeck, probably datable to the Roman Imperial period.[1]
An accurate parallel may be made with an earring from the former Cafiero Collection, in the Barletta Museum.[2]

First - third centuries AD.

1. *Collection de Monsieur le Comte X, Vente Hotel Drouot - Salle n° 8*, 17/11/1972, Paris 1972, no. 37.
2. van den Driessche 1975, pp. 11-12, no. 8, pl. II; see quoted comparison with a new specimen at the Museo di Siracusa.

59. Pair of earrings

Gold. Height 4.1; Width 1.5

These earrings are composed of an umbonate elliptical shield decorated with two confronting spirals and an underlying arched row of granules. They are equipped with an apical ring where the movable suspension hook is inserted. Suspended below is a cluster of hollow spheres edged with granules that surround the spheres and fall downward in rectangular strips.

This pair of earrings belongs to a type widespread in the Roman Imperial period and peculiar to the Oriental provinces, particularly documented in Syria, Lebanon, Palestine and Egypt[1]. Various specimens are known in the Museums of Damascus and Beirut;[2] one comes from Hauran, in northern Syria.[3]

A dated context is supplied by a tomb in Jaffa from the third century AD.[4]

A variant form of the same type, lacking the double spiral on the shield, is documented by a specimen said to come from Turkey[5] and by a pair from the Huston Collection in San Francisco.[6]

Second - third centuries AD.

1. Cf. Zahn 1929, p. 38, no. 71a-b; Segall 1938, no. 132, pl. 34; Amandry 1953, I, nos 308-309; *Antike Kunstwerke, Auktion II (14/05/1960), Ars Antiqua AG Luzern,* Luzern 1960, p. 64, no. 187, pl. 72; von Bothmer 1961, p. 73, pl. 102, no. 286, from Palestine; Zouhdi 1971, p. 99, pl. XV, no. 14, from Zawieh (Syria); Rudolph, Rudolph 1973, p. 102, no. 78b; Hackens 1976, pp. 116-118, no. 52; *Galerie Günter Puhze, Katalog 5,* Freiburg 1983, no. 66; *Galerie Günter Puhze, Katalog 6,* Freiburg n.d., no. 108; *Galerie Günter Puhze, Katalog 8,* Freiburg 1989, no. 46; *Sotheby's,* 13th-14th Dec. 1990, p. 74, no. 95; Zouhdi 1989, p. 562, no. 16, Fig. 210d; Galerie Günter Puhze, Katalog 9, Freiburg 1991, no. 32; *Galerie Günter Puhze, Katalog 10,* Freiburg 1993, no. 46; *Christie's London, Antiquities and Souvenirs of the Grand Tour, 27 October 1993,* pp. 24-25, no. 106; Rudolph 1995, pp. 239-240, no. 66.B.1-2; *Christie's,* 21 April 1999, p. 59, no. 140; *Christie's,* 13 December 2002, pp. 58-59, no. 639, later republished in *Christie's,* 11 December 2003, p. 52, no. 418; *Christie's,* 11 December 2003, p. 45, no. 395.
2. Hoffmann, von Claer 1968, pp. 139-141, no. 90, Hamburg, Museum für Kunst und Gewerbe.
3. *Collection de Monsieur le Comte X... Bijoux d'or, orfèvrerie, vases phéniciens antiques. Vente Hotel Drouot, Salle 8,* 17/11/1972, Paris 1972, nos 46-47, pl. 1.
4. Higgins 1980, p. 178, pl. 54, D.
5. Deppert Lippitz 1985, no. 50, pl. 24.
6. Greifenhagen 1967, pp. 88-89, Figs 17-20.

60. *Pair of earrings with lion protome (?)

Gold. Height 4.8/4.6; width 1.5/1.8
One conical pendant missing.

Each earring is composed of a rectangular shield with concave edges, bordered by a double twisted wire that forms two symmetrical loops. The interior is decorated with plain wire circles. Attached to the shield is a lion (?) protome with open jaws, made from two symmetrical die-formed valves soldered together at the seams. Suspended from below are two hollow conical elements with embossed decorations similar to the biconical beads on necklace no. **76**: a frieze of small circles with radiating rays (solar symbol) alternating with a plain band and a row of small bosses. The tubular suspension hook has a thickened extremity decorated with a small ring of double twisted wire.

61. *Pair of earrings with monstrous mask

Gold and gems. Height 4.0/3.7; width 1.4/1.2

The body of each earring consists of a die-formed sheet gold mask of a monstrous creature. The plain wire suspension hook is inserted in the top and is fastened with a double knot. Suspended from below is a pendant made from a wire wound into a spring and rings, to the bottom of which is fastened a green gem.

62. *Pair of earrings

Gold. Height 4.5/4.2; width 1.9

The elliptical body is decorated centrally with a flower composed of seven beaded wire circles

Fig.16. Female head wearing earrings with pendants and a crown of pearls. From Cerveteri, 1828 excavations. Second half fourth – first half third century BC. Vatican City, Vatican Museums, inv. 13806. Terracotta. Height 25 cm.

surmounted by granules, flanked by two similar circles located on the main axis. The border is decorated with beaded wire and a row of circles without granules. Suspended from the center is an acorn pendant, made from two die-formed and soldered valves, fixed to the body by a braided wire rod with annular terminals. Two hollow drop-shaped pendants hang from either side.

63. *Pair of earrings

Gold. Height 3.3; width 1.9/2.0

The body of each earring consists of an elliptical

bezel, edged with granules forming a fringed border. Applied to the front is a die-formed frog confronting a wire snake. Three pendants are suspended from below: in the center, a twisted strip terminating in a granule, and on either side a moulded rod. The suspension hook is a simple pin.

64. *Pair of earrings

Gold. Height 5.7; width 2.6/2.7

The body of each earring consists of an elliptical bezel, edged with granules forming a fringed bor-

der. Cut-out sheet gold flowers with central granules are applied to the front, and three granules are located on the main axis. Suspended from below are three pendants terminating in granules. The suspension hook is a simple pin.

65. *Pair of earrings

Gold. Height 3.3; width 1.6

The body of each earring consists of an elliptical

bezel, bordered by a denticulated rod with a hammered imitation of spooled wire and a fringed border consisting of a row of triangles. On the front is a sinuous wire surrounded by granules arranged in an almond shape.

66. **Pair of earrings

Gold. Height 9.7/9.8; max. width 4.2/4.5

Each earring is composed of a wire with hook-shaped ends shaped into a circle, along which are disposed four hollow sheet gold spheres decorated along the soldered seams with circular flowers alternating with granules. Four graduated wire rings arranged concentrically and fixed in the slots of a medial tongue are suspended from the

lunate pendant, decorated with circular flowers. A row of four granules hangs from either extremity of the lunate pendant.

For classification, cf. no. **67.

67. **Pair of earrings

Gold. Height 9.6/11.0; width 4.2/4.0

Each earring is composed of a wire circle with hook-shaped ends, along which are inserted four hollow sheet gold spheres, decorated along the soldered seams with double twisted wire circles. A lunate pendant is fastened to the center, decorated with a twisted wire that outlines the seams and forms V-shaped designs and circles. Suspended from the pendant are four graduated wire circles arranged concentrically and inserted in the openings of a twisted wire. Hanging from either extremity of the lunate pendant are two twisted wire pendants: one consists of a succession of five circles, while the other is a rod with an apical circle.

This is probably a fake, inspired by typologies of Roman earrings widespread in Cyprus, in the form of a flattened lunar crescent, with plain or twisted wire decoration, dated to the second century AD.[1] For the shape of the hoop with inserted spheres, a comparison may be made with two pairs of earrings from Thebes, found in a tomb dated to the first century AD, featuring hollow spheres decorated with filigree circles, similar also in dimension;[2] further analogous compositions have been seen in later Byzantine earrings with small globes from the ninth to eleventh centuries AD.[3]

1. Marshall 1969, nos 2454, 2458, 2461-2462, pl. LIII.
2. Marshall 1969, nos 2565-2567, pl. LIII.
3. D'Angela 1989, pp. 34-35, no. 10.

NECKLACES

68. Necklace with anchor and vase pendants

Silver. Anchor pendants: height 2.5; width 2.7; thickness 0.7
Vase pendants: height 2.3; width 1.4/0.6

Reassembled from four anchor-shaped pendants and two hollow vase-shaped pendants. The former, consisting of two die-formed sheet gold valves, are decorated along the seams with a double twisted wire. The cylindrical suspension tubes

are made from coiled wire. The vase pendants have plain wire rings at either extremity of the cylindrical neck. The top is sealed by a soldered disc to which is attached the cylindrical suspension tube, also in this case consisting of a tube of coiled wire.

Plain anchor pendants were found in tomb II at Banditella in Marsiliana D'Albegna, dated to the first quarter of the seventh century BC.[1]
Analogous anchor pendants, but in gold and decorated with granulation, are attested in Vulci throughout the seventh century BC, as may be observed on a necklace in Munich from the former L. Bonaparte Collection.[2] Pendants similar to those on the Monaco necklace, with the same decorative attributes, make up the Louvre necklace, from the former Campana Collection.[3]
The anchor motif appeared in the punched decoration on a gold pectoral from the Guerriero tomb in Tarquinia, dated to the end of the eighth century BC,[4] and may also be seen in the decoration on bronze shields from the Regolini Galassi Tomb in Cerveteri,[5] as well as on specimens from the Avvolta tomb in Tarquinia,[6] the Grande Tomba 3 in Fabriano,[7] and those attributed to the Barberini Tomb in Palestrina, from the second quarter of the seventh century BC.[8]
Vase-shaped pendants in precious materials are documented in Cerveteri on a necklace from the Regolini Galassi Tomb,[9] as well as in Palestrina, on a reassembled necklace in the Villa Giulia Castellani Collection,[10] and in Falerii.[11] Analogous silver pendants are strung on necklaces on the art market.[12]

First half seventh century BC.

1. von Hase 1975, p. 128, note 144, pl. 26 top left.
2. Becatti 1955, pl. LXIV, no. 259; Cristofani, Martelli 1983, pp. 131, 278, no. 90.
3. von Hase 1975, pp. 128-129, note 147, pl. 27 top left.
4. Strøm 1971, pp. 68-69, 77, Fig. 84; von Hase 1975, p. 128, pl. 25 top.
5. Pareti 1947, pl. XXXV, no. 247; von Hase 1975, p. 128, pl. 25 bottom.
6. Strøm 1971, Fig. 21.
7. Strøm 1971, Fig. 22.
8. Strøm 1971, pp. 21-22, 48, 174, Figs 12-14.
9. Pareti 1947, p. 212, no. 140, pl. XIV.
10. Caruso 1988, no. 68, pl. X.
11. Karo 1905, p. 154, Fig. 18.
12. *Art of Ancient Italy* 1970, no. 23t, 23cc.

69. Biconical bead with granulation

Gold. Length 1.3; Max. diameter 1.1

Biconical bead made from two valves of moulded sheet gold, whose junction is concealed by an applied gold wire. The surface is decorated with granulation in a meander pattern. The perforations at either extremity are trimmed with a plain wire ring. This is most likely a necklace bead, readapted in modern times as a pendant with the insertion of

a circular-section pin shaped into a handle.

Beads similar in manufacture and of the same dimension (1.3 cm long) may be observed on a necklace from Narce, Monte Cerreto, at the Museo di Villa Giulia, dated around the mid-seventh century BC,[1] and recur, in the same site, on a second specimen from tomb 33 in the Pizzo Piede necropolis, of which three single beads survive.[2]
A further parallel may be made with a necklace from the former Castellani Collection at the British Museum, thought to be of Praenestine provenance.[3]

First half seventh century BC.

1. Karo 1905, p. 155, no. 11, pl. I, 6; Cristofani, Martelli 1983, pp. 132-133, 278-279, no. 91.
2. F. Barnabei, A. Pasqui, *Degli oggetti di ornamento personale, delle armi e degli altri istrumenti del corredo funebre*, in *MAL* 4, 1894, cols. 349-350, Fig. 173; Karo 1905, p. 155, no. 12, pl. I, 1
3. Marshall 1969, no. 1453, pl. XXII; Higgins 1980, pl. 33A; Cristofani, Martelli 1983, pp. 130, 277-278, no. 88.

70. Necklace with glass paste beads

Gold and glass paste. Length 16.5; diameter of gold beads 1.1/0.7; diameter of glass paste beads 1.2/0.6

Reassembled from glass paste beads of various forms, typologies (lenticular, cylindrical, and globular beads decorated with white circles on blue such as *etched beads*) and dimensions, alternating with hollow gold beads, both spherical and lenticular, made from two stamped hemispheres soldered along the seams.

Plain stamped beads are found on different necklaces, sometimes reassembled from intrusive or modern elements, such as the necklace from the former Castellani Collection at the British Museum, in which an analogous association with glass paste beads recurs,[1] or in another necklace from the same Museum reassembled from smooth beads, decorated with filigree and granulation,[2] or a specimen from Vulci in the Gregorian Etruscan Museum.[3]
For lenticular beads, a parallel may be made with a reassembled necklace from the 1835 Vulci excavations in the Gregorian Etruscan Museum.[4] The chronology of these beads, dated to the second half of the seventh century BC,[5] undoubtedly creates some uncertainty regarding the shared significance of the various elements on the necklace in question.
With regards to the glass paste beads, in addition to those on the Castellani Collection necklace at the British Museum, one may recall the specimens found in Vetulonia[6] and Cerveteri, former Castellani Collection, at the Museo di Villa Giulia,[7] as well as countless anonymous elements from the art market.[8]
Spherical beads in stamped sheet gold, both plain and decorated with granulation and filigree, may be observed on a necklace from Cetona, dated to the end of the sixth century BC,[9] and on one from the former Candelori Collection.[10] A chronological reference is supplied by a necklace composed of smooth, spherical beads alternating with rings of granules, found at Polverosa di Orbetello in a sarcophagus from the first half of the fifth century BC.[11]
A further parallel may be made with a specimen found in tomb 85 in the Aleria necropolis, whose context, dated to 460-400 BC, also permits a chronological qualification for the granulated spheres.[12]
The type was also widespread in southern Italy: a necklace from Ruvo is reassembled from granulated and filigreed spheres associated with others decorated with repoussé bosses.[13]

Second half seventh century BC (lenticular beads); late sixth - fifth centuries BC.

1. Marshall 1969, no. 1450, pl. XXI.

2. Marshall 1969, no. 1456, pl. XXIII.
3. *Musei Etrusci...monimenta* 1842, pl. CXXV, 2; Scarpignato 1985, p. 61, no. 68, with further comparisons.
4. *Musei Etrusci...monimenta* 1842, I, pl. CXXIV, 3; Scarpignato 1985, p. 60, no. 65.
5. *Ibid.*
6. I. Falchi, *Nuovi scavi nella necropoli di Vetulonia,* in *NotSc* 1887, p. 517; von Bissing 1938, pp. 299-300, nos 60-61, 63; Camporeale 1969, p. 101, pl. XXXV, 1-2
7. Bordenache Battaglia 1980, no. 73; Caruso 1988, p. 41, no. 75.
8. For example: *Christie's,* 11 December 2003, p. 51, no. 416.
9. Becatti 1955, pl. F, 2; Greifenhagen 1970, p. 87, pl. 66, nos 3-4; Cristofani, Martelli 1983, pp. 172, 293-294, no. 154.
10. J. Sieveking, Bericht der *Antikensammlungen in München,* in *AA* 44, 1929, cols. 32-34, Fig. 31 bottom.
11. *Magie des Goldes* 1996, pp. 60-61, no. 59.
12. Jehasse 1973, p. 411-413, no. 1593b, pl. I.
13. Breglia 1941, no. 23, pl. IV.

71. Necklace reassembled from 50 beads of sheet gold

Gold. Length 44.5; diameter of beads 1.1/0.5

Reassembled from 50 beads of various dimensions regularly disposed, the large ones alternating with the smaller ones. The beads are hollow, made from two stamped sheet gold hemispheres soldered along the seams. The decoration, in filigree and openwork, consists of volutes, double rows of circular perforations bordered by wire circles, and double rows of circles intersected by a wire spirally wound around a second straight wire.

A necklace with beads decorated in filigree and *pulviscolo* granulation, which in two cases features also the spring-coiled wire decoration that characterizes the specimen in question, is now in Berlin (Staatliche Museen Preussischer Kulturbesitz, Antikenabteilung), purchased by Campanari, and is dated to the sixth century BC.[1] Beads decorated with spring-coiled wire may also be seen on two reassembled necklaces in the British Museum.[2] An analogous technique is also found on certain elements from a reassembled necklace in the Gregorian Etruscan Museum dated to the end of the sixth-fifth centuries BC.[3] Very similar beads also make up a necklace at the Liverpool Museum.[4]

A necklace known from the antique market was reassembled from spheroid beads, both plain and decorated with granulation, with interposed rings ornamented with spring-coiled wire.[5] Generally, necklaces with spheroid beads decorated with filigree are widely documented, known also in Magna Graecia between the sixth and fourth centuries BC, with an apparent hiatus in the course of the fifth century BC.[6] Still in southern Italy, a sphere not unlike these beads decorates the catchplate of a gold fibula from tomb 62 in Teano, safely datable to the last decade of the fourth century BC, confirming the duration and extent of the technique.[7]

Probably fifth - fourth centuries BC.

1. Greifenhagen 1970, p. 87, pl. 66, no. 2.
2. Marshall 1969, pl. XXIII, nos 1454 (Castellani Collection), 1456.
3. Scarpignato 1985, p. 61, no. 68.
4. Johnstone 1932, p. 444, no. 10322, pl. XX.
5. *Christie's,* 6 December 2000, no. 77.
6. Guzzo 1993, p. 190, type I.B, no. 7 (from Taranto), no. 8 (from Oppido Lucano: cf. Lissi Caronna 1980, pp. 245-247, no. 2, Figs 180-181, from a monetary treasure dated between 320 and 269 BC); *ibid.,* p. 201, type V.C, no. 1, from Taranto, first half fourth century BC.
7. E. Gabrici, in *MAL* 20, 1910, col. 41, Fig. 22; for the chronology: Trendall 1967, pp. 550, 559-560, Teano-Tübingen Group.

72. Necklace with flattened links and lunar crescent amulet

Gold and pearl. Length 41.0

Composed of a chain of flattened figure-of-eight links, within which is suspended a large ribbed ring with a pendant in the form of a lunar crescent *(lunula)*. The clasp is made from a hook-shaped wire that corresponds on the opposite terminal with a moulded wire element terminating in rings at either end and decorated with an irregular pearl set between two rings of granules.

The type of necklace with flattened figure-of-eight links, both closed and open as in this case, is well-documented with different examples from the Vesuvian area, generally datable to the first century AD: Pompeii, House of the Blacksmith[1] and Oplontis, Villa B.[2] A close parallel for the chain type with individually pinched and soldered links is a necklace at the Brooklyn Museum.[3] Both the type of chain and the *lunula* pendant are widely documented throughout the Roman world.[4]

For the *lunula* pendant, cf. also no. **109.**

Rings of granules are strung like partitions between beads on a necklace from Cetona dated to the end of the sixth century BC.[5] Analogous rings are interposed between beads on a necklace from Vulci in the Gregorian Etruscan Museum, currently dated to the fourth-third centuries BC,[6] and on two other reassembled necklaces from the same Museum, datable, on the whole, between the second half of the sixth and the first half of the fifth centuries BC.[7]

Fig.17. Statuette of Aphrodite-Isis wearing a necklace with a central lunar-crescent pendant. Unknown provenance; probably from Roman Egypt. Late first century BC – first century AD. Vatican City, Vatican Museums, inv. 18373. Bronze. Height 40.7 cm.

Considering the chronological gap between the necklace (chain and pendant) and the rings of granules, it is likely that the necklace in question was assembled from heterogeneous elements. Even the asymmetrical position of the pendant, which normally occupies the mid-section, could be the result of a modern recomposition. It should be noted, however, that Roman-British necklaces had *lunula* pendants, associated with the Celtic solar symbol, that were placed in analogous decentralized positions.[8]

Second half sixth – fifth centuries BC (rings of granules); first century AD (necklace and pendant).

1. D'Ambrosio, De Carolis 1997, p. 32, no. 31, pl. III.
2. *Magie des Goldes* 1996, pp. 110-111, no. 152; D'Ambrosio, De Carolis 1997, p. 65, no. 190, pl. XVIII.
3. Davidson, Oliver 1984, p. 137-138, no. 189.
4. Breglia 1941, pl. XXXVII, 1, no. 501 (unknown provenance), pl. XXXIV, 9, no. 502 (from Scafati), pl. XXXVII,4, no. 503 (= Cantilena 1989, pp. 218-219, no. 86, unknown provenance); Deppert Lippitz 1985, p. 11, no. 4, pl. 3 (supposed provenance Asia Minor); D'Ambrosio 2001, p. 977, Fig. 5, from Pompeii - Moregine; Pavesi, Gagetti 2001, pp. 45-46.
5. Becatti 1955, pl. F, 2; Greifenhagen 1970, pl. 66, nos 3-4, p. 87; Cristofani, Martelli 1983, pp. 172, 294, no. 154.

6. Cristofani, Martelli 1983, pp. 238, 316, no. 266.
7. Scarpignato 1985, pp. 61-62, nos 67, 70.
8. Johns 1996, pp. 92-93, Figs 5.5-5.6 and Johns 1997, p. 82, Fig. 11.

73. Necklace with chain, gems and colored stones

Gold, carnelian (?) and rock crystal (?). Length approx. 55

The necklace is composed of a chain of double links made from moulded wire and twisted closed, in which are inserted regularly alternating translucent white globular beads and intense red beads. A double-faced bivalve sheet gold scarab joins the terminals.

This type of chain, made from segments of twisted wire alternating with colored gems and stones, is characteristic of Roman Imperial goldwork, with examples dating from the first to the third centuries AD.[1] Similar necklaces, however, had a much longer tradition, as in the case of a Byzantine necklace from Antinoe, in Egypt, dated to the fifth-seventh centuries AD, which adopts the same type of chain with inserted sapphires alternating with pearls.[2]

For the scarab clasp (*see infra* nos **199-222**), a parallel is known only from collection material, dubiously dated to the Roman period.[3]

First - second centuries AD.

1. Davidson, Oliver 1984, p. 140, no. 192, first century AD; Greifenhagen 1975, p. 33, no. 2, pl. 30, from southern Russia; Deppert Lippitz 1985, pl. 4, no. 7, from Hungary, late first - second century AD; Greifenhagen 1975, pl. 30, no. 4; Deppert Lippitz 1985, pl. 4, nos 5-6, second century AD; *Arte e cultura in Croazia* 1993, p. 155, no. 194, from Sisak, Croatia, second - third centuries AD; Pavesi, Gagetti 2001, pp. 95-108, type VII; cf. also: Barini 1958, p. 51 and Fig. n/n, from Ostia; Böhme 1974, p. 43, Fig. 18, at the Museum of Mainz; Caliò 2000, pp. 67-68, no. 90, at the Gregorian Etruscan Museum.
2. Baldini, Lippolis 1999, p. 136, no. 18.
3. van den Driessche 1975, p. 15, no. 19, Fig. 18, former Ferdinando Cafiero Collection, at the Museum of Barletta.

74. *Bulla* pendant

Gold. Height 5.1; width 4.1

Suspended from necklace no. **73** is a *bulla* pendant of lenticular section in repoussé sheet gold, backed with a flat sheet of gold. Pictured frontally is a mythical episode, most likely the murder of Troilus by Achilles: a naked male figure is on the point of stabbing a sitting naked man with his sword, grabbing him by the hair. An abandoned shield lies behind the second figure. A continuous wave motif outlines the scene; the background is thickly stippled. The juncture of the two valves is decorated with beaded wire. The cylindrical suspension tube has upturned, spool-shaped extremities and is decorated with a central annular beaded wire ridge.

Given the chronological and cultural gap between the two elements of this necklace, it is evident that the *bulla* was added to the chain in recent times.
The illustrated, discoid *bulla* with repoussé mythological scenes is a typical product of Etruscan goldwork, which asserted itself throughout the first half of the fourth century BC. With its numerous active workshops, the city of Vulci produced splendid examples and represents one of the most active centers,[1] followed by other areas such as Todi[2] and Populonia.[3] Other examples were found in the Piceno area but are thought to be imported from Vulci.[4]
The specimen in question may be paralleled, notwithstanding certain compositional and typological differences (such as Achilles wearing a *chlamys*), with two of the seven *bullae* that make up a necklace from Vulci, now at the Gregorian Etruscan Museum.[5] It is worth noting that the smaller *bullae* on this necklace have the same type of decoration on the suspension tubes. Returning to decorative attributes, a similar layout may also be observed on two of the three *bullae* on a necklace in the British Museum, which picture two confronting male figures.[6]
This type of jewel is also documented with other examples of unknown provenance, respectively in London, at the British Museum;[7] at the Louvre in Paris;[8] and in the antique market.[9]

Fig. 18 . Female votive statue from Pratica di Mare wearing a cloak that completely wraps her body, leaving her hands free – the right, pressed against her chest, bears an offering – and wearing a necklace and an illustrated *bulla* pendant. Late fourth – early third centuries BC. Rome, Soprintendenza Archeologica per il Lazio, inv. P77.2. Terracotta. Height 93.5 cm.

First half fourth century BC.

1. Becatti 1955, nos 359-361; Cristofani, Martelli 1983, nos 221-222, 260; Buranelli 1992, p. 94, no. 56.
2. G. Bendinelli, *Antichità tudertine del Museo Nazionale di Villa Giulia,* in *MAL* 23, 1914, cols. 615-616, Fig. 3, pl. II, 4; Becatti 1955, no. 364.
3. Cianferoni 1992, pp. 28-29, Figs 45-47.
4. Becatti 1955, no. 363, from Filottrano; Coen 1998, pp. 85-97, from Osimo - Monte Petrano.
5. Andrén 1948, p. 95, Fig. 1; Becatti 1955, no. 359, pl. XCII, with bibliography; Cristofani, Martelli 1983, no. 260; Buranelli 1992, p. 94, no. 56, with further bibliography.
6. Interpreted as Herakles and Iolaus by Marshall 1969, no. 2285, pl. XLVI.
7. Cristofani, Martelli 1983, no. 261.
8. Higgins 1980, pp. 151-152, pl. 42,B = Cristofani, Martelli 1983, no. 264; Cristofani, Martelli 1983, nos 262-263.
9. *Antike Kunstwerke Nachlass Dr. Jacob Hirsch, Teil II, Ars Antiqua AG Luzern, Auktion 2,* Mai 1959, p. 48, no. 137, pl. 65.

75. Necklace

Gold, pearls and emeralds (?). Length approx. 17.0

The chain is composed of twisted wire rings to which are fastened, alternately, green gems of cylindrical or irregular prismatic form and pearls. Inserted centrally is an elliptical medallion bordered by a double row of granules, inlaid with a red cabochon-cut stone (garnet?).

This type of chain, made from twisted wire and containing colored gems and stones, is character-

istic of Roman Imperial goldwork, with examples dated to the first-second centuries AD.[1] In northern Italy and in the imperial provinces[2] gold necklaces with emerald prisms or rough, irregular emeralds are also documented, occasionally combined with pearls and sapphires, distinguished by a type of chain that is very similar to this one, and placed in a later period, in the second-third centuries AD.[3] This tradition survived in seventh-century Byzantine creations, which also proved to be stylistically akin to the more ancient versions of Roman jewelry.[4]
For the medallion, possibly with typological precedents from the Hellenistic period,[5] an iconographic parallel may be found around the middle of the second century AD.[6]

Second - third centuries AD.

1. Greifenhagen 1975, p. 33, no. 2, pl. 30; Deppert Lippitz 1985, pl. 4, no. 7, from southern Russia, late first - second centuries AD; Greifenhagen 1975, pl. 30, no. 4; Deppert Lippitz 1985, pl. 4, no. 6, second century AD; Davidson, Oliver 1984, p. 140, no. 192, first century AD; Deppert Lippitz 1985, pl. 4, no. 5, second century AD; Moratello 1999, pp. 262-263, no. 1, pl. XCII,1, first century AD. Also compare: Barini 1958, p. 51 and Fig. n/n, from Ostia; *Antike Kunstwerke, Nachlass Dr. Jacob Hirsh II. Teil und anderen Besitz,* Auktion 2. Mai 1959, Ars Antiqua AG Luzern, Luzern 1959, p. 50, no. 143, pl. 64, from the antique market; Böhme 1974, p. 43, Fig. 18, at the Museum of Mainz.
2. Oliver 1996, p. 136, Fig. 8, no. 62, from Bonn, found with a monetary treasure dated to 247-251/252 AD.
3. Pavesi, Gagetti 2001, pp. 95-108, type VII; *ibid.*, pp. 104-105, no. 33, pl. VI, from Aquileia, second - third centuries AD; *ibid.*, pp. 105-106, no. 34, pl. VII, from Arco di Trento, late second - early third centuries AD; *ibid.*, pp. 106-107, no. 35, pl. VIII, from an unspecified location in the Trentino, third century AD.
4. Baldini, Lippolis 1999, p. 137, no. 31.
5. Cf. Alexander 1928, pl. I, top; Christie's NewYork, 5 Dec. 2001, no. 70.
6. Allason-Jones 1989, pl. 10, panel with female portrait from Hawara.

76. *Necklace with biconical beads

Gold and glass paste. Total length 25.0; length of gold beads 1.8; height of pendant 3.3

The necklace is reassembled from eleven biconical beads in sheet gold, alternating with the same number of blue glass paste beads decorated with white circles. The closing mechanism is missing. One extremity bears a small bronze spiral. The biconical beads have repoussé decorations consisting of a frieze of small circles with radiating rays (solar symbol), alternating with a plain band and a row of studs. The drop-shaped pendant, made from bivalve sheet gold, is decorated with a central die-formed owl and a row of small bosses along the border. A chain of double braided wire borders the junction of the two valves.

Biconical beads, although larger in size, were generally adopted as early as the Orientalizing period.[1] In a reassembled necklace from the art market,[2] this type of bead is associated with a gold repoussé disc pendant (*see infra*, nos **24-28**).

A solar motif, analogous to that on the biconical beads on this necklace, is incised on a ring from Herculaneum dated to the first century AD.[3] Biconical beads may be observed, for instance, on a Roman necklace from the market, reassembled with carnelian beads and pendants.[4] In any case, the biconical shape enjoyed a long-lasting tradition, as documented by a Byzantine necklace from Egypt, dated to the late sixth-seventh centuries AD.[5]

1. For example Cerveteri, Regolini Galassi Tomb: Pareti 1947, p. 205, no. 66, pl. XII; Tarquinia: Karo 1902, p. 125, Fig. 106; cf. also: G. Pinza, *Materiali per la Etnologia antica Toscano Laziale,* I, Milano 1915, p. 176, note 1.
2. *Classical Antiquities,* Münzen und Medaillen A.G. Basel 14, 19/06/1954, p. 13, no. 45.
3. D'Ambrosio, De Carolis 1997, p. 97, no. 303, pl. XXX.
4. *Christie's*, 6 December 2000, no. 112.
5. Baldini, Lippolis 1999, p. 136, no. 19: Washington-Dumbarton Oaks Collection.

77. Necklace with top-shaped beads

Gold. Length 31.3

The necklace is reassembled from a sequence of three top-shaped beads with striated bodies, made from two stamped sheet gold valves decorated at either extremity with a double braided wire, alternating with a cylindrical bead decorated with three rings of double braided wire, placed at the center and at either extremity.

For cylindrical beads, one may compare a reassembled necklace from the antique market, thought to be from the Roman Imperial period, second-third centuries AD (?).[1]

1. *Christie's*, 6 December 2000, no. 138.

PENDANTS

78. Disc pendant

Gold sheet over die-formed bronze sheet. Preserved height 8.7; diameter 8.4

Repoussé necklace pendant equipped with a suspension cylinder. At the center is a boss inscribed by three concentric raised circles, which are inscribed in turn by the following decorative ele-

ments distributed on concentric tiers and separated by ridges: a series of raised circles with central bosses, a series of small arcs with three bosses, zig-zag patterns, and circles with a central boss. The suspension cylinder is decorated with zig-zag patterns.

Cf. no. **82**.

79. Disc pendant

Gold sheet over die-formed bronze sheet. Max. diameter 6.0
Missing suspension element.

Repoussé necklace pendant. At the center is a boss inscribed by three concentric raised circles, followed by a decoration of concentric tiers consisting of a series of double circles with central bosses, a ridge of false rope, zig-zag patterns, and a double ridge of false rope.

Cf. no. **82**.

80. Disc pendant

Gold sheet over die-formed bronze sheet. Max. diameter 7.0
Missing suspension element.

Repoussé necklace pendant. At the center is a boss inscribed by three concentric raised circles, followed by a decoration of concentric tiers consisting of: a plain broken meander pattern, a series of double circles with central bosses, a

ridge of false rope, a zig-zag pattern and a double ridge of false rope.

Cf. no. **82**.

81. Disc pendant

Gold sheet over die-formed bronze sheet. Height 7.1; Max. diameter 7.0

Necklace pendant equipped with a suspension cylinder made from a folded-over strip of sheet gold, decorated with repoussé designs. At the center is a boss inscribed by three concentric raised circles, followed by a decoration of concen-

tric tiers consisting of: a plain broken meander pattern, a series of double circles with a central boss, a ridge of false rope, a zig-zag pattern and a double ridge of false rope.

Cf. no. **82**.

82. Disc pendant

Gold sheet. Diameter 6.2
Portions missing.

Repoussé necklace pendant. Starting at the center and in concentric tiers: a central boss inscribed by two concentric raised circles, a double row of raised dots, two rows of circled bosses and a double row of raised dots.

This type of jewel (nos **78-82**), peculiar to the feminine and infantile spheres, was widespread in Etruria, ancient Latium and Campania from the early Iron Age to the Orientalizing period, and reveals an evident parallel affinity with examples from Rhodes dated to the second half of the eighth century BC.[1]
Dated to the second quarter of the eighth century BC is the gold disc from tomb XLIII in Tivoli, decorated with a circled stud in the center and concentric rows of raised dots.[2] These are followed, in the second half of the eighth century BC, by specimens with sober geometric decorations from the necropolis of Veio - Quattro Fontanili, tomb Yα[3] and tomb KKLL 18-19.[4]
Placed in the same period is a pendant from tomb 110 in Castel di Decima, distinguished by the representation of the lunar crescent and solar disc (the first rendered with an amber bezel, the second with a repoussé *bulla*), a motif of ancient Oriental origin.[5] This Oriental motif also recurs in Bisenzio, in tomb 22 at Olmo Bello, dated to the last quarter of the eighth century BC,[6] in tomb 10 at Bisenzio-Bucacce, dating to the early seventh century BC,[7] and during the same period in Vulci, with the rich version of the Munich specimen,[8] as well as in Palestrina.[9] A reflection of this astral theme may be recognized in the circular, semicircular or lunate bezels that recur on openwork bracelets from the same period (*see infra* no. **130**).
The above-mentioned tomb 10 at Bisenzio-Bucacce contained the pendant type with an elaborate geometric layout, including bosses with raised circles, swastikas, and a series of S-shaped designs inscribed by roped ridges,[10] which finds an immediate parallel in the specimen at Hamburg's Museum für Kunst und Gewerbe.[11]
The pendants in question reveal close analogies, in form and in decorative syntax, with those on a necklace from tomb 2 in Bisenzio-Olmo Bello at the Museo di Villa Giulia, where repoussé discs

alternate with amber beads.[12]
For the decorative recurrence of inscribed bosses, circles and dots, these pendants are broadly comparable to a well-known specimen from Cumae, Stevens Collection.[13] Furthermore, various examples of unknown provenance have appeared on the art market[14].

Third quarter eighth century BC.

1. von Hase 1975, pp. 123-124, Fig. 11 (Veio-Quattro Fontanili EE 7-8B), p. 124, pl. 22 bottom right (Kamiros), pl. 23 (Tarquinia and Vetulonia); general notes on the diffusion, Cristofani, Martelli 1983, p. 30.
2. *Civiltà del Lazio Primitivo* 1976, p. 198, no. 11, pl. XXXV, late Latial period II - early Latial period III.
3. Cristofani, Martelli 1983, pp. 250-251, no. 4.
4. Cristofani, Martelli 1983, pp. 250-251, no. 5.
5. A. Bedini, *L'ottavo secolo nel Lazio e l'inizio dell'Orientalizzante antico alla luce di recenti scoperte nella necropoli di Castel di Decima*, in *La parola del Passato* 32, 1977, p. 306.
6. Cristofani, Martelli 1983, p. 251, infra no. 7.
7. E. Galli, *Il sepolcreto visentino delle Bucacce*, in *MAL* 21, 1912, col. 449, Fig. 36.
8. Cristofani, Martelli 1983, p. 278, no. 90.
9. Cristofani, Martelli 1983, p. 279, no. 92; for notes on the motif in general, ibid., p. 36.
10. E. Galli, *Il sepolcreto visentino delle Bucacce*, in *MAL* 21, 1912, col. 450, Fig. 38; von Hase 1975, p. 126, pl. 23 top right.
11. Hoffmann, von Claer 1968, pp. 78-79, no. 49.
12. *Ori e argenti* 1961, p. 24, no. 10; von Hase 1975, p. 124, note 133, pl. 22 top and bottom left; Cristofani, Martelli 1983, pp. 76, 251-252, no. 7.
13. Siviero 1954, p. 7, no. 1; von Hase 1975, pp. 99-182, pl. 21; Guzzo 1993, p. 219, type I.B, no. 1.
14. *Classical Antiquities, Münzen und Medaillen A.G. Basel,* 14, 19/06/1954, p. 13, no. 45, subsequently published in *Kunstwerke der Antike, Münzen und Medaillen* 22, 13/05/1961, Basel 1961, no. 205; *Christie's London* 06/06/1994, p. 101, no. 300.

83. Scarab pendant

Silver and white steatite. Width 2.7; height 2.2; bezel 2.0 x 1.5

Rotating bezel pendant with a scarab, consisting of a plain wire with tapered ends that locate into two hook-shaped clasps soldered to the bezel. Soldered to the top of the pendant is a tubular coiled wire suspension element. The elliptical bezel is formed from a smooth gold plate with folded-in edges that contains the scarab, fixed with a gold cut-out ring soldered to the base. The scarab has a high back and marked head; the prothorax is separated from the elytra by an incised curved line. Incised hieroglyphs decorate the flat side.

84. Scarab pendant

Silver and white steatite. Width 2.7; height 2.4; bezel 2.1 x 1.5
Same as previous.

85. Scarab pendant

Silver and white steatite. Width 2.8; height 2.3; bezel 2.0 x 1.5
Same as previous.

86. Scarab pendant

Silver and white steatite. Width 2.7; height 2.3; bezel 1.8 x 1.5
Same as previous.

87. Scarab pendant

Silver and white steatite. Width 2.6; height 2.2; bezel 1.9 x 1.4
Same as previous.

88. Scarab pendant

Silver and white steatite. Width 2.7; height 2.5; bezel 1.9 x 1.3

Similar to previous. The clasps are ring-shaped, while the bezel has a moulded gold plate that partially encases the scarab.

These pendants (nos **83-88**) derive from Oriental Phoenicio-Cypriot prototypes[1] first introduced in Pithecussae and Cumae in the last quarter of the eighth century BC.[2]
Given the presence in this period at Pithecussae of scarabs from the Lyre Player Group, created in various shades of serpentine (red, green, gray-brown or black) from northern Syria or other parts of the Near East and mounted on silver pendants of a similar typology,[3] it is thought that the introduction to Etruria and southern Italy of this particular shape of pendant occurred starting in the last quarter of the eighth century BC.[4]
Throughout the seventh century BC, purely ornamental reworkings saw the substitution of Levantine seals with scaraboids in amber or rock crystal,[5] or the creation of gold bezels with fine granulation and *pulviscolo* decoration, as may be observed in a well-known pendant from Vulci picturing hunting scenes, now at Munich's Antikensammlungen, from the mid-seventh century BC.[6] The case of the specimen from tomb XI at Colle del Forno, dated to the second half of the seventh century BC, shows a reworking of the pendant's setting with the insertion of a wingless two-headed sphinx.[7]
The pendants in question reveal numerous affinities with those found in Vetulonia and Marsiliana d'Albegna, where Egyptian-style scarabs with analogous settings were found.[8] In particular, a specimen from the Circolo dei Monili in Vetulonia is very similar to these, which may, by analogy, be hypothetically referred to such a context.[9]
Similar pendants, limited only to the silver setting and found without the scarab, figure among materials from the Falcioni Collection in the Gregorian Etruscan Museum.[10]

Probably seventh century BC.

1. Boardman, Scarisbrick 1977, p. 42, no. 89, Harari Collection; Higgins 1980, pp. 141-142, Fig. 22; various specimens from Cyprus in the Cesnola Collection (Culican 1973, pp. 40-41, pl. IIIA) and from tomb 62 in Marion (*CypSwEx* II, p. 370, pl. LXX,40), probably of northern Syrian origin.
2. Guzzo 1993, pp. 68-69, 221-222.
3. J. Boardman, G. Buchner, *Seals from Ischia and the Lyre-Player Group*, in *JDAI* 81, 1966, pp. 11, 42-43, Fig. 16.
4. Culican 1973, pp. 40-42, Fig. 1,d-e (from Cumae and Vetulonia); Ruxer, Kubczak 1975, pp. 96-98, no. 2, Fig. 2 (from Etruria); Boardman, Vollenweider 1978, p. 49, nos 208-209, pl. XXXVI (from Tarquinia, with an Egyptian scarab); see also: E. Galli, *Il sepolcreto visentino delle "Bucacce"*, in *MAL* 21, 1912, col. 431, Fig. 18 = D. Randall Mac Iver, *Villanovans and Early Etruscans*, Oxford 1924, pl. 32 = *Ori e argenti* 1961, p. 26, no. 18, with previous bibliography (Bisenzio, Bucacce, tomb 3); *Materiali di antichità varia, III, Scavi di Vulci. Materiale concesso a Francesco Paolo Bongiovì*, Roma 1964, p. 27, no. 623; von Bissing 1933, p. 373-376, nos 8-15, pl. XXII and Camporeale 1969, p. 100, pl. XXXIV, 3-8 (Vetulonia); von Bissing 1933, pp. 376-381, nos 16-23, pl. XXIII, from Marsiliana d'Albegna.
5. Cristofani, Martelli 1983, p. 37.
6. Becatti 1955, no. 258b, pl. LXIV; Cristofani, Martelli 1983, p. 279, no. 94.
7. P. Santoro, *Colle del Forno. Loc. Montelibretti (Roma). Relazione di scavo sulle campagne 1971-1974 nella necropoli*, in *NotSc* 1977, pp. 265-266, no. 27, Figs 69-70,c.
8. On scarabs, see *infra: A Note on Scarabs*, by M. Cappozzo.
9. Camporeale 1969, p. 100, pl. XXXIV, 6.
10. Caliò 2000, p. 92, nos 145-147.

A NOTE ON SCARABS

By Mario Cappozzo

The scarab, to the ancient Egyptians, was a sacred animal that was identified with the symbol of the sun god Ra at the moment of rising. A hieroglyph in the form of a scarab, in fact, carries the meaning "to become," "to rise again," or "to renew oneself." This meaning led to the use of the scarab, particularly during the Late Period, in funerary contexts. The larger scarabs, so-called "heart scarabs," inscribed on their underside with chapter 30 of the Book of the Dead, were placed over the heart of the mummy, while the smaller ones were used as propitiatory amulets or seals, and were often set in rings[1] or strung on necklaces. On their undersides these small objects present figures and symbols of divinity, synthetic formulae of various types, animals, names of pharaohs and, very rarely, names of individuals. The cryptography of the god Amon's name also appears on many scarabs, particularly during the Third Intermediate Period.

The scarab enjoyed exceptional favor not only in Egypt, but throughout the entire Mediterranean basin. In addition to the near Syro-Palestinian coast, scarabs were found also in Persia, on the shores of the Black Sea, in Cyprus, Rhodes, Crete, Greece, Magna Graecia, Sardinia,[2] Etruria, Malta, Carthage and Ibiza.[3] In the Mediterranean area the scarab was generally used as an amulet, but also as an ex-voto or funerary deposit, while scarabs with yet another purpose were found in the sacrificial ditch of the Veio sanctuary.[4] Also worth noting are several scarabs with known archaeological contexts, found in the tombs of children.

The vast area of diffusion of scarabs in the Mediterranean basin suggests a large network of commercial trade with Egypt, which took place between the end of the ninth and the sixth centuries BC, when the production of scarabs ceased (in Egypt the production ceased after the end of the 26th dynasty).[5]

It is, however, problematic to date this type of artifact due to the frequent absence of information on the context in which it was found, and also because today there still exist no safe stylistic dating criteria. In this regard, an important criterion for attempting to date a scarab is related to the characteristics of the clypeus, the elytron and the protothorax.[6] The Late Period, for example, produced small scarabs (particularly in steatite) with very high backs.[7] The names of pharaohs, if present, are not a valid dating criterion, since, especially during the Late Period, manufacturers of these artifacts often used the names of past pharaohs, which carried greater magical powers, to increase the magical effect of their amulets.[8]

Scarab no. **83** bears three unintelligible marks in between two *nb* marks, denoting the word "Lord," and is decorated with a series of vertical parallel lines. Its unnaturalistic appearance, which only vaguely outlines the head and the elytra (which, separate from the protothorax, are not excessively marked), suggests a placement in the Late Period.[9]

Scarab no. **84** pictures on its base a group of five hieroglyphs which may be read *Imn-R' nb(.i)*, or "Amon-Ra is my Lord". The same group of hieroglyphs (without the *nb* mark) appears on a scarab from Pithecussae.[10]

Scarab no. **85** bears the name of the god Amon. The name of the Theban god recurs frequently in scarabs from the Late Period, both written uncoded and in puzzle form, using the acrophonic principle of many hieroglyphs, probably intended to increase the amulet's magical value. Despite the mention of a god of Upper Egypt, the Delta is the likely area of origin for these artifacts. It is worth noting, in fact, that Bosticco hypothesizes a Naukratite origin for certain scarabs from Pithecussae and underlines that Vercoutter hypothesized a similar origin for certain scarabs found in Punic necropoles.[11] Furthermore, Bosticco points out, the Conca area in Etruria also produced a series typical of Naukratis, a Greek city in Egyptian territory that boasted, in the sixth century, an active production of scarabs for export.

Figures and symbols of divinity are present on the base of scarab no. **86**. Two urei are symmetrically disposed underneath a winged solar disc.[12] The signs are engraved in a perfunctory manner and are not well characterized.

Scarab no. **87** presents the inscription *Imn-nfr*, or "Amon is good". The form of the hieroglyphs appears, also in this case, to be cursory. Late Period.

A decorated oval flanked by two papyrus plants is pictured on the base of scarab no. **88**. Papyrus plants are very often seen as decorative elements on scarabs. In a specimen cited by Hornung, two papyrus plants flank a cartouche with the name of Thutmosis II, but a single plant may also be found as the only decorative element.[13] Late Period.

1. Hölbl 1979, vol. II, pls 80-94, shows numerous scarabs with bezels from Vulci, Bisenzio, Marsigliana, Vetulonia.
2. Scandone Matthiae 1975
3. For Italy cf. Hölbl 1979.
4. Bosticco 1976, pp. 214-215 with bibliography.
5. Cf. Hall 1913, p. XVI.
6. An early classification was attempted by Rowe 1936 and Newberry 1906, who listed numerous types in their respective works.
7. Giveon 1984, p. 975.
8. Hornung 1976, p. 28.
9. Hall 1913, type J 1, XXXIII.
10. Bosticco 1957, p. 218; Hornung 1976, p. 289, no. 489.
11. Bosticco 1957, p. 228.
12. Cf. for similar types Bosticco 1957, p. 227, no. 17; Guidotti 1994, p. 76, no. L 64.
13. Hornung 1976, p. 248, no. 292; pp. 349-351.

89. **Female head pendant

Gold. Height 3.3; width 3.2

Discoid, die-formed pendant picturing a female head with wavy hair and central parting, decorated below by a collar made up of a sequence of radiating ridges, and framed by a pair of volutes. The pendant is equipped with a sheet gold suspension cylinder with folded-in edges, made separately and soldered to the disc.

90. **Female head pendant

Gold. Height 3.4; width 3.1

Same as previous.

91. **Female head pendant

Gold. Height 3.4; width 3.2

Same as previous.

92. **Female head pendant

Gold. Height 3.4; width 3.3

Same as previous.

93. **Female head pendant

Gold. Height 3.0; width 3.0

Same as previous.

94. **Female head pendant

Gold. Height 3.3; width 3.2

Same as previous.

95. **Female head pendant

Gold. Height 2.8; width 3.2
Missing suspension cylinder.

Same as previous.

These pendants (nos **89-95**) in the form of a frontal

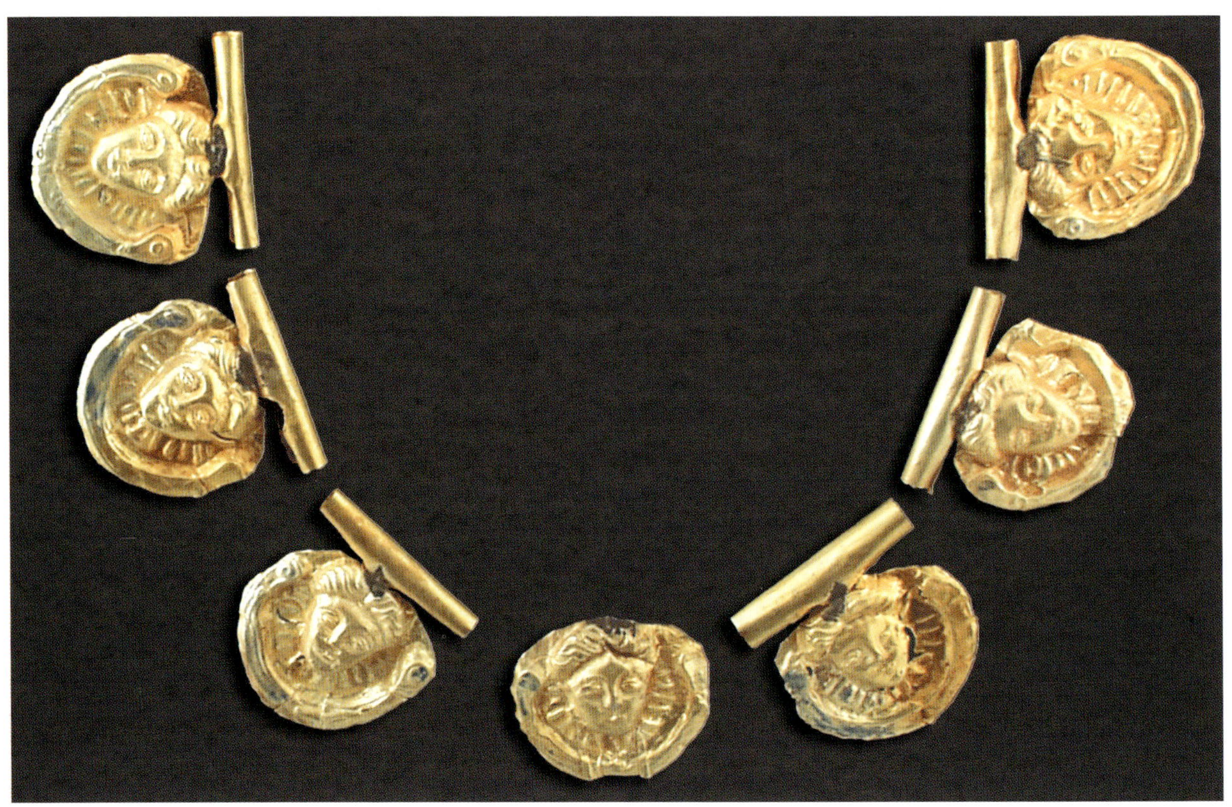

female head with a hathoric hairstyle, a high ridged collar, and framed between volutes, seem to be inspired, with misinterpretations and vague reproductions, by typologies established throughout the course of the seventh century BC in Vetulonia, as documented in peripheral tombs II[1] and IV in the Pietrera Tumulus,[2] in the Leoncini d'Argento Tomb,[3] as well as in Narce.[4] Also worth recalling are two specimens of unknown provenance in the British Museum.[5] The inspiration for these pendants is an iconography of clearly eastern origin, most likely Cypriot, appearing in close relation with the theme of the winged divinity with hathoric hair, characterized by phytomorphic endings and/or leonine protomes.[6] A further stylization of this theme may have led to the definition of the well-known anchor symbol, highly recurrent both in Orientalizing goldwork and bronzes.[7]
These pendants differ from the above-mentioned examples from Vetulonia in the "classic" typology of the female faces with radiate hair which in this case appears to be extrapolated, with evident anachronisms, from more recent creations, among which may be cited, for example, the pendants on a necklace from Vulci in the Gregorian Etruscan Museum, dated to the first half of the fourth century BC, with female protomes inspired by the Gorgonic mask.[8]
To these stylistic considerations, themselves indicative of a falsification, others of a technical nature must be added, such as the sketchy repoussé decoration on an open plate of gold, with the absence of a support, as well as the characteristics of the suspension element, which appears to be unrefined, disproportionate, fragile and visibly juxtaposed.

1. Karo 1902, p. 126, Fig. 108; Becatti 1955, p. 178, pl. LXV, 260.
2. Becatti 1955, pl. LXV, 261.
3. A. Talocchini, *Le oreficerie ed il vasetto configurato del circolo dei Leoncini d'Argento di Vetulonia,* in *StEtr* 31, 1963, pp. 82-84, pl. XIII; cf. also *Magie des Goldes* 1996, pp. 36, 38, no. 21, dated to the third quarter of the seventh century BC.
4. Karo 1905, p. 12, no. 8, pl. I, 4.
5. Marshall 1969, nos 1449, 1453, pls XXI-XXII.
6. W. Culican, *A Foreign Motif in Etruscan Jewellery,* in *BSR* 39, 1971, pp. 1-12.
7. Cf. *ibid.*, pls I-III, IVc.
8. Becatti 1955, pl. XCII, no. 362; Scarpignato 1981, pp. 12-13; Cristofani, Martelli 1983, pp. 211, 307, no. 220, with further bibliography and comparisons.

96. Illustrated *bulla*: four-horse chariot driven by Zeus/Tinia

Gold. Diameter 5.8; height 6.7
Missing the rear backing plate.

In general, cf. no. **74**.

Pictured in repoussé on the front are four winged horses in flight, led by a bearded figure (Zeus/Tinia) whose bare bust emerges. He is wearing a *chlamys*, and holding a stylized thunderbolt in his right hand. The border is decorated with beaded wire. The suspension cylinder, in rolled-over sheet gold, is decorated externally with linear designs and tongues made alternately

with plain, twisted and beaded wire. Six spheres of various sizes are disposed along the junction with the *bulla*.

This *bulla*, in its subject of the four-horse chariot driven by Zeus, finds a particular parallel in two analogous examples from Vulci at the Gregorian Etruscan Museum.[1] This pair has the same layout, but with the inclusion of a second figure, identified as Athena, beside Zeus/Tinia, and it also has the same decoration on the suspension cylinder; these elements may contribute to the recognition of a related workshop. However, certain differences in iconography (omission of the chariot, fluttering *chlamys*, slightly three-quarter view of the face) as well as in style (rendering of the face, the anatomy and the wing plumage) contribute to the exclusion of the possibility that the *bulla* in question was made by the same hand responsible for the above-mentioned examples from Vulci.

Early or first half fourth century BC.

1. *Musei Etrusci...monimenta* 1842, I, pl. CXXIII, 3; *Monumenti del Museo Etrusco...* 1842, I, pl. LXXVIII, 3; Andrén 1948, p. 95, pl. II, 1; Becatti 1955, no. 360, a-b, pl. XCII; Scarpignato 1981, pp. 10-11, Fig. 5; Cristofani, Martelli 1983, pp. 212, 307-308, no. 221.

97. *Female head pendant

Gold. Height 3.4; width 2.8

98. *Female head pendant

Gold. Height 3.7; width 2.9

99. *Female head pendant

Gold. Height 3.7; width 2.9

100. *Female head pendant

Gold. Height 3.8; width 2.9

101. *Female head pendant

Gold. Height 3.5; width 2.9

102. *Female head pendant

Gold. Height 3.6; width 2.6

These six pendants (nos **97-102**) are made of die-formed sheet gold open on the rear, each equipped with a rolled-over sheet gold peg. Framed within a double row of small bosses is a frontal female head with bipartite hair that waves slightly upward and backward. A diadem adorns the head, with its rounded face, turgid cheeks, low brow and severe expression.

There are no specific parallels for these pendants. The use of the female mask, in a typology that conforms stylistically to Classical tradition, may be found in Etruscan goldwork from the second half of the fourth century BC, which derives in turn from Magno-Graecian tradition.[1] The theme of the human mask, made in the repoussé technique, may be seen on a pair of earrings from the

Melvin Gutman Collection.[2] More generally, for the female mask typology, comparisons may be made with Etruscan antefixes dated from the mid-fourth century BC, such as those found in Tarquinia,[3] Vulci,[4] Orvieto[5] and particularly Civita Castellana.[6] The use of the female protome may also be traced to Apulian pottery, where it recurs in both plastic vases[7] as well as in volute-kraters; in the latter class, the innovation of the medallion with a frontal female portrait was introduced in the second quarter of the fourth century BC by the Iliupersis Painter,[8] and persisted throughout the second half of that century.[9] In Etruscan ceramography, the theme of the female head is plastically reproduced in the *Head Kantharoi* from the last quarter of the fourth century BC,[10] preceded by the Attic female head *oinochoai* from the Basle Group (440-420 BC) which, with their low brow and bipartite hair truncated above the ears, also constitute a valid iconographic reference for the pendants in question.[11]

Probably second half of the fourth century BC.

1. Compare, for example, pendants on a necklace from Pescia Romana: Cristofani, Martelli 1983, pp. 237, 316, no. 265.
2. Parkhurst 1961, p. 122, no. 50.
3. Andrén 1940, p. 69, pl. 23:82; M. Cataldi Dini, in *Gli Etruschi di Tarquinia,* Modena 1986, pp. 363-364, no. 913, Fig. 359.
4. F. Buranelli, *Gli scavi a Vulci della società Vincenzo Campanari - Governo Pontificio (1835-1837),* Roma 1991, pp. 203-206, nos 22-23.
5. Andrén 1940, p. 181, pl. 68:224.
6. Andrén 1940, p. 103, pl. 34:119, Vignale-Tempio Piccolo; *ibid.*, p. 92, pl. 27:98, Celle.
7. C. Albizzati, *Kantharos plastico di fabbrica etrusca,* in *Dissertazioni della Pontificia Accademia Romana di Archeologia* 14, 1920, p. 277, Fig. 6 on left, p. 230, Fig. 9.
8. A.D. Trendall, A. Cambitoglou, *The red-figured vases of Apulia,* I-II, Oxford 1978-1982, p. 188, pl. 61,3-4, no. 8/11.
9. *Ibid.*, nos 14/120, 16/41, 17/9, 18/1, 18/41, 18/287, 18/289-290, 23/231, 23/239, 27/13, 28/1, 28/18, 28/39, 28/87, 28/96, 28/118 and *passim*.
10. M. Harari, *Il "Gruppo Clusium" della ceramografia etrusca,* Roma 1980, pp. 159-176, pl. XLII,2B, Chiusi workshop, pls LII,11B, LIII,12B-13B, LIV,14B, LV,15B, southern workshop - Tarquinia (?).
11. J.D. Beazley, *Charinos Attic Vases in the Form of Human Heads,* in *JHS* 49, 1929, pp. 71-72, Figs 23-24.

103. *Hollow palmette pendant

Gold. Height 5.0; width 2.7

Hollow pendant, made from two die-formed valves joined at the seams, with repoussé and incised decoration picturing a seven-leaved palmette. The suspension element consists of a hoop-shaped sheet gold band decorated centrally with a row of repoussé bosses and edged with twisted wire at the attachment point.

There are no specific comparisons for this piece. It was probably inspired by the "acorn" type *bulla* pendants, which may be observed in the recomposition of the Castellani necklace in the British Museum, dated to the first half of the fourth century BC, in this case characterized by a repoussé palmette decoration on the side, while a profile of a head is pictured frontally.[1] The seven-petalled palmette recurs as a characteristic theme in acorn-shaped pendants on necklaces from Filottrano, in the Piceno, dated around the mid-fourth century BC.[2]

1. Marshall 1969, no. 2271; Cristofani, Martelli 1983, pp. 209, 306, no. 216; J. Swaddling, A. Oddy, N. Meeks, *Etruscan and Other Early Gold Wire from Italy,* in *Jewellery Studies* 5, 1991, pp. 18-19, Fig. 39.
2. Coen 1998, p. 85, no. 7, Figs 9a-b, Santa Paolina, tomb XXI; cf. also pp. 85-87, no. 2, Figs 1-7, Santa Paolina, tomb 2.

104. *Olla*-shaped pendant

Gold. Height 1.6; width 1.1. Missing collar.

The body is made from two die-formed sheet gold valves, soldered at their widest point. Three grains are attached to the underside. A corrugated handle with volutes at the joints is attached to the mouth of the vessel.

105. *Olla*-shaped pendant

Gold. Height 1.5; width 0.8

The body is made from two die-formed sheet gold valves, soldered at their widest point. Three grains are attached to the underside. A corrugated handle with a central row of granules is attached to the mouth of the vessel.

Olla-shaped pendants similar to these (nos **104-105**) may be observed on a necklace from Orvieto, former Castellani Collection, at the Museo di Villa Giulia, in which they alternate with plain *bullae*, pomegranates, gold beads and glass paste beads. The necklace, possibly the result of an arbitrary 19th-century reconstruction, is currently dated to the fourth century BC.[1]
Similar pendants alternate with beads of various typologies in a reassembled necklace in the British Museum, also from the Castellani Collection.[2]

Fourth century BC.

1. Cristofani, Martelli 1983, no. 258; *Magie des Goldes* 1996, pp. 62-63, no. 62.
2. Marshall 1969, no. 1454, pl. XXIII.

106. Pomegranate-shaped pendant

Gold. Height 2.9; diameter 1.7

Pomegranate-shaped pendant composed of a hollow sphere decorated with granulation and filigree, with circles of twisted wire and granules and equipped with a suspension ring.

Similar pendants have an ancient tradition in the eastern Mediterranean, being documented in Cyprus as early as the Mycenaean period. A hollow, pomegranate-shaped pendant decorated with granulation was found in Enkomi.[1] Another example from the same location, in the Cyprus Museum, is decorated with a series of triangles in granulation and dated to 1440-1230 BC, or "Late Cypriote II".[2]
From western Anatolia (Ionia or Lydia) there derives a pomegranate-shaped pendant with no decoration and with a cylindrical suspension element, dated to the second half of the seventh century BC.[3]
In Etruria, plain pomegranate-shaped pendants from Orvieto may be seen in a reassembled necklace from the former Castellani Collection at the Museo di Villa Giulia.[4]
Pomegranate-shaped pendants, plain or decorated with impressed studs, appear on a necklace

from Vulci at the Gregorian Etruscan Museum, currently dated to the fourth – third centuries BC.[5]
Also in Etruria, elements similarly shaped as pomegranates are recurrent as terminals on hairpins dated to the sixth century BC.[6] A gold brooch with a globular head decorated with granulation was found among grave goods from the Littore Tomb in Vetulonia.[7]

Probably fourth – third centuries BC.

1. Marshall 1969, p. 41, no. 623, pl. V = Karo 1899-1901, p. 277-278, Fig. 45.
2. A. Pierides, *Jewellery in the Cyprus Museum*, Nicosia 1971, p. 18, no. 5, pl. VIII.
3. Rudolph 1995, p. 71, no. 12.
4. Caruso 1988, p. 40, no. 72, pl. X.
5. Cristofani, Martelli 1983, pp. 238, 316, no. 266.
6. C. Alexander, *Jewelry. The Art of Goldsmith in Classical Times*, New York 1928, p. 44, no. 93; Marshall 1969, nos 1347-1353, pl. XVII, former Castellani Collection, from Chiusi no. 1350; Greifenhagen 1970, p. 92, nos 8-9, pl. 70, from Chiusi.
7. C. Benedetti, *La tomba vetuloniese del "Littore"*, in *StEtr* 27, 1959, p. 246, no. 46, pl. XXIa.

107. Medallion with intaglio portrait

Gold and glass paste. Height 4.7; width 3.3

Transparent elliptical gem worked with an intaglio design picturing a frontal nude male bust with short hair rendered in small curls, dressed in the manner of Hermes with a caduceus on his left shoulder. A likely product of modern manufacture, the openwork setting, trimmed with spooled wire, is equipped with a suspension element with oblique sides and upturned edges.

The intaglio portrait on this remarkable medallion is a near-perfect replica of the incision on an amethyst in Vienna (measuring 2.84 x 2.27 cm)

attributed to the engraver Eutyches and dated to 30-20 BC[1] .The close similarity with the Viennese intaglio is perceivable in the typology of the face - characterized by puffy cheeks, full and com-

Fig.19.Cast of engraved amethyst with frontal portrait, attributed to the engraver Eutyches. 30-20 BC. Vienna, Kunsthistorisches Museum. 2.84 x 2.27 cm.

Fig.20. Carnelian with frontal portrait of Gaius Caesar. From the Mainz area. Not later than 4 AD. Vienna, Kunsthistorisches Museum, inv. IXa 72. 1.7 x 1.9 cm.

pressed lips, incised irises - and in that of the hair, which is analogous even in the form and distribution of the curls. The caduceus is rendered in the same detail, in the wings, for example; the only appreciable difference in the Viennese amethyst is in the bust, which is larger toward the bottom and has drapery resting on the right shoulder.

Contributing to a possible attribution of this intaglio to the Augustan period are a number of analogies that may be made with other incisions of portraits of the imperial family:[2] a carnelian in Vienna with the portrait of Gaius Caesar, who died in 4 AD[3] , a sardonyx in Florence picturing the two confronting busts of Gaius and Lucius Caesars, also with curly hair and *barbulae*[4] , and the portrait attributed to Germanicus on the Vienna cameo, known as Gemma Augustea, dated to 4-14 AD.[5]

In terms of statuary, the young figure on this intaglio appears to be equally associable with portraits of Gaius[6] and Lucius Caesars,[7] or more generically with Tiberian-age portraits of Nero Caesar (?), son of Germanicus,[8] and Caligula (?).[9] The classic configuration of the face, with its slightly open, fleshy mouth, paired with the short and curly animated hair typical of Hellenistic tradition, may also be found in a portrait of Juba II, King of Mauritania (25 BC - 23 AD), dated to the Augustan period, early first century AD.[10]

The possible identification of a prince from the Augustan period is further corroborated by the iconography: the assimilation to Hermes, in fact, draws on a recurrent theme in the art and literature of the period, as in the case of the Luni Altar in which Augustus is assimilated to Mercury. The caduceus pictured on this gem assumes a prominent place among imperial symbols evoking peace and prosperity.[11] The use of "deification," specifically with the identification of Hermes through the portrait's association with the caduceus, was already affirmed by the end of the Republic, in the second half of the first century BC, with a particular interest around 40 BC.[12]

The assimilation to Mercury subsequently registered a concentration in the course of the second century AD, contrasted by more sporadic documents from the following century.[13] From a general perspective, the youthful bust associated with the caduceus evokes an iconography characteristic of the funerary realm, contiguous to the private sphere, and as such was occasionally pictured on the tympana of gravestones,[14] with an

Fig.21. Sardonyx [sard intaglio] with the confronting busts in profile of Gaius (20 BC-4 AD) and Lucius Caesar (17 BC-2 AD). Florence, Museo Archeologico Nazionale, inv. 14914.

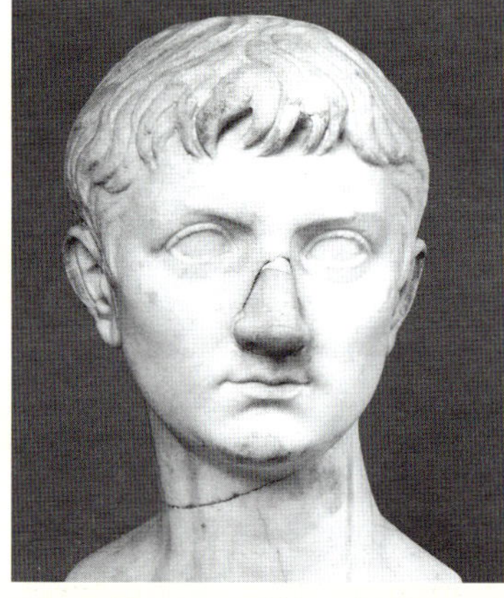

Fig.22. Portrait of Gaius (20 BC-4 AD) or Lucius Caesar (17 BC-2 AD). Claudian-Age copy of Augustan original. 41-54 AD. Modern bust. Vatican City, Vatican Museums, inv. 1228. Marble. Height 50 cm.

Fig.23. Portrait of a young Caligula (?). Tiberian Age, 14-37 AD. Modern bust; later reworking of hair. Vatican City, Vatican Museums, inv. 1978. Marble. Height 58 cm.

Fig.24. Portrait statue with caduceus from the Tomba dei Manili. From a 360 BC prototype. 100 AD. Vatican City, Vatican Museums, Greek Cross Room, inv. 187. Marble. Height 129 cm.

evident symbolic allusion to Hermes Psychopompos.[15] A similar subject, for its bust with a caduceus assimilated to Hermes, but wearing a *chlamys* and pictured in profile, may also be seen on a later carnelian from Istanbul, dated to the age of Marcus Aurelius.[16]
With the support of the considerable analogies found with the Viennese amethyst, it is possible to recognize in this intaglio the hand of the same Eutyches or of a master very close to him. Eutyches, who is also responsible for a rock crystal from the Berlin collection picturing the frontal bust of Pallas Athena, continued, with his brothers Herophilos and Hyllos, the tradition of his father Dioskurides, most likely remaining in service for the same imperial family.[17] It is to be considered that creations of such value and refinement may only be traced back to a prestigious and exclusive commission such as this.

30-20 BC.

1. Zwierlein Diehl 1973, p. 137, no. 420, pl. 70 and p. 17.
2. For stylistic and iconographic considerations on portraits in Augustan-age glyptics, cf. Rocco 2001.
3. Megow 1987, p. 273, C5, pl. 7, 3.
4. Pollini 1987, pp. 9, 35-38, pl. 1, 1.
5. Megow 1987, pp. 155-163, pl. 6, 5.
6. Massner 1982, pp. 53-60, pls 15c, 16c; Pollini 1987, p. 98, no. 11, pl. 13, p. 99, no. 13, pl. 15; Rose 1997, no. 49, pl. 122.
7. Massner 1982, pp. 53-60, pls 15d-16d; Pollini 1987, p. 105, no. 32, pl. 33, p. 106, no. 36, pl. 37; Rose 1997, no. 49, pl. 123, no. 96, pl. 198.
8. Rose 1997, no. 52, pl. 164.
9. *Museo Chiaramonti* 1, pp. 128-129, no. 715.
10. Smith 1988, pl. 68, 3-4, type 2 = Johansen 1994, pp. 42-43, no. 9.
11. A. Frova, *Scavi di Luni* I, Roma 1973, p. 54, pl. 15,1; Wrede 1981, p. 280, no. 224.
12. Wrede 1981, p. 28; for the gems: Vollenweider 1972-1974, p. 285, s.v. *Mercur*; pls 93,1-3 (44-35 BC), 99,5 (early second century AD), 101,1-3 (40 BC), 127,1 (mid-first century BC), 148,16,18 (Octavian, 44-40 BC).
13. Wrede 1981, pp. 273-283.
14. Wrede 1981, no. 217, pl. 32,1, 100-120 AD, Vatican Museums, Lapidary Gallery; Wrede 1981, no. 218, pl. 33,3, 115-135 AD, Torino.
15. Wrede 1981, pp. 116-117.
16. *AGDS* I,3, no. 2530, pl. 232.
17. For engravers of the Augustan age, cf. Vollenweider 1966, pp. 67-69.

108. *Bulla*

Gold. Height 4.9; width 3.5

This *bulla* is made from two fused valves of smooth sheet gold, bordered at the seams with beaded and spooled wire. Spiral-beaded wire is applied to the edges and along the central axis of the trapezoidal suspension element. The upper portion of the body is decorated with short rows of grains.

The *bulla* has strong symbolic connotations of recognized Etruscan origin, following the tradition transmitted to the Roman world during the Regal Period in which it was worn by young aristocrats in the age of puberty.[1]
Plain *bulla* elements were quite common in Etruscan goldwork from the fourth century BC. One may cite, for example, a necklace from Tarquinia,[2] or a specimen from Orvieto (former Castellani Collection), now in Rome at the Museo di Villa Giulia, of dubious recomposition,[3] both of which fall within a typology also attested iconographically.[4]
For its shape, however, this specimen is compara-

Fig.25. Statue of youth wearing toga with *bulla*. The head is ancient but not pertinent. Mid-first century AD. Head: 220-230 AD. Vatican City, Vatican Museums, inv. 10451. Marble. Height 144 cm.

ble to *bullae* from the Roman era, dated prevalently to the first century AD, a period to which iconographic documentation may also be referred, which in some cases significantly derives from Etruria.[5] Of these examples, several were found in the Vesuvian cities,[6] Herculaneum[7] and Pompeii.[8]

In Rome, an example is known from Via Tiburtina, former Castellani Collection,[9] while from the city's suburbs one may recall a *bulla* from a burial ground in Ariccia, at the Madonna di Galloro sanctuary, dated by its association with a coin of Vespasian from 73 AD.[10] Another example, without knurled wire decorations, dated to the Augustan age, comes instead from Ostia and is corroborated by late-Etruscan iconographic documentation.[11]

Other examples are present in collections or on the art market.[12]

First century AD.

1. Cf. in general: Gregory Warden 1983.
2. Marshall 1969, no. 2271; Higgins 1980, pl. 44.
3. Cristofani, Martelli 1983, pp. 233, no. 258.
4. Cristofani, Martelli 1983, p. 19, pl. VIII.
5. E.g.: Giuliano 1957, p. 20, no. 25, pl. 15, from Veio; Claudian or Flavian period with unrelated head from 220-230 AD.
6. Siviero 1954, pls 200-205.
7. Breglia 1941, p. 90, no. 916, pl. XL,1; Siviero 1954, no. 338.
8. Breglia 1941, nos 917-918, pl. XXXIII,10; Siviero 1954, nos 339-340; Cantilena 1989, p. 214, no. 57; Pirzio Biroli Stefanelli 1992, no. 69, Fig. 114.
9. Caruso 1988, pp. 45-47, no. 86.
10. Bordenache Battaglia 1983, pp. 34-39, no. 1.
11. Cristofani, Martelli 1983, pp. 239, 316, no. 267; Buranelli 1992, p. 87, no. 45.
12. L. Berge, K. Alexander, *Ancient gold work from Chicago Collections*, in *AncWorld* 11, 1985, p. 30, no. 149: Field Museum of Natural History; *Christie's*, 6 July 1994, p. 101, no. 301 and *Christie's*, 11 December 1996, p. 62, no. 115.

109. Lunar crescent pendant

Gold. Height 1.2

Lunula-shaped pendant with separate terminals and central ridge, equipped with a suspension ring with raised ridges at either extremity.

The shape of this pendant, which evokes a lunar crescent, while boasting distant Oriental origins dating to the second millennium BC, asserted itself during the late-Classical and Hellenistic periods. A necklace with a lunar-crescent pendant, associated with a pair of inverted-pyramid earrings (cf. no. **28**), adorns the female protome on a Tarantine antefix dated to the first half of the fourth century BC,[1] while an actual example was found in Delos in a context dated to 122-88 (or 122-69) BC.[2]

The use of *lunula*-shaped pendants is attested throughout the early Imperial period, when they were preferentially given to children as amulets to protect their growth, safeguarding at the same time their mother's life.[3]

A specimen from Naxos is dated by context to the last quarter of the first century BC.[4]

Numerous examples, both isolated and in association with necklaces, generically dated between the first century BC and the first century AD were found in Vesuvian locations such as Pompeii,[5] Oplontis[6] and Herculaneum.[7] Also dated to the first century AD is a pendant presumably from Asia Minor, at the Römisch-Germanischen Zentralmuseum in Mainz.[8] A *lunula* pendant, strung on a silver collar, was originally worn by a statuette from the baths at the Vindonissa (Windisch) military camp, dated to the first century AD.[9]

The type appears to have persisted until the second century AD,[10] as documented also by a gold and emerald necklace with a *lunula* pendant found in a sarcophagus in Vallerano (Rome), dated to 150-180 AD.[11] Also dated around the mid-second century AD is the Roman-British Snettisham treasure which included several *lunula* pendants.[12] Further parallels may be made with materials of uncertain provenance and from the art market[13].

Cf. no. **72.**

Second half first century BC - first/second centuries AD.

1. *Magna Graecia* 2002, pp. 146-147, no. 10.
2. E. Lévy, *Tresor hellenistique trouvé à Délos en 1964. Les bijoux,*

in *BCH* 89, 1965, pp. 555-556, pls XVII, XXII; Davidson, Oliver 1984, pp. 76-77, no. 74 = Williams 1924, p. 184, pl. XXVIII, 123.
3. Barini 1958, pp. 50-52; Scatozza Höricht 1989, pp. 57-61.
4. Bacci Spigo 1984, pp. 64-65, pl. III, b.
5. Breglia 1941, pl. XXXII, 4, no. 480.
6. D'Ambrosio, De Carolis 1997, pp. 32-33, no. 32, pl. III p. 66, nos 195-196, pl. XIX, p. 160, no. 190, pl. XVIII.
7. Scatozza Höricht 1989, pp. 57-58, no. 78, pp. 60-61, nos 83-85.
8. Deppert Lippitz 1985, p. 11, no. 4, pl. 3.
9. *Ori degli Elvezi* 1991, p. 154, no. 242.
10. Pfeiler 1970, p. 71, pl. 19; Greifenhagen 1975, p. 25, pl. 17, no. 3; pl. II, 7.
11. *Mistero di una fanciulla* 1995, pp. 31-33, 43, Fig. 10.
12. Johns 1997, pp. 42-43, p. 113, nos 320-322. For examples without contexts, one might additionally refer to the following comparisons: Arneth 1850, S IV, G61; Gramatopol, Craciunescu 1967, p. 143, nos 70-71, pl. IX, 1-2; Hoffmann, von Claer 1968, pp. 66-68, no. 43; Metzger 1976, p. 12, no. 17; *Ori e argenti* 1990, pp. 6, 31, no. 56; Rudolph 1995, p. 274, no. 81; from the antique market: *Ancient Art of the Mediterranean World & Ancient Coins,* NAAG Numismatic & Ancient Art Gallery AG, 7 April 1991, Zurich 1991, no. 177; *Christie's* 2002, pp. 44-45, no. 601.

110. Harpokrates pendant or amulet

Silver. Height 4.2; width 2.3
Missing suspension loop.

The pendant, or amulet, is in the form of Harpokrates as a winged boy with a lunar crescent on his head, pictured in the act of holding his right hand to his mouth, while carrying a cornucopia in his left hand.

Amulets picturing Harpokrates (cf. no. **153**), the son of Isis, in infantile guises were widespread throughout the Mediterranean during the Roman Imperial period.[1] Versions of this pendant are known in gold, silver and bronze.[2] A pendant from the Thames in London pictures a silver Harpokrates with a gold chain crossed over his body and a gold suspension loop.[3] Specimens in both bronze and silver, very similar to the one in question, were also highly recurrent in Herculaneum;[4] these were reproductions of cult statues particularly common in Herculanean lararia.[5] A similar example in gold is known from the market.[6]

Fig.26. Alexandrian-style statuette of Harpokrates. Former Grassi Collection. Roman Imperial period, second-third centuries AD, from Hellenistic original. Vatican City, Vatican Museums, inv. 15620. Bronze. Height 16 cm.

First century AD.

1. Tran Tam Tinh, B. Jaeger, S. Poulin, s.v. *Harpokrates*, in *LIMC* IV, Zürich-München 1988, pp. 419-424, cf. particularly no. 118d.
2. Lusingh Scheurleer 1996, pp. 152-171.
3. Johns 1996, p. 106, Fig. 5.18.
4. Scatozza Höricht 1989, no. 71-78.
5. V. Tran Tam Tinh, *Le culte des divinités orientales à Herculanum,* Leiden 1971, p. 72, nos 31-33, Fig. 21; V. Tran Tam Tinh, *Essai sur le culte d'isis a Pompéi,* Paris 1964, pp. 12 ff.; V. Tran Tam Tinh, *La vita religiosa,* in *Pompei 79,* Collection of Studies edited by F. Zevi, Napoli 1979, pp. 56 ff.
6. *Christie's*, 6 December 2000, no. 34.

111. *Olla*-shaped pendant

Gold. Height 1.3; width 0.8

Pendant in the form of a globular *olla*, with diagonal ridges on the body, a widened mouth, and equipped with a suspension ring.

A similar pendant is associated with a bracelet found in La Stella,

Ariccia, in a sarcophagus dated to the middle or third quarter of the first century AD.[1] A second example of analogous workmanship is strung on a plain wire hoop (earring?) from tomb 67 in Voghenza, dated to the second century AD (?).[2]

Second half first century AD - second century AD.

1. Bordenache Battaglia 1983, pp,. 31-33, Fig. 1.
2. *Voghenza* 1984, pp. 166-167, 197, Fig. 134. Cf. also: Pollak 1903, pl. XIII, no. 352; Marshall 1969, pl. LXXI, n.no, in the British Museum.

112. Pendant with radiate male portrait

Gold. Height 2.3; width 1.3

Elliptical pendant composed of a repoussé plate picturing a highly stylized, frontal radiate male portrait (*Sol?*), bordered by a circular-section plain wire terminating in a grain at either extremity (*lunula?*) and equipped with a ridged suspension loop.

Pendants or amulets picturing the radiate bust of the god Sol and with a border possibly inspired by the lunar crescent shape (cf. no. **109**) were very common during the early Roman Imperial period.[1] An example, circular in shape, was found in the ancient marina of Herculaneum.[2]

Fig.27. Embossed disc picturing Sol on a chariot. From Rome, Domus Flavia on the Palatine. Late second century AD. Vatican City, Vatican Apostolic Library, Medagliere, inv. 552. Bronze. Diameter 9.5 cm.

First - second centuries AD.

1. Greifenhagen 1975, p. 104, pl. 72, no. 20.
2. D'Ambrosio, De Carolis 1997, p. 105, no. 352, pl. XXXIII.

113. Amulet with eye and magical symbols

Gold. Diameter 1.8

Composed of a repoussé gold disc, outlined with a row of embossed dots and equipped with a small ring on the rear. The design pictures a central eye surrounded by barely intelligible symbols and animals.

In spite of difficulties in the interpretation of the pictured symbols, this pendant appears to be undoubtedly comparable to amulets with symbols against the evil eye from the mid- to late-Imperial periods, dated to the second-third centuries AD, that picture a central eye surrounded by magic and apotropaic symbols: elephants, scorpions, felines, serpents, thunderbolts, and phalluses[1]. The design is of Egyptian origin and represents the eye of Horus, who took on various forms after being lacerated by the god Thoth into 64 different parts. This iconographic type registered a remarkable popularity in the Greek and Roman eras and was also adopted by the Judaic and Christian realms, perpetuating itself well into the late-Antique and Byzantine periods.[2]
A finding from a tomb in Massa Marittima, dated to the final decades of the first century AD, perhaps still in Flavian times, constitutes the only chronological reference for a class of amulets otherwise composed of a considerable number of

specimens of undocumented provenance[3].

Late first - third century AD.

1. Cf: Arneth 1850, S IV,G69; Cesnola 1903, pl. IV, no. 5; Segall 1938, pp. 137-138, no. 213, pl. 42; *SwCypEx* IV,3, p. 118, Fig. 36,12, p. 121; Marshall 1969, nos 2887-2889, pl. LXVIII; *Christie's* Catalogue, November 28, 1979, p. 31, no. 129, pl. 22; M. Kohlert-Németh, *Archäologische Reihe römische Bronzen I aus Nida-Heddernheim. Götter und Dämonen*, Frankfurt am Main 1988, pp. 9-10, Fig. 4; *Ori e argenti* 1990, pp. 5, 29, no. 45; *Christie's*, 6 July 1994, p. 101, no. 302; Caliò 2000, pp. 90-91, no. 141.
2. C.W. King, *Antique Gems and Rings*, London 1872, p. 72, pl. LVI, no. 9; C. Daremberg, E. Saglio, *Dictionnaire des antiquités grecques et romaines*, II,2, Paris 1896, s.v. *Fascinum*, p. 987, Fig. 2888; D. Levi, *The Evil Eye and the lucky Hunchback*, in AA.VV., *Antioch on the Orontes III. The Excavations of 1937-1939*, Princeton 1941, pp. 220-232, Fig. 101a-b; Bonner 1950, p. 97-100; Goodenough 1953, pp. 238-241, Figs 1049-1050, 1063-1066; J. Engemann, *Zur Verbreitung magischer Übelabwehr in der nichtchristlichen und christlichen Spätantike, in Jahrbuch für Antike und Christentum* 18, 1975, pp. 22-48; K.M.D. Dunbabin, *The mosaics of Roman North Africa. Studies in Iconography and Patronage*, Oxford 1978, pp. 161-162, pl. LXV,163-164; P.W. Schienerl, *Ein Goldamulett aus der Walters Art Gallery in Baltimore*, in P.W. Schienerl, *Schmuck und Amulett in Antike und Islam*, Aachen 1988, pp. 82-89.
3. G. Camporeale (ed.), *L'Etruria mineraria*, exhibition catalogue (Portoferrario, Massa Marittima, Populonia), Milano 1985, pp. 168, 180, no. 398; A. Parrini, in *Museo Archeologico Massa Marittima*, Firenze 1993, pp. 80, 122-123, Fig. 170, pl. XX.

114. Pair of Antonine bust pendants

Silver. Height 3.0; width 1.7

Each pendant is in the form of a draped female bust, the hair fastened behind the head and wearing a diadem. A three-leaved palmette with lateral volutes is attached to the top of the head, frontally concealing the suspension hoop.

A pair of similar busts is known from the market, similar in their small size (19x11x10 mm) but made of stone (green chalcedony or prasio quartz) and featuring Antonine-age hairstyles.[1] The hairstyle on the pendants in question, gathered in a bun with a smooth crown, also seems to recall a late-Antonine typology, which may be observed in portraits of Faustina Minore, or those inspired by her, from the period between 160 and 180 AD.[2]

Fig. 28. Female portrait from the Antonine period. 138-193 AD. The bust is modern. Vatican City, Vatican Museums, inv. 1812. Marble. Height 48 cm.

1. *Ancient Art of the Mediterranean World & Ancient Coins*, NAAG Numismatic & Ancient Art Gallery AG, 7 April 1991, Zurich 1991, p. 33, no. 136.
2. Fittschen, Zanker 1983, nos 22-23, 116, pls 31-32, 147-148.

115. Pendant with embossed decoration: feline with prey (?)

Gold. Diameter 2.7; height 0.7

Cylindrical sheet gold pendant, open in back and equipped with a suspension ring. A three-wire braid design, flanked by two beaded wires, decorates the border. Pictured frontally is a feline pouncing on its prey (?), barely intelligible due to its state of conservation.

The object is generically comparable to clasps[1] or necklace pendants[2] documented in the Roman Imperial period and datable to the first-second centuries AD. Similar elements may also be found in later ancient goldwork, such as a medallion of Theodosius I,[3] and in Byzantine goldwork, documented in a necklace terminal[4]

and parts of a belt with a hook and double eye.[5]

Probably second century AD.

1. D'Ambrosio, De Carolis 1997, p. 32, no. 32, from Pompeii.
2. Marshall 1969, no. 2897, pl. LXVIII; Greifenhagen 1975, p. 32, nos 1-6, pl. 27.
3. de Ridder 1911, no. 1416.
4. Ross 1965, no. 4,A.
5. Ross 1965, nos 37-38, pls XXX-XXXI.

116. Pendant

Stone and gold. Height 1.6; diameter 1.1

Composed of a perforated globular blue/violet stone bead strung with a gold wire moulded into a suspension hoop.

Similar beads make up a necklace from Kastell Aalen, in the Aalen Limesmuseum, dated to the second-third centuries AD.[1]

1. Böhme 1974, pp. 4-5.

117. Lunar crescent pendant with carnelian bead

Gold and carnelian. Height 1.4; diameter 0.6

Composed of a pendant in the form of a lunar crescent, with separate ends that locate into a perforated globular carnelian bead.

The shape of the gold pendant finds a parallel in an earring type documented in the Roman era.[1]

1. Lindsay Allason Jones 1989, p. 4, p. 79, no. 176, pl. 31, type 2e.

118. Acorn pendant

Gold. Height 1.5; width 1.0

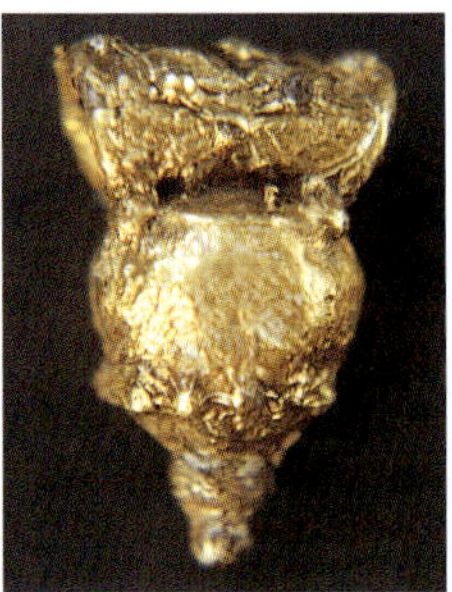

Acorn-shaped pendant terminating in two stacked grains of decreasing diameter, and equipped with a cylindrical suspension hoop with oblique sides.

119. Pendant or Amulet

Silver. Length 4.2; width 2.9

Composed of a die-formed sheet gold disc picturing a three-quarter view of a draped female bust. Applied to either extremity of the vertical axis are two rectangular plaques, decorated in repoussé with a row of beads between two ropes, which conceal the suspension tubes, made from a folded-back portion of the disc.

In the absence of close parallels, a distant analogy may be made with an impressed sheet gold disc decorated with a cloaked female divinity with a sceptre, from southern Russia, dated to the first century AD.[1] A medallion picturing a crowned female divinity, from the former Burton Y. Berry Collection, comes from the eastern Mediterranean, possibly Syria.[2]

1. Greifenhagen 1970, p. 50, no. 25, pl. 26; cf.: E.H. Minns, *Scythians and Greeks*, Cambridge 1913, p. 407, Fig. 295.
2. Rudolph 1995, p. 218, no. 60D.

120. **Acorn pendants

Gold. Width 2.4/2.0

Each pendant is composed of three acorns of die-formed sheet gold, each decorated with a shell of small squares in relief, open in back, and fastened to one another by a terminal ring with a rear peg.

The acorns on these pendants are anomalous in shape, in that the shell appears to be volumetrically more contained than the fruit. Such a peculiarity is observable in the pendants in Bientina, composed of two valves, in the Museo di Villa Guinigi in Lucca, dated to the second quarter of the fifth century BC.[1]

Acorn pendants are found strung in various ways on different jewels. The type originates in Asia Minor where it developed between the mid-sixth and fourth centuries BC.[2]

In the Italian peninsula, acorn pendants may be observed on a necklace from Vulci of dubious recomposition, from the former L. Bonaparte Collection in Munich's Antikensammlungen, dated to the end of the sixth century BC,[3] and in a necklace from Armento dated to the fourth century BC.[4]

The anomalies with respect to typologies of the period, as well as technological peculiarities such as the wire made by drawing and not by twisting, and the suspect regularity of the suspension ring, similar to those of modern-day trinkets, suggest that these pendants are fakes, although inspired by originals dated between the end of the sixth and the fourth centuries BC.

1. Cristofani, Martelli 1983, pp. 163, 291, no. 138,a-b.
2. Davidson, Oliver 1984, pp. 12-13, no. 3.
3. Cristofani, Martelli 1983, pp. 172, 294, no. 155.
4. Breglia 1941, no. 91, pl. XV,2.

FIBULAE

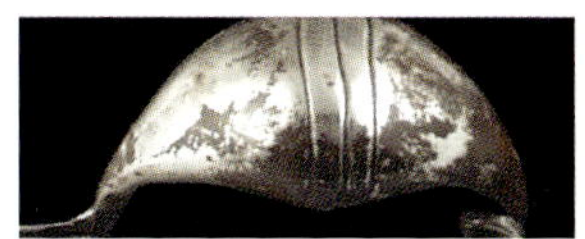

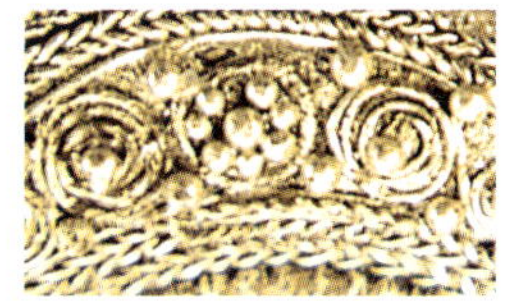

121. Leech-shaped fibula

Gold. Length 7.2; height 2.1
A few dents; a scratch near the spring.

The bow, with its slightly laterally expanded extremities, is hollow and made from sheet gold.

Soldered to one extremity is the long pin, equipped with a two-coil spring. The long, canal-type catch-plate is tapered at the end.

122. Leech-shaped fibula

Gold. Length 5.8; Height 2.1
A few dents; a small hole on the bow.

The bow, with its slightly laterally expanded extremities, is hollow and made from sheet gold.

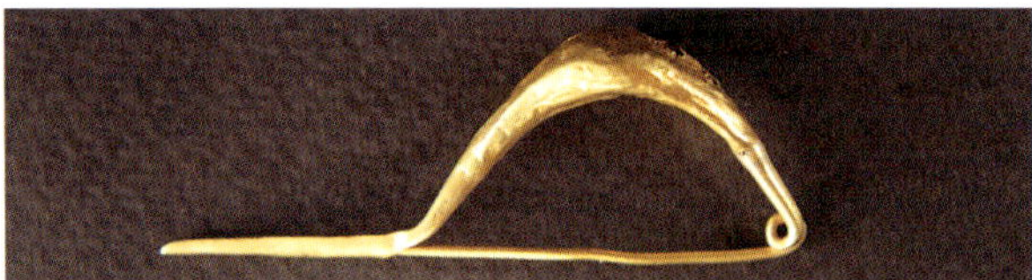

Soldered to one extremity is the long pin, equipped with a two-coil spring. The long, canal-type catch-plate is tapered at the end.

These two fibulae (nos **121-122**) find a close parallel in the example from Cumae, fondo P. Scala, tomb LVI, in silver and with a full bow.[1] The type also appears in the area of the Alban hills, still in silver but in the sheet version.[2] Finally, an analogous specimen appeared in the Baurat Schiller Collection.[3]

Last quarter eighth - seventh century BC.

1. Gabrici 1913, cols. 260-261, Fig. 102; Sundwall 1943, p. 226, type GIIIßa 20; Guzzo 1993, p. 144, type IIB, no. 3; for chronology, *ibid.*, pp. 13-15.
2. F. Arietti, B. Martellotta, *La Tomba Principesca del Vivaro*, Città di Castello 1998, pp. 55-57, no. 16a, Fig. 15.
3. Zahn 1929, p. 45, no. 91, pl. 43.

123. Leech-shaped fibula

Silver. Length 9.2; height 3.1; width 2.5
Integral.

The bow, rounded and with laterally expanded extremities, is made from a single sheet and is decorated orthogonally with three parallel lines incised in the center. The pin, with its single-coil spring, is soldered to the bow. The catch-plate is elongated and tapered toward the end.

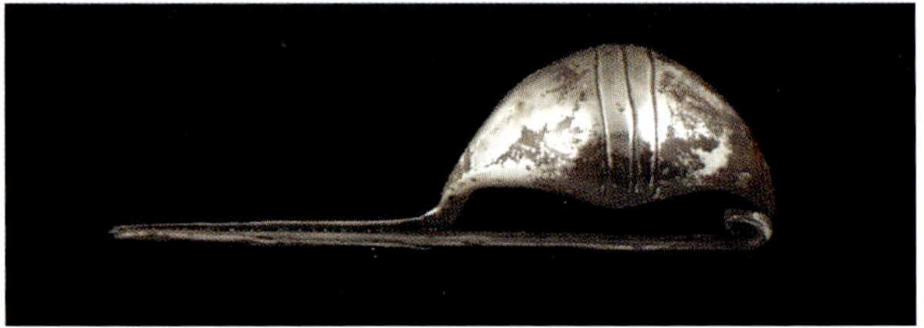

This fibula finds a parallel in specimens from Cumae-Maiorano, tomb 16, also in silver and with analogous lateral expansions.[1]
For Etruria, one might compare the fibulae from Vetulonia - Poggio alla Guardia[2] and from the tomb in Volterra - Gesseri,[3] in gold with a smooth body, to which may be added, for the Agro Falisco, the Narce specimen from the Monte Cerreto necropolis.[4] Versions in gold with decorations in filigree[5] and granulation[6] are also known in Etruria.
The type is dated from the last quarter of the eighth through the entire seventh century BC.

Fig.29.
Anthropomorphic cinerary vase with iron fibula on the shoulder. The fibula, according to the ancient custom, originally fastened the garment worn by the anthropomorphic vase, only traces of the fabric of which survive. From tomb 72 in Tolle. Late seventh century BC. Chianciano Terme, Museo Civico delle Acque, inv. 72/1. Impasto ceramic. Height 51 cm; width 35 cm; length of fibula 10 cm.

1. Gabrici 1913, cols. 226-27, Figs 70-71; Guzzo 1993, p. 143, type IIA, nos 1-4; for chronology, *ibid.*, pp. 13-15.
2. Karo 1899-1901, p. 261, Fig. 29.
3. Cristofani, Martelli 1983, pp. 122, 274, no. 72; *Magie des Goldes* 1996, pp. 34-35, nos 15-18, third quarter seventh century BC.
4. Cristofani, Martelli 1983, pp. 141, 282, no. 104, mid-seventh century BC.
5. Vetulonia - Secondo Circolo delle Pellicce: Karo 1899-1901, p. 250, Fig. 16a.
6. Cristofani, Martelli 1983, pp. 98, 262, no. 33, Cerveteri, Regolini Galassi Tomb; L. Berge, K. Alexander, *Ancient Gold work from Chicago Collections*, in *The Ancient World* 11, 1985, p. 11, no. 28, Kenneth Parvin Memorial Collection.

124. Fibula with decorated bow

Gold and glass paste. Length 5.4; height 2.0; bead diameter 0.9

Fibula with a plain bow, consisting of a rectangular-section rod, onto which is strung a blue glass paste bead. The circular-section pin is equipped with a two-coil spiral. The elongated catch-plate is tapered toward the end.

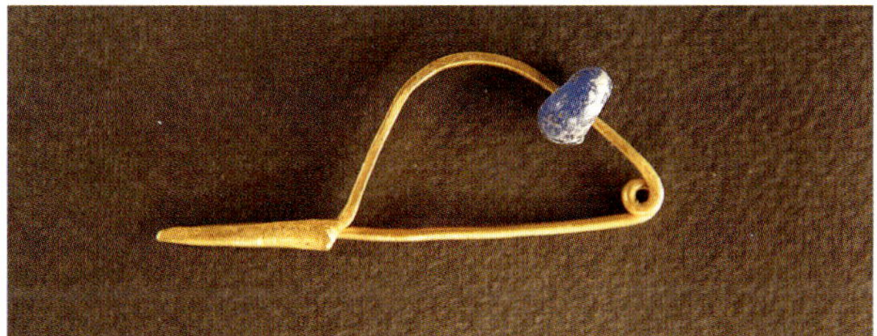

This has the same shape as the covered-bow fibulae that were widespread in the Orientalizing period both in Latium[1] and southern Etruria,[2] in the style of the specimen from the Guerriero Tomb in Tarquinia, datable to the last quarter of the eighth century BC.[3]
From collection material, a comparison may be made with a specimen in gold, with an uncovered bow, from the former Baurat Schiller Collection[4] and of unknown provenance; another appears in the Terrosi collection.[5]

Last quarter eighth – third quarter seventh century BC.

1. Bietti Sestieri 1992, type 39h, pl. 38, p. 372, period IV, or possibly IVA, 730/20 - 630/20 BC.
2. K. Raddatz, Bisenzio II. *Eisenzeitliche und frühetruskische Funde aus Nekropolen von Bisenzio (Capodimonte, prov. Viterbo)*, in *Hamburger Beiträge zur Archäologie* 9, 1982, pp. 140, 171, pl. 2,7-8; Toms 1986, p. 81, Fig. 29, type II.6, Veio phases IIB - IIC or III; cf. Sundwall 1943, p. 206, type GIßb.
3. Strøm 1971, pp. 141-145, Fig. 87.
4. Zahn 1929, p. 45, pl. 43, no. 90.
5. Paolucci 1991, p. 137, no. 181.

125. Dragon fibula

Gold. Length 6.7; height 3.1

The bow is articulated into two segments of rhomboidal profile, with lateral protrusions. The pin, bearing no spring, forms a wide arc, marked at the midpoint by an annular knot which serves to fasten folds in the cloth. The long catch-plate is slightly tapered.

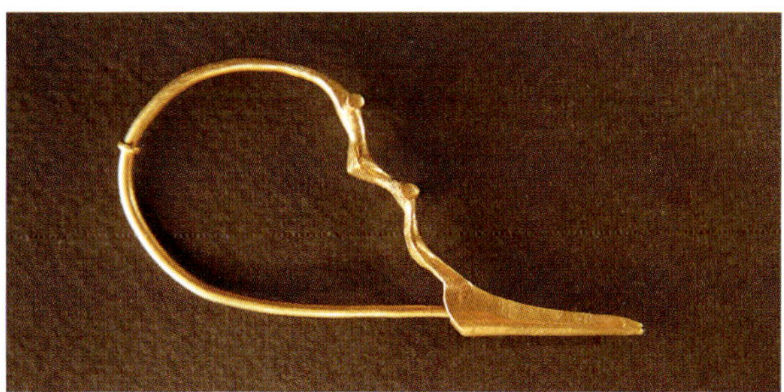

This fibula is similar to specimens in silver, equipped however with two- or three-turn springs, datable to the second quarter of the seventh century BC: Marsiliana d'Albegna - Banditella, tomb LXIII;[1] Vetulonia - Circolo degli Acquastrini;[2] former Castellani collection, in the British Museum.[3]
For the rigid arc with no spring, the fibula finds a close parallel in bronze specimens from Marsiliana d'Albegna - Banditella, tomb XXXII,[4] and tomb XCIII.[5]
An identical example may be seen in New York's Metropolitan Museum of Art.[6]

Second quarter seventh century BC.

1. Minto 1921, p. 116, pl. XII,9; Sundwall 1943, p. 237, no. 5; G.C. Cianferoni, in *Schätze der Etrusker* 1986, p. 162, no. 10, Fig. on p. 6.
2. Karo 1899-1901, p. 241, Fig. 5.
3. Marshall 1969, pl. XIX, no. 1374.
4. Minto 1921, p. 69, pl. XXIII,7.
5. Minto 1921, p. 147, pl. XXIII,12.
6. Alexander 1928, pp. 39, 41, no. 91.

126. *Navicella* fibula

Gold. Length 10.0; height 1.5; width 1.4

The bow, open on the underside, is made from a single sheet of uniform thickness. Its widely

expanded extremities cause it to have a rhomboidal profile on the dorsal face. The catch-plate is very elongated and is of the canal-type variety.

The fibula corresponds to Sundwall's GIIßa type and finds a particular parallel in a specimen from Vulci[1] as well as in those found in Marsiliana d'Albegna: Banditella, tomb XXXIV,[2] tomb XVII[3] and tomb XXXIX.[4] The fibula from tomb 3 in Bisenzio[5] is also of a similar typology.
Further comparisons may be made with an example from the former Campanari Collection, in the British Museum,[6] and with a second of unknown provenance in the Gregorian Etruscan Museum.[7] Very similar anonymous specimens are also known from the market,[8] such as an inscribed version richly decorated with granulation, referable to Caere and dated to 660-640 BC.[9]

Second – third quarter seventh century BC.

1. Sundwall 1943, p. 218, no. 15, Fig. 348, from Vulci, in Munich.
2. Minto 1921, p. 73, pl. XIV,2.
3. G.C. Cianferoni, in *Schätze der Etrusker* 1986, p. 161, no. 4, Fig. on p. 4, second quarter seventh century BC.
4. *Ibid.*, p. 161, no. 5, Fig. on p. 4.
5. E. Galli, *Il sepolcreto visentino delle "Bucacce"*, in *MAL* 21, 1912, col. 430, Fig. 16; *Ori e argenti* 1961, p. 24, no. 12.
6. Marshall 1969, pl. XIX, no. 1378.
7. Scarpignato 1985, p. 22, no. 2.
8. *Werke* 1970, p. 48, no. 122; *Christie's*, 11 December 2003, p. 41, no. 385, from the Marcel Ebnöther – Les Arcs Collection.
9. M. Cristofani, *Appunti di epigrafia etrusca arcaica*, in *ArchCl* 25-26, 1973-74, pp. 153-155, pl. XXXVIII.

127. Fibula fragment with four-faced bow

Silver. Length 2.1; width 1.0

Only the bow is preserved from this fibula, made from a smooth sheet in the form of a leech, and encased on all four sides by a second sheet, richly decorated with filigree and granulation. On the convex face, three large beaded wires alternate with plain and spiral-beaded wires. On the lateral faces, two spiral-beaded wires, placed side by side to form a braid, frame a spiral design of plain wire with alternating granules and a central flower composed of nine grains.

This fibula is characteristic of the Hellenistic necropoles of Campania, particularly documented in Teano, where it also recurs in tombs 32 and 58.[1]

Third century BC.

1. Gabrici 1910, col. 78, Fig. 47 = tomb 32; *ibid.*, col. 39, Fig. 21 = tomb 58; *passim*, also tombs 9, 23-24, 27-28, 38, 46, 58, 69, 71, 74, 76.

128. **Fibula

Gold. Length 6.1; width 1.4

The body is hollow and in the form of a tortoise shell, open on the underside, made from a single sheet and decorated with two repoussé confronting double volutes. The long, closed-case catch-plate is smooth on three sides, decorated on top with a sequence of symmetrical repoussé

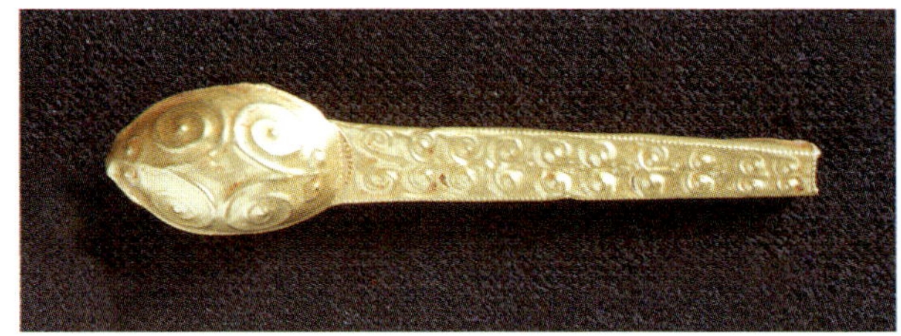

volutes terminating in small studs. Beaded wire decorates the edges of the body and catch-plate.

129. **Fibula

Gold. Length 6.0; width 1.5

The body is hollow and in the form of a tortoise shell, open on the underside, made from a single sheet and decorated with a sequence of repoussé radial lobes. The long, case-like catch-plate is decorated with flowers composed of five small bosses. The lateral faces bear a continuous rectangular meander pattern; beaded wire decorates the edges of the body and catch-plate.

BRACELETS

130. Openwork bracelet

Silver. Length 14.3; height 3.6

Composed of six strips of silver sheet edged in plain wire, alternating with five bands decorated with openwork filigree in a serpentine pattern. The extremities are capped by a hammered plate, decorated in front with a hollow semisphere outlined by a plain wire ring and flanked by two semicircular bezels made from a thin strip of cut-out and soldered silver sheet, made to hold a convex amber stone, preserved only in one case. The clasp is made from the extension of the three central strips, capped by a hammered band and terminating, on one extremity, in a pair of small hollow cylinders.

Openwork bracelets analogous to this in form and technique are particularly common in Vetulonia,[1] where tombs have prevalently revealed gold specimens. Entirely non-iconic bracelets of a more simple structure, with filigree decoration alternating with plain strips, were documented in this necropolis at an early stage with gold specimens: Circolo dei Monili,[2] Circolo di Bes[3] and Pietrera Tumulus – tomb I;[4] in addition to these, a pair of bracelets in white electrum or silver from Poggio alla Guardia was defined by Karo as "the most archaic."[5] Analogous bracelets were also found in Marsiliana d'Albegna, where only the gold version recurs: Banditella, tomb II.[6] Also from Vetulonia, and also in gold, a variant form is documented that has illustrated sheets with repoussé work at the extremities,[7] documented in the Migliarine Tumulus,[8] in the Pietrera Tumulus – tomb II[9] and peripheral tomb IV[10] as well as in a cremation tomb discovered in 1903 and not further specified[11] and in an isolated specimen purchased by Milani in 1898.[12] The variant form with applied repoussé sheets, characterized additionally by a meander-pattern filigree design, is also attested in Populonia.[13]

Worth noting is a pair of gold bracelets from the former Campanari Collection, in the British Museum since 1841, with repoussé plaques on a structure of strips and openwork filigree, but featuring a different type of clasp.[14]

In addition to the piece from the Circolo dei Monili (see above), this bracelet finds a very close parallel in a specimen from the former Campana Collection, in the Louvre Museum,[15] which constitutes convincing evidence for a provenance in southern Etruria, an area which may also be home to the specimen from Munich purchased by Louis I of Bavaria, also in gold.[16]

The parallel distribution of this class in southern Etruria is documented by the discovery in Tarquinia of two openwork bracelets that stand out for being, like the piece in this collection, one of the few versions in silver.[17] Another version of the bracelet, also documented in Tarquinia, is made without the alternating strips and filigree: it preserves, however, the shape, and features inserted figures at the terminals as well as repoussé and granulated decoration.[18]

The gold specimen in the Czartoryski collection in Cracow, of unknown provenance, features repoussé plaques at the extremities.[19] Its erroneous attribution to Tarquinia, based only on

comparison, has generated a misunderstanding in the subsequent bibliography in which it is indicated as Tarquinian.[20]

The wide and parallel diffusion of the openwork bracelet in southern Etruria, which seems to have established itself despite the uncertain provenance of some materials, contributed to the attribution of the type to this area,[21] considering also the early presence of the technique in southern Etruria, which counts precedents as early as the ancient Orientalizing period. In this regard, one may recall the two silver openwork bracelets from Bisenzio, from the last quarter of the eighth century BC,[22] that have the same filigree work as a group of hair fasteners found in Cerveteri,[23] Rome,[24] Castel di Decima,[25] Palestrina [26] and in the princely Vivaro tomb.[27] Also in Caere (Cerveteri), spiral bracelets from the Castellani Collection are made with an openwork technique featuring filigree alternating with strips, similar to the Vetulonia specimens.[28]

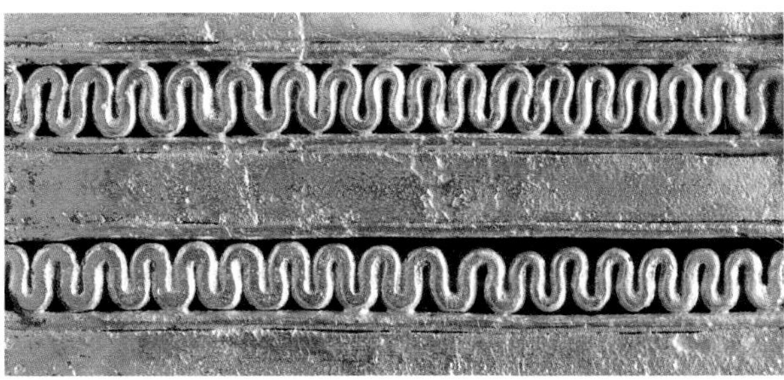

The southern limit for the diffusion of this type is currently represented by the discovery in Pontecagnano of a bracelet in gilt silver, which, based on tests, was made with more complex instruments and different methodologies with respect to those used on the gold bracelets from Vetulonia.[29]

The use of silver filigree, more complex from a technological point of view than its gold counterpart, is attested in Vetulonia, both in a pair of openwork bracelets from Poggio alla Guardia[30] and in a fastener from the Straniera Tomb, which also shares with our bracelet the peculiarity of the bezel-set amber buttons.[31] At the same time, the openwork technique with silver filigree appears to have been known in southern Etruria at an early stage, as documented by the above-mentioned bracelets from Bisenzio and Tarquinia. It is to this area, and more generally to the southern Etruria/Latium area, that the princely goods of Pontecagnano largely refer.[32]

For comparanda of uncertain provenance one might recall the Cracow example (see above) and that in Baltimore's Walters Art Gallery.[33]

First quarter seventh century BC.

1. I. Falchi, *Nuovi scavi della necropoli di Vetulonia*, in *NotSc* 1887, pp. 472-531.
2. Karo 1902, p. 103, Fig. 56; Montelius 1895-1910, pl. 182,2; Giglioli 1935, pl. XXI,2; Becatti 1955, pl. LXVI, no. 262; *Mostra dell'Etruria padana e della città di Spina*, Bologna 1960, p. 262, no. 856, pl. XV; *Ori e argenti* 1961, p. 32, no. 47; L. Banti, *Il mondo degli Etruschi*, Roma 1969, p. 321, pl. 64,c; Camporeale 1969, p. 70, pl. XLVII,2; O.J. Brendel, *Etruscan Art*, Hamondsworth 1978, p. 72, Fig. 43.
3. Karo 1902, p. 105, Fig. 59; Montelius 1895-1910, pl. 181,9; Mc Iver 1924, p. 110, Fig. 29; K. Kilian, *Zum Beginn der Halstattzeit in Italien und im Ostalpenraum*, in *Jahrbuch des Römisch-Germanischen Zentralmuseums Mainz* 17, 1970, p. 81, Fig. 8,5.
4. Karo 1902, p. 107, Fig. 61; Montelius 1895-1910, pl. 200,4.
5. Karo 1902, p. 102, Fig. 54.
6. Minto 1921, pp. 202-203, pl. XIV,20; Camporeale 1969, p. 70, pl. XXI,4; Cristofani, Martelli 1983, p. 266, no. 47; G.C. Cianferoni, in *Schätze der Etrusker* 1986, p. 164, nos 16-17, Fig. on p. 11; *Magie des Goldes* 1996, p. 24, no. 1.
7. See also: P.G. Guzzo, *La collezione etrusca del Museo Nazionale di Atene*, in *StEtr* 37, 1969, pp. 289-290, pl. LX,a.
8. Karo 1902, p. 106, Fig. 60; Montelius 1895-1910, pl. 203,3; Mc Iver 1924, pp. 147, pl. 28,5-6; Giglioli 1935, pl. XXI,3; *Ori e argenti* 1961, p. 32, no. 48; von Hase 1975, p. 132, note 156, pl. 42 bottom left, with bibliography.
9. Karo 1902, p. 107, Fig. 62; Montelius 1895-1910, pl. 201,1; Mc Iver 1924, pp. 153-154, pl. 29,5; Strøm 1971, p. 91, N 2-3, Fig. 64.
10. Karo 1902, p. 107, Figs 63-64; Montelius 1895-1910, pl. 202,6; Mc Iver 1924, pp. 153-154, pl. 29,3; Strøm 1971, p. 91, nos 6-7, Fig. 65; M. Cygielman, in *Schätze der Etrusker* 1986, p. 184, nos 1-2, Fig. on p. 27, dated to the second quarter of the seventh century BC; *Magie des Goldes* 1996, pp. 27-29, no. 7.
11. G. Karo, *Vetuloneser Nachlese*, in *StEtr* 8, 1934, pp. 49-50, pl. XXIII,1; von Hase 1975, p. 132, note 157, pl. 41 on right.
12. Karo 1902, p. 107, Fig. 65; von Hase 1975, p. 132, note 158, pl. 42 bottom right, with bibliography; M. Cygielman, in *Schätze der Etrusker* 1986, p. 184, nos 3-4, Fig. on p. 28, dated to the first half of the seventh century BC.
13. A. Minto, *Populonia. Relazione degli scavi archeologici governativi eseguiti nel 1923*, in *NotSc* 1924, p. 28-29, Fig. 14.
14. Marshall 1969, nos 1362-3, pl. XVII.
15. Karo 1902, p. 104, Fig. 58; Coche de la Ferté 1956, pp. 13, 15, 37, 39, 77, 119, pl. XXIX,1-2; Higgins 1980, p. 144, pl. 37B.
16. Karo 1902, p. 104, Fig. 57.
17. W. Helbig, *Oggetti trovati nella parte più antica della necropoli tarquiniese*, in *AnnInst* 1883, p. 290; I. Undset, *L'antichissima necropoli tarquiniese*, in *AnnInst* 1885, p. 100; *MonInst* 11, 1883, pl. LX,8-9; Karo 1902, p. 102, Fig. 55.
18. Karo 1902, p. 114, Fig. 74; Marshall 1969, nos 1358-1359, pl.

XVIII; Strøm 1971, p. 68, S 34-35, Fig. 56, with previous bibliography; Coche de la Ferté 1956, pp. 42, 75, pl. XXVII,1-2, p. 81; Higgins 1980, pl. 36, A-B; Stary 1981, pl. 19,5.

19.Ruxer, Kubczak 1976, pp. 107-109, no. 2, Fig. 1, compared with Marshall 1969, nos 1358-1359. It is worth noting that the half-moon design and repoussé sheets recur equally in examples from Vetulonia, while the openwork is entirely absent in the Tarquinian specimen from the British Museum with which the Cracow bracelet has been compared.

20.Cristofani, Martelli 1983, *infra* no. **47**.

21.Cristofani, Martelli 1983, p. 37.

22.Cristofani, Martelli 1983, pp. 77, 252, no. 8, with further comparisons.

23.Karo 1902, p. 117, Fig. 85f, in gold.

24.G. Pinza, *Monumenti primitivi di Roma e del Lazio antico,* in *MAL* 15, 1905, cols. 161, 451, pl. XIV, no. 14, Esquiline tomb C, in silver.

25.A. Bedini, *L'ottavo secolo nel Lazio e l'inizio dell'orientalizzante antico alla luce di recenti scoperte nella necropoli di Castel di Decima,* in *ParPass* 32, 1977, pp. 305-307, Fig. 14a-b, tomb 101, in gold.

26.R. Garrucci, *On the discovery of Sepulchral Remains at Veii and Praeneste,* in *Archaeologia* 41, 1867, p. 205, no. 3; probably to be identified with Marshall 1969, p. 125, no. 1360-1361, pl. XVIII, said however to come from Caere/Cerveteri.

27.F. Arietti, B. Martellotta, *La tomba principesca del Vivaro di Rocca di Papa,* Città di Castello 1998, pp. 47-51, pls A, III, in gold.

28.Marshall 1969, no. 1364, pl. XVII, in gold.

29.E. Formigli, *L'antica tecnica dei bracciali a filigrana,* in *StEtr* 44, 1976, pp. 203-210, pls XXXVII-XXXIX, particularly pl. XXXVIIId.

30.Karo 1902, p. 102, Fig. 54.

31.I. Falchi, in *NotSc* 1887, p. 520, pl. XIX,1; I. Falchi, *Vetulonia e la sua necropoli antichissima,* Firenze 1891, pl. V,16; Karo 1899-1901, pp. 269-270, Fig. 38.

32.B. D'Agostino, *Tombe "Principesche" dell'orientalizzante antico da Pontecagnano, MA,* serie miscellanea II, 1, Roma 1977, pp. 51 ff.

33.J.V. Canby, D. Buitron, A. Oliver, *Ancient Jewelry in Baltimore,* in *Archaeology* 32,5, 1979, p. 56, Fig. on bottom left; *Walters Art Gallery. Jewelry: Ancient to Modern,* New York 1979, p. 70, Fig. 222.

RINGS AND GEMS

131. Ring

Silver. Diameter 2.2

Composed of a plain, circular-section hoop.

132.Ring

Gold. Diameter 2.2

Composed of a plain, circular-section hoop.

Rings of this shape, given their simplicity, registered a wide diffusion, which also spanned an extensive chronological period.[1] In southern Italy, specimens in gold or silver are attested as early as the sixth century BC.[2] Plain rings of thick gold wire are known from the Spina necropolis, where they were found in contexts dated to the first half of the fifth century BC[3] and to the mid-fifth century BC.[4] A gold specimen was found in association with grave goods from an unspecified location in Etruria, dated to 530-490 BC, in the Rhode Island School of Design's Museum of Art.[5]

Similar shapes persist in the late Classical era,[6] lasting through Hellenism[7] and the early Imperial period, [8] from which derive, among others, specimens found in the Vesuvian area.[9]

1. For an example from collection material, of unspecifiable chronology, cf. Caliò 2000, p. 82, no. 82.
2. Guzzo 1993, pp. 44-45, 181-182, type XI A, nos 1 (Drapia-Torre Galli), 2-5 (Francavilla Marittima), 6 (Metaponto), 7-8 (Taranto), 9-16 (Melfi), 17-18 (Cumae), 19-21 (Taranto); L. Masiello, in *Arte e Artigianato* 1996, p. 157, no. 100, in silver, from Taranto, associated with middle-Corinthian remains, second quarter sixth century BC.
3. Valle Pega, tomb 27C: *Ori Emilia* 1958, no. 78, Fig. 21.
4. Valle Trebba, tomb 579: Becatti 1955, pl. H2; *Ori Emilia* 1958, no. 52, Fig. 16.
5. Hackens 1976, p. 35, no. 1.
6. A. Alessio, in *Ori di Taranto* 1985, p. 302, nos 247-248, second half fourth century BC.
7. *Ibid.*, p. 302, no. 249, first century BC.
8. Henkel 1913, p. 212, nos 1-2, pl. I.
9. D'Ambrosio, De Carolis 1997, p. 40, nos 72-73, pl. VII; D'Ambrosio 2001, pp. 970-971, no. 1, Fig. 1 on right.

133. Ring with incised bezel

Silver. Diameter 1.8; bezel 1.3

The narrow, D-section hoop terminates in a circular bezel, engraved in low relief, which is unintelligible as a result of corrosion.

Despite the state of conservation, the ring is comparable to an archaic Greek type, dated to the mid-sixth century BC.[1] These probably gave rise to the later circular-bezel rings that were common in southern Italy.[2]

1. Boardman 1975, no. 68, type M.
2. Hoffmann, von Claer 1968, p. 177, nos 114-115; Guzzo 1993, pp. 33, 163-165, type IIA, nos 1-4 (Capua- fourth century BC), 5 (S. Maria del Cedro), 7 (Reggio Calabria), 8 (southern Italy).

134. Ring with swivel scarab

Gilt silver sheet and carnelian. Diameter 2.3; bezel 1.0 x 0.8; diameter hoop 0.2

The circular-section silver hoop, overlaid in sheet gold, terminates in circular collars at the attachment to the bezel. The walls of the elliptical bezel are decorated with granulation and filigree, consisting, from the bottom upward, of consecutive rows of granules, twisted plain wire, spirally coiled plain wire, twisted plain wire, and another row of granules. The scarab is mounted with triangular teeth covered in granulation.

This is comparable to a specimen from Cyprus, in a private collection, datable to 530 BC,[1] and to a second ring, from the former Castellani Collection in the British Museum, dated to the early fifth century BC.[2]

1. Deppert Lippitz 1985b, pp. 134-135, Fig. 86.
2. Marshall 1907, p. 54, no. 299, pl. VIII.

135. Ring with incised oval bezel

Silver. Diameter 2.2; bezel 1.1 x 0.5

Consists of a twisted hoop terminating in an incised lozenge-shaped bezel, bordered by a row of punched dots, and picturing a bird in flight.

This is a ring type of Greek production, usually made in silver, that was widespread in Etruria from the mid-sixth century BC through the entire fifth century BC,[1] and during the same period in southern Italy, where it seems to have persisted, within the limits of votive contexts, until the fourth century BC.[2] A specimen is known from Praeneste that was found in a cist from the early fifth century BC.[3] Other examples in the J.P. Getty Museum in Malibu are said to be from Gela[4] or more generally from Sicily or southern Italy.[5]

Mid-sixth - fifth centuries BC.

1. Marshall 1907, p. 8, no. 35, pl. I and p. 147, no. 907, pl. XXIII, both Castellani Collection; Boardman 1967, pp. 18-20, group F; Boardman 1970, p. 155, pls 429-431, p. 187; Boardman 1975, nos 66-67, pp. 93-94, type F.
2. Guzzo 1993, pp. 41-43, 175-176, type VIIIA, nos 1 (Posidonia), 2-3 (Oliveto Citra), 4 (Francavilla Marittima), 5-6 (Drapia - Torre Galli), 7 (Naples), 8 (Armento = Boardman, Vollenweider 1978, no. 98), 9-12 (Vico Equense).
3. Boardman, Vollenweider 1978, no. 100.
4. Spier 1992, pp. 25-31, nos 31-43.
5. *Ibid.*, p. 33, nos 48-49. Cf. also: Henkel 1913, p. 51, pl. XIX, no. 376, but with an objectionable dating to the Augustan age; Hoffmann, Davidson 1965, p. 247, no. 105, Melvin Gutman Collection; Greifenhagen 1975, nos 3-4, pl. 62.

136. Ring with incised oval bezel

Silver. Diameter 2.3; bezel 1.7 x 1.0

The circular-section hoop terminates in a flat, amygdaloid bezel, outlined by a punched groove, bearing an incision picturing a helmeted female figure in a standing pose and carrying a shield, identifiable as Athena.

The ring represents a type of Greek origin, attested from the sixth century BC in the Dodecannesus,[1] in Rhodes[2] and variously diffused in the Mediterranean basin,[3] where it seems to have persisted throughout the fourth century BC.[4] It was also present in Etruria, in Vulci[5] and in Tarquinia,[6] during the sixth - first half of the fifth centuries BC, while in southern Italy, in documented cases, it is dated to the second half of the fourth century BC.[7]
The subject of Athena Promachos, which seems to be the inspiration for the incision on this ring, may be observed on a bronze specimen with a pointed oval bezel from Nemea, dated to the late fifth century BC.[8]

Late sixth - fifth centuries BC.

1. Greifenhagen 1975, p. 85, nos 1-2, pl. 62.
2. L. Laurenzi, *Necropoli ialisie (scavi dell'anno 1934)*, in *Clara Rhodos* 8, 1936, p. 160, Fig. 146, from Ialysos, mid-sixth century BC.
3. Marshall 1907, nos 44-45, 47.
4. Hoffmann, Davidson 1965, nos 108-114. For more on the type and for further comparisons: Boardman 1967, pp. 25-27, pl. 7, group N, in particular cf. N 43 dated to the early fifth century BC; Boardman 1970, pp. 212-215, 296, pls 656-660, type I, Penelope Group, second quarter fifth century

BC; Boardman 1975, no. 72, late sixth century BC.
5. Hoffmann, von Claer 1968, pp. 172-173, no. 109.
6. Marshall 1907, p. 10, no. 43, pl. II.
7. Guzzo 1993, pp. 43-44, pp. 179-180, type IX C, nos 1 (southern Italy), 2 (Capua).
8. S.G. Miller, *A Miniature Athena Promachos*, in *Studies in Athenian Architecture, Sculpture and Topography Presented to H.A. Thompson*, Princeton 1982, pp. 93-99, pl. 14a-c.

137. Ring with elliptical bezel

Gold. Diameter 2.2; bezel 1.6 x 0.8

The ring is composed of a circular-section hoop to which is attached a smooth, elliptical bezel with tapered extremities and rounded edges.

This finds a close parallel in a specimen from Spina, found in tomb 392, dated to the fifth century BC.[1] A very similar second specimen bearing the inscription *palartas* was found in the Pisciarelli district of Civitavecchia and is now in the Museo di Villa Giulia in Rome.[2]

Fifth century BC.

1. Becatti 1955, pl. H, 3.
2. Becatti 1955, pl. LXXXV, no. 345.

138. Ring with elliptical bezel

Gold. Diameter 1.85; bezel 1.6 x 1.2

The flattened, rectangular-section hoop terminates in a smooth, elliptical bezel with tapered extremities and rounded edges.

Rings of this form have a long tradition, being documented in the Mediterranean area since the Minoic-Mycenaean age, 1700-1600 BC.[1]
Specimens with pointed oval bezels, but also bearing incisions, are documented in Sicily (Stosch Collection), in southern Italy (Stevens Collection) and in southern Russia (Olbia), beginning in the second half of the fifth century BC,[2] and in Magna Graecia[3] and Taranto throughout the fourth century BC.[4] A specimen from Praeneste is dated to the third century BC;[5] the same chronology is attributed to a ring from the Castellani Collection, with a hollow hoop, and thus intended for funerary use.[6] A similar ring, of probable Egyptian provenance, is dated to the first century AD.[7]

Probably fourth - third centuries BC.

1. Higgins 1980, pl. 8,A-B, from Knossos, Ailias necropolis, tomb 7.
2. Becatti 1955, pl. LXXX, nos 321-324.
3. *Ibid.*, no. 325.
4. Becatti 1955, no. 320, no. 327; *Ori di Taranto* 1985, p. 284, no. 195.
5. Boardman 1966, pp. 7-8, no. 16, pl. II.
6. Marshall 1907, nos 921-922, pl. XXIII.
7. Rudolph 1995, p. 261, no. 72.F.

139. Ring bezel with repoussé decoration

Gold. Width 2.75; height 2.1

Only the amygdaloid-shaped bezel is preserved, composed of a repoussé plate closed on the underside by a second smooth plate, with no traces of the attachment to the original hoop. Pictured is a speeding four-horse chariot with a driver bending toward the horses. The outer border is outlined with a frame composed of a doric *kyma*, a plain listel and a row of grains.

Despite its incomplete state, the ring is associated with the so-called Fortnum Group, of Etruscan production, in which themes tied to the heroic world are known to recur.[1]
The ring is a second-rate, simplified replica of a more complex iconography, the original version of which may be seen on the bezel of a ring from the Bibliothèque Nationale in Paris, which pictures a chariot of four winged horses with an underlying figure of a marine divinity with the body of a fish and brandishing a sceptre.[2] Despite Boardman's suggestion that the figure may be recognized as Helios, with underlying Okeanos, it is also possible that this ring may picture the episode of Pelops riding the chariot drawn by the horses he received from Poseidon, with which he takes flight over the sea, symbolized by the fish-bodied divinity, after having defeated Oenomaus in the fatal chariot race. The theme recurs again on the Attic hydria by Polygnotus from tomb 271 in Spina, dated around 440 BC and thus nearly contemporary with our rings.[3] A second copy, also in the Bibliothèque Nationale, shows a more simplified version, with the chariot drawn by normal horses,[4] which might have given rise to the ring in question.
A chronological reference for this class of rings, variously dated, is represented by tomb 559 at Valle Trebba in Spina, dated to around 450 BC.[5]

Second half fifth - first half fourth century BC.

1. Boardman 1966; Cristofani, Martelli 1983, pp. 242, 318, no. 277, from Populonia. For the type in general, cf. also: Marshall 1907, nos 213-215, 217, pl. VI; Vollenweider 1984, pp. 85-87, nos 132-133.
2. Boardman 1966, p. 12, no. XXIX, pl. VI.
3. I. Triantis, *Pelops*, in *LIMC* VII, p. 283, no. 3.
4. Boardman 1966, p. 12, no. XXX, pl. VI.
5. *Ori Emilia* 1958, p. 46, no. 45, Figs 32-33; cf. Boardman 1966, pp. 12, 15, no. xxiii, for placement in the second half of the fifth century BC and further bibliography.

140. Ring with carnelian scarab

Gold and carnelian. Diameter 1.9; bezel 0.6 x 0.7

The hoop is composed of a central twisted wire and two plain wires that spread out at the top to hold the elliptical bezel, flanked by two circles of twisted wire, each decorated with three grains.

The bezel, whose smooth edge is decorated with two symmetrical granules, is outlined in twisted wire. Contained within is a red carnelian in the form of a scarab.

For its soldered wire workmanship, this ring recalls a Cypriot example from Poli-tis - Chrysokhou, equipped with a double bezel with scarab, dated to the fifth - fourth centuries BC.[1]

1. Marshall 1907, no. 702, pl. XVIII.

141. Ring with incised scarab

Silver and carnelian. Diameter 1.9; scarab 0.9 x 0.65

The circular-section hoop is wrapped at the extremities with a spirally coiled silver wire. The carnelian scarab has an incised base picturing an unintelligible subject (crouching animal?).

This finds a close parallel in a specimen from tomb 9 in Roccagloriosa, dated to 360-350 BC.[1]
This type of ring is also attested in Etruria.[2]
For the subject engraved on the base, one may compare Etruscan carnelian scarabs picturing crouching or running animals.[3]

Fourth century BC.

1. *Bellezza e lusso* 1992, pp. 58-60, no. 3, Fig. 13.
2. Marshall 1907, no. 701, pl. XVIII, dated to the fifth-sixth centuries BC.
3. Boardman 1975, p. 110, no. 194, nos 195-196. Cf: Zwierlein Diehl 1973, no. 89; Sena Chiesa 1978, p. 49, no. 1, pl. I, dated to the third century BC.

142. Ring

Gold and stone. Diameter 1.7

The smooth, circular-section hoop has tapered ends wrapped in coiled wire and terminates in a cylindrical red stone bead.

A similar ring, but with a scarab, was found in tomb 9 in Roccagloriosa, dated to 360-350 BC.[1]
The type seems to be documented both in the fourth and third centuries BC.[2]

1. *Bellezza e lusso* 1992, pp. 58-60, no. 3, Fig. 13.
2. Deppert Lippitz 1985, no. 119, pl. 47. Cf. also: Marshall 1907, nos 330, 335, pl. IX; Siviero 1954, no. 71, pl. 90,a, from Cumae, Stevens Collection, fourth century BC.

143. Ring

Silver. Diameter 1.8; bezel 1.0

Composed of a lenticular-section hoop with a circular bezel, raised and slightly convex, on which is incised a dog facing right, surmounted by a lunar crescent.

This type of ring and subject find parallels in Greco-Western examples that were common in southern Italy throughout the fourth century BC or in early Hellenism.[1] A variant form with a much larger bezel, such as may be seen in the rings from Capua Vetere[2] and in the Stevens Collection,[3] is dated to the third century BC. These may be correlated to the type with an elliptical bezel that is raised and separated from the hoop, examples of which are known from Teano[4] and Naples.[5]

Also worth noting is a similar specimen, but with a concave bezel, in the British Museum[6] as well as a second one in gold, with the same subject but without the lunar crescent, in the Vatican's Gregorian Etruscan Museum, from the Falcioni Collection.[7]

Fourth – first half third century BC.

1. Boardman 1970, p. 229, pls 786-793, type VIII; Boardman, Scarisbrick 1977, nos 11-12, 14.
2. Breglia 1941, no. 155, no. 6, pl. XXIV,6; Becatti 1955, no. 342, pl. LXXXV.
3. Breglia 1941, no. 154, pl. XXIV,4; Becatti 1955, no. 343, pl. LXXXV.
4. Guzzo 1993, pp. 169-170, type VA, nos 2-5.
5. *Ibid.*, no. 6.
6. Marshall 1907, no. 106, pl. IV.
7. Caliò 2000, p. 73, no. 97.

144. Ring with gem

Bronze and carnelian. Diameter 1.9; bezel 0.6 x 0.9

The very fine, D-section hoop widens toward the top to form a distinct oval bezel, to which is fixed a cabochon-cut stone (orange carnelian).

The type, although comparable to a Hellenistic-period specimen from Taranto,[1] is more appropriately assimilable to Roman material from the early Imperial period.[2]

1. *Ori di Taranto* 1984, p. 297, no. 229, Arsenale tomb 150, first quarter third century BC.
2. Henkel 1913, p. 261, nos 1126-1127, pl. XLIV, in bronze; Marshall 1907, p. 213, no. 1373, pl. XXXII, from Hod Hill; D'Ambrosio, De Carolis 1997, p. 42, no. 89, pl. IX, from Pompeii, in bronze, found without its gem.

145. Ring with false bezel in relief

Gilt bronze and stucco. Diameter 2.2; bezel 1.8 x 1.5

Composed of a very flattened, D-section, ribbon-like hoop, terminating in a slightly raised elliptical bezel, which contains a false gem (green stucco) decorated in relief, picturing a head in profile facing left.

The ring is Roman Hellenistic, dated from the first century BC through the entire Augustan age[1] and draws on earlier styles in gold that were established as early as the Hellenistic period, in the third-second centuries BC.[2]
Consistent with the ring's chronology is the false gem, which reproduces the incisions of heads of beardless youths in profile, with laurel wreaths, which were recurrent throughout the first century BC.[3]

1. Henkel 1913, p. 19, no. 115, pl. VII.
2. Marshall 1907, pp. 21-22, nos 110-114, Fig. 27.
3. *AGDS* I,3, no. 2235, first century BC; *AGDS* II, no. 477, last quarter first century BC.

146. Ring with gem

Gilt bronze and garnet. Diameter 2.4; width 1.3

The circular-section hoop expands progressively toward the top, terminating in a sunken, elliptical bezel, which contains a red carnelian with a convex surface, incised with a helmeted female head in profile (Athena).

The form of the ring has late-Hellenistic precedents, such as that from a tomb in Taranto dated

to the first half of the first century BC,[1] and eventually grew common by the first century AD.[2] The type is dated by Henkel to the Flavian period[3] and at the same time falls within Guiraud's type 1c for rings from Roman Gaul.[4] The gem is datable, like the ring, between the second half of the first century BC and the first century AD.[5]

Second half first century BC - first century AD.

1. *Ori di Taranto* 1985, p. 301, no. 245.
2. D'Ambrosio, De Carolis 1997, p. 73, no. 237, pl. XXIV, from Oplontis - Villa B.
3. Henkel 1913, p. 262, nos 145-146, pl. VIII.
4. Guiraud 1989, pp. 179-180, Figs 9c-10c, first century BC - first century AD.
5. Furtwängler 1900, pl. XL, no. 48; A. De Ridder, *Collection de Clercq. Les bijoux et les pierres gravées,* VII,2, Paris 1911, pl. XXI, nos 2919-2927; Walters 1926, pl. XIX, no. 1376; Fossing 1929, no. 273, pl. IV; *AGDS* II, no. 369, mid-first century BC; *AGDS* III, p. 88, no. 92, pl. 37, first century AD; *AGDS* I,3, nos 2183-2186, pl. 189, second half first century BC; Maaskant Kleibrink 1978, no. 651, first century AD; Sena Chiesa 1978, no. 97, pl. XIV, late first century BC; Zwierlein Diehl 1979, nos 635-636, mid-first century BC - first century AD; U. Pannuti, *Museo Archeologico Nazionale di Napoli, Catalogo della collezione glittica,* I, Roma 1983, p. 19, no. 22; *Galerie Günter Puhze, Katalog 5,* Freiburg 1983, no. 60; Vollenweider 1984, no. 251, mid-first century BC; Spier 1992, p. 108, no. 272, first century AD.

147. Ring with gem

Gold and agate. Diameter 2.4

The ring's semicircular-section hoop expands progressively toward the top to a sunken, elliptical bezel, which holds a cabochon-cut eye agate with an unintelligible incision.

This is a well-documented ring type of Vesuvian production from the first century AD,[1] and more generally, close to Guiraud's type 2c.[2]

First century AD.

1. D'Ambrosio, De Carolis 1997, p. 44, no. 97, pl. IX, from Boscoreale; *ibid.*, p. 98, no. 308, pl. XXX, from the ancient marina of Herculaneum; for the gem, *ibid.*, p. 98, no. 307, pl. XXX.
2. Guiraud 1989, pp. 181-182, Fig. 11c, Fig. 14, first century AD - first half third century AD. Cf.: Marshall 1907, no. 450, pl. XIII; Henkel 1913, p. 262, no. 156, pl. VIII, Flavian age; *Christie's*, 11 December 2003, p. 65, no. 456.

148. Ring

Silver. Diameter 2.1; thickness 0.3

The ring has separate terminals, with a progressively thickening section toward the top. The terminals are in the form of serpent's heads rendered with stippling and incision.

This type of ring was highly recurrent in silver, but was also made in gold and in bronze,[1] and registered a wide popularity in the Vesuvian area. Various examples are known from Pompeii,[2] Herculaneum[3] and Oplontis - Villa B.[4]

First century AD.

1. Cf.: Henkel 1913, pp. 47-48, pl. XVII,337-338; Siviero 1954, p. 61, no. 219, pl. 169; Pfeiler 1970, p. 29, pl. 4,4; Laffineur 1980, pp. 428-429, no. 124, Figs 136-137, Canellopoulos Collection; Higgins 1980, p. 183, pl. 64,I = Marshall 1907, p. 180, Fig. 139, no. 1135; Caliò 2000, p. 83, no. 124.
2. Breglia 1941, p. 79, no. 669, pl. XXXIX,2; D'Ambrosio, De Carolis 1997, p. 37, nos 52-53, pl. VI.
3. Siviero 1954, p. 61, nos 216, 218, pl. 169,c-d; Scatozza Höricht 1989, pp. 52-54, nos 57-62, in silver, pp. 55-56, nos 69-70, in bronze; D'Ambrosio, De Carolis 1997, pp. 94-96, nos 287-295, pl. XXX.
4. D'Ambrosio, De Carolis 1997, pp. 68-69, nos 207-209, pl. XXII.

149. Ring

Silver alloy. Diameter 2.7

The semicircular-section hoop widens progressively toward the top, terminating in a sunken, elliptical bezel, bordered by a lunar crescent in relief, currently missing its stone.

The type is dated to the early Imperial period, between Tiberius and the Flavians,[1] and finds parallels among material of Pompeian provenance.[2]

A ring with a raised lunar crescent comes from Alexandria, in Egypt, and is dated to the Roman period.[3] Further comparisons may be made with material from the market.[4]

First century AD.

1. Henkel 1913, no. 162, pl. IX.
2. D'Ambrosio, De Carolis 1997, p. 41, no. 84, pl. VIII.
3. Marshall 1907, no. 248, pl. VI.
4. *Galerie Günter Puhze, Katalog 6*, Freiburg n.d., no. 96, in gold.

150. Ring with incised palmette

Gold. Diameter 1.5; bezel width 0.5

Very thin, ovo-rectangular-section hoop, terminating in a flat oval bezel on which is incised a palm branch.

This type of ring was especially common in the Vesuvian area in the early Imperial age.[1] The palm was thought to bring good luck, considered a symbol of victory, and consequently, of well-being and peace.[2]

First century AD.

1. For the type: Henkel 1913, pp. 8-9, 235-236, nos 60, 45-46, pl. III; Hoffmann, von Claer 1968, p. 184, no. 124; Caliò 2000, p. 76, no. 104.
2. Siviero 1954, no. 510; Scatozza Höricht 1989, pp. 42-43, nos 33-35 (Herculaneum); D'Ambrosio, De Carolis 1997, p. 39, no. 65, pl. VII (Pompeii); *ibid.*, p. 71, nos 224-225, pl. XXIII (Oplontis, villa B); *ibid.*, p. 97, nos 297, 299, pl. XXX (Herculaneum).

151. Ring with incised carnelian

Gold and carnelian. Diameter 1.7; bezel 0.7 x 0,55

Composed of a thin wire hoop and an elliptical bezel, which holds an incised stone (red carnelian), with a barely intelligible design, probably a butterfly.

For the ring type, a comparison may be made

with a specimen found in a cinerary urn from Rome, Abbey of the Three Fountains, datable to the first half of the first century AD.[1] The type is documented in the same period also in the Vesuvian area: Oplontis, Villa B.[2] The form, which appears to derive from late-Hellenistic examples from the third quarter of the first century BC,[3] is dated by Henkel to the Augustan age.[4]
The subject of the flying butterfly finds parallels in Greek gems beginning in the third century BC[5] and is found in Roman gems dated to the early first century AD, consistently with the ring's chronology.[6]

First half first century AD.

1. Bordenache Battaglia 1983, pp. 23-24, no. 2.
2. D'Ambrosio, De Carolis 1997, p. 73, no. 236.
3. A. Alessio, in *Ori di Taranto* 1985, p. 301, no. 246.
4. Henkel 1913, p. 21, no. 128, pl. VII, p. 259; cf. also: Marshall 1907, p. 81, no. 469, pl. XIII; Guiraud 1989, p. 181, Fig. 11a, p. 182, Fig. 12, type 2a.
5. *AGDS* I,1, no. 429.
6. *AGDS* III, p. 151, no. 547, pl. 75; cf. also Richter 1971, no. 383, dated to the Roman Imperial period.

Fig.30. Statue of a crowned Venus and cherub with a helmet ("Venus the Victorious"). Imperial Roman period. The legs on the two figures are of modern restoration. Vatican City, Vatican Museums, inv. 2959. Marble. Height 112 cm.

152. Ring with incised paste bezel

Bronze and glass paste imitating striated agate. Diameter 2.7; bezel 1.6 x 1.2

A very thin, D-section hoop terminates in a sunken elliptical bezel, which contains a gem incised with the figure of Venus the Victorious (*Venus Victrix*) standing next to a pillar, while the little Amor in the background stands by a shield resting on the ground.

For its form, the ring finds a parallel in a specimen from Herculaneum,[1] falling more generally within a category attested between the end of the Republic and the Augustan age.[2]

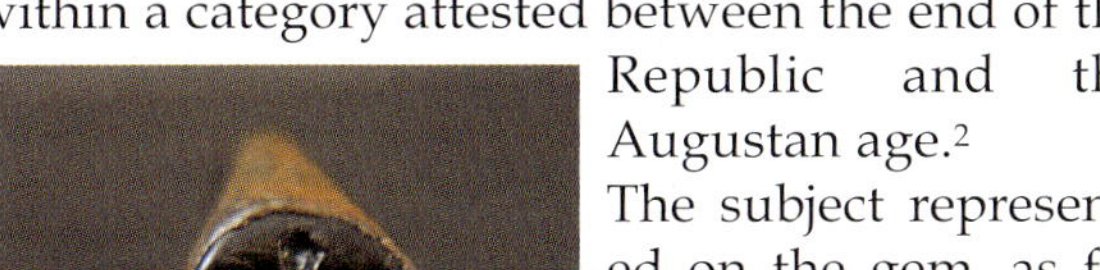

The subject represented on the gem, as far as concerns *Venus Victrix* in general, recurs in incisions dated throughout the Imperial period, from the first to the third centuries AD.[3] However, the variant form with the figure of Amor, such as in this case, appears to be restricted to the early Imperial age, consistently with the ring's chronology.[4]

First half first century AD.

1. Scatozza Höricht 1989, p. 50, no. 55.
2. Henkel 1913, pl. VII, nos 115, 118; cf. also Guiraud 1989, p. 181, Fig. 11a, p. 182, Fig. 12, type 2a.
3. Fossing 1929, nos 695-709, pl. IX; Richter 1956, no. 300; M. Henig, *A Corpus of Engraved Gemstones from British Sites*, Oxford 1978, no. 279; Vollenweider 1984, nos 379-385; Spier 1992, p. 101, no. 244, first century AD.
4. Richter 1956, no. 301, pl. XLII; *Frank Sternberg AG Zürich. Antike Münzen, Renaissancemedaillen, Geschnittene Steine und Schmuck der Antike, Antike Kleinkunst*, Auktion XXVII, 7. und 8. November 1994. Zürich 1994, p. 102, no. 734.

153. Ring with incised carnelian

Gold and carnelian. Diameter 2.1; bezel 1.2 x 0.7

Composed of a lenticular-section hoop which expands to form an elongated, sunken oval bezel, containing an incised red gem (carnelian), picturing a frontal view of a semi-draped standing figure (Harpokrates, cf. no. **110**), with a bare chest, a cornucopia on the right and the left arm flexed as

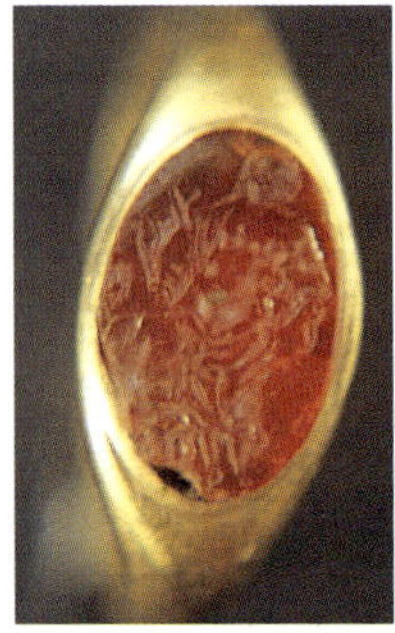

though the figure were leaning against a pillar.

The ring may be compared with types that were popular in the course of the first century AD[1], while the gem with Harpokrates is more extensively attested between the late first and third centuries AD[2].

Second half first century AD.

1. Henkel 1913, p. 262, no. 138, pl. VIII (Tiberius-Caligula), p. 263, no. 172, pl. IX (second half first century AD); Scatozza Höricht 1989, p. 35, no. 14, from Herculaneum; D'Ambrosio, De Carolis 1997, pp. 45-46, nos 103-104, pl. X, from Pompeii.
2. A. Furtwängler, *Beschreibung der geschnittenen Steine im Antiquarium*, Berlin 1896, no. 6483, pl. 45, no. 8718, pl. 62; Furtwängler 1900, XLIII,57, XLIV,43, LXII,3; Walters 1926, no. 1799, pl. XXIII; Fossing 1929, nos 1736-1737, pl. XX; *AGDS* I,3, pl. 328, no. 3492; Zwierlein Diehl 1979, nos 1364-1366 (late first-second century AD), 1367-1368 (third century AD), pls 128-129.

154. Ring with incised carnelian

Gold and carnelian. Diameter 2.2; bezel 1.6 x 0,95

A wide, D-section hoop expands to form a large, elongated elliptical bezel, which holds an incised red carnelian, picturing a standing helmeted warrior armed with spear and shield (Mars).

The form numbers Hellenistic precedents, widespread throughout the Mediterranean as early as the third century BC.[1] The type may, however, be placed in the early Imperial age.[2]
The subject in general is pictured, in an inverse layout, on gems dated from the early first century BC[3] to the end of the first - first half of the second centuries AD.[4]

First century AD.

1. Marshall 1907, p. 68, no. 373, pl. XI, from Italy, third century BC; *Ori di Taranto* 1985, no. 237, from Taranto = Guzzo 1993, pp. 34-36, p. 166, type IIIAc, no. 1, first half second century BC.
2. Henkel 1913, p. 261, no. 138, pl. VIII (Tiberius-Caligula); Guiraud 1989, pp. 181-182, Figs 11a-12, type 2a, first century BC-first century AD; D'ambrosio, De Carolis 1997, p. 43, no. 93, pl. IX (Pompeii, Zosimus Taberna).
3. Zwierlein Diehl 1979, no. 1095, pl. 84.
4. Platz Horster 1987, no. 115, pl. 22.

155. Ring with incised red jasper

Gold and red jasper. Diameter 1.7; bezel 0.9 x 0.7

The D-section hoop expands to form an elliptical bezel, which contains a red gem with an engraved cantharus with two birds resting on the edges.

The ring type is documented between the first century BC and the first century AD[1].
Representations of elaborate vases, with or without birds, are fairly recurrent in the early Roman Imperial age. For the gem, a close parallel may be made with a specimen from the Harari Collection.[2]

First century AD.

1. Marshall 1907, p. 75, nos 421-422, pl. XIII; Henkel 1913, p. 261, no. 137, pl. VIII (Tiberius-Caligula), p. 263, no. 172, pl. IX (50-79 AD); Guiraud 1989, pp. 181-182, Figs 11a-12, type 2a, first century BC-first century AD; D'Ambrosio, De Carolis 1997, p. 44, no. 95, pl. IX, from Pompeii.
2. Boardman, Scarisbrick 1977, p. 28, no. 34.

156. Ring with silver bezel

Bronze and silver. Diameter 2.3; bezel 0.8 x 0.5

The D-section hoop widens progressively toward the top, terminating in a hollow that holds a rectangular silver bezel with a slightly convex surface, decorated with rows of punched dots.

The type is generally attested in the early Imperial age.[1] Parallels may be found in examples from the Vesuvian area: Pompeii's Porta Marina;[2] Herculaneum's Ancient Marina;[3] Suburban Baths.[4]

Probably first century AD.

1. Henkel 1913, pp. 27, 262, no. 179, pl. IX; also close to type 2c in Guiraud 1989, pp. 181-182, Fig. 11c, 14, first century-first half third century AD.
2. D'Ambrosio, De Carolis 1997, p. 40, no. 77, pl. VIII.
3. D'Ambrosio, De Carolis 1997, p. 101, no. 324, pl. XXXI, in gold and emerald.
4. Scatozza Höricht 1989, pp. 34-35, no. 16.

157. Ring with Victory incision

Gold. Diameter 2.1; width 0.7

A ribbon-like, D-section hoop expands toward the oval bezel with a flat surface on which is incised a Victory bearing palm and wreath, flanked by the inscription "MAXIM."

The type is attested throughout the first century AD.[1] Examples are known from Pompeii featuring smooth bezels without inscriptions.[2] Other specimens, comparable to this, were found both in Oplontis, Villa B[3] and in Herculaneum's Ancient Marina.[4] A very similar ring figured among the Grottarossa sarcophagus goods, in Rome, dated between the late age of Hadrian[5] and the Antonine age, 160-180 AD.[6] Similarly shaped rings are attested in Britain in contexts dating from the early first century AD[7] to the beginning of the third century AD.[8]

First - early third centuries AD.

1. Henkel 1913, p. 236, no. 57, pl. III; Moratello 1999, p. 281, nos 18-19, pl. CIII,18-19.
2. D'Ambrosio, De Carolis 1997, nos 59-61, pls VI-VII.
3. D'Ambrosio, De Carolis 1997, p. 70, no. 221, pl. XXII.
4. D'Ambrosio, De Carolis 1997, pp. 96-97, no. 301, pl. XXX.
5. M. Sapelli, in A. Giuliano, *Museo Nazionale Romano. Le Sculture,* I,1, pp. 318-324, no. 190
6. Bordenache Battaglia 1983, pp. 100-123, no. 10.
7. Henig 1978, no. 784, pl. LVIII.
8. Henig 1978, no. 771, pl. LVIII.

158. Ring with Herakles knot

Silver. Diameter 1.85

Composed of a circular-section wire ring, with terminals shaped into a Herakles knot.

This type of ring registers a wide documentation in the Roman world which, chronologically, reaches at least as far as the third or possibly the fourth century AD.[1] The Herakles knot may also be observed on bracelets found in Lyon in a second-century AD context,[2] while a gold wire ring with a knot on top was found in Cologne in association with a coin of Severus Alexander, 222-235 AD.[3] Similar examples figure in the Castellani Collection in Rome's Museo di Villa Giulia[4] and in Athens' Benaki Museum.[5]

Probably second - third century AD.

1. Henkel 1913, p. 230, no. 329, pl. XVII, in silver; Siviero 1954, p. 63, no. 230, pl. 171d; Guiraud 1989, p. 193, Fig. 36f, p. 194, Fig. 38f, type 6f, first century BC-fourth century AD.
2. A. Comarmond, *Description de l'écrin d'une dame Romaine trouvé a Lyon en 1841,* Lyon 1844, pp. 17-19, nos 5-7, pl. 3.
3. Henkel 1913, p. 6, no. 26, pl. II.
4. Bordenache Battaglia 1980, p. 348, no. 81; Caruso 1988, p. 51, no. 101, hypothetically dated to the third-second centuries BC.
5. Lymperopoulos 1999, p. 276, no. 105.

159. Ring with incised Fortune

Gold. Diameter 2.3; bezel 1.9 x 1.6

The hoop is made from a square-section wire and a double twisted wire wrapped together. Pictured by incision on the elliptical bezel is Fortune in a standing pose, shown frontally but with her face in profile, draped and bearing a cornucopia in her right

Fig.31. Statue of Fortune, from Rome, Church of S. Marco. Roman copy of late-Hellenistic original from the late second century BC. 150-200 AD. Vatican City, Vatican Museums, Greek Cross Room, inv. 202. Marble. Height 118 cm.

hand while holding a helm with her lowered left hand. On her head is a disc (?), possibly an Isiac attribute.

The subject, quite recurrent in engraved gems from the Roman Imperial era, appears on a Greco-Hellenistic gold ring with an oval bezel dated to the second century BC, in a syncretistic iconography, in which Tyche-Fortune is assimilated to Isis.[1] Fortune is a highly recurrent subject in engraved gems, beginning with specimens dated to the first and early second centuries AD.[2]
For its typology and for certain stylistic and iconographic characteristics, this specimen is more readily comparable to engraved gems dated to the second-third centuries AD.[3]
The same subject appears on a gold ring from the market[4] and on a gold ring with an engraved bezel from the A. Ollivier Collection.[5]

Second-third centuries AD.

1. Boardman, Scarisbrick 1977, no. 15.
2. A. Krug, *Römische Gemmen und Fingerrings im Museum für Vor- und Frühgeschichte Frankfurt a.M.*, in *Germania* 53, p. 124, no. 23, pl. 34, first century BC - first century AD; Maaskant Kleibrink 1978, no. 751; Zwierlein Diehl 1979, no. 1075; Dimitrova Milceva 1980, no. 81; Vollenweider 1984, no. 405; Maaskant Kleibrink 1986, pp. 44-45, nos 90-91.
3. *AGDS* I,3, nos 2604-2610, second - early third centuries AD; *AGDS* II, nos 527-528, third - fourth centuries AD; *AGDS* III, pp. 95-96, nos 149, 151, 155, pl. 41; *ibid.*, p. 208, no. 46, pl. 91; AGDS IV, nos 1506-1511; C. Weiß, *Die antiken Gemmen der Sammlung Friedrich Julius Rudolph Bergau im Germanischen Nationalmuseum, Nürnberg*, Nürnberg 1996, nos 142-144; Zwierlein Diehl 1979, nos 1538, 1541; Vollenweider 1984, no. 406, second century AD; Zahlhaas 1985, p. 41, no. 43, second century AD; Chadour-Sampson 1997, p. 122, no. 25.
4. *Christie's*, 5 October 1988, pp. 9-10, no. 306.
5. Chadour-Sampson 1997, pp. 132-134, no. 28, late second - third centuries AD.

160. Gem with magic intaglio: Abrasax

Black jasper with green highlights. Height 2.5; width 2.0. Scratched edges.

The gem is elliptical, with an incision of Abraxas or Abrasax in its iconography of a snake-footed giant with a cock's head, wearing a cuirass and armed with a shield and whip, surrounded by magical inscriptions in the Greek alphabet.

This is the representation of a divine power, frequently invoked in late-Ancient magical papyri and in amulets of this type that were generally set in rings or necklaces. The divinity is the result of a syncretistic process, which blends conceptual and iconographic elements of eastern (Iranian, Syrian, Egyptian) and Greek origin, performed particularly, but not exclusively, in a Judaeo-Christian realm, within the Gnostic sects that thrived between the second and third centuries AD. The cosmic and solar meaning is inherent even in the word Abrasax, composed of the succession of the mystic numbers whose numerical value adds up to 365, the days of the solar year and the number of skies according to Gnostic speculation: $\alpha=1 + \beta=2 + \rho=100 + \alpha=1 + \sigma=200 + \alpha=1 + \xi=60$.[1]
This type of amulet was particularly widespread

in Egypt, Palestine, Syria and Anatolia between the second and third centuries AD,[2] but later examples are also known, such as that found in a late-Roman villa in La Olmeda, Spain, in a fourth-century AD context.[3]
In addition to gems, the subject of Abrasax is found pictured on the rear of a bronze medallion in Rome's Antiquarium Comunale, dated to the fourth - early fifth centuries AD, a replica of which exists in a private collection in Sicily.[4]
These gems - originals, and perhaps even copies - were also used in the Middle Ages in altogether peculiar contexts: curiously, a ring with a Gnostic gem was found in the tomb of Bishop Seffrid in the Chichester Cathedral, dating to 1151, while an analogous second specimen was found in the tomb of Archbishop Walter of Canterbury, dated to 1205.[5]

Second-third centuries AD.

1. A.A. Barb, *Abraxas - Studien,* in *Hommages à Waldemar Deonna, collection Latomus* 28, 1957, pp. 67-86; A.A. Barb, s.v. *Gnostiche Gemme,* in *EAA* III, 1960, pp. 971-974; M. Le Glay, s.v. *Abraxas,* in *LIMC* I, pp. 2-7.
2. Cf.: Carnegie 1908, pp. 138-140, pl. XIII, N1; Fossing 1929, nos 1858-1859, 1862-1863, pl. XXI; Bonner 1950, pp. 123-139, p. 278, pl. VII, 152, pp. 280-282, pl. VIII, 162-176, pp. 283-284, pl. IX,184-185; Goodenough 1953, pp. 245-258, Figs 1078-1096, 1098-1115; *Bedeutende Kunstwerke aus dem Nachlass Dr Jacob Hirsch,* Auktion 07/12/1957, Luzern 1957, p. 38, no. 109, pl. 51, set in a necklace pendant; A. Delatte, Ph. Derchain, *Les intailles magiques gréco-égyptiennes,* Paris 1964, pp. 25-39, nos 1-38; G. Sena Chiesa, *Gemme del Museo Nazionale di Aquileia,* Padova 1966, p. 421, nos 1540-1542, pl. LXXVIII; *AGDS* I,3, nos 2907-2912; *AGDS* III, p. 53, nos 186-187, pl. 23, pp. 226-229, nos 127-137, pls 100-102; Henig 1978, no. 367, pl. XLII; Maaskant Kleibrink 1978, nos 1097-1098, 1104; P. Zazoff, *Die antike Gemmen. Handbuch der Archäologie,* München 1983, pls 113,7-8, 114,1-2, 116,70; H. Philipp, *Mira et Magica. Gemmen im Ägyptischen Museum der Staatlichen Museen Preussischer Kulturbesitz Berlin-Charlottenburg,* Mainz am Rhein 1986, pl. 41, nos 158-160, pl. 42, nos 161-164, pl. 43, nos 166-169; A.R. Mandrioli Bizzarri, *La collezione di gemme del Museo Civico Archeologico di Bologna,* Bologna 1987, p. 131, nos 262-263; *Frank Sternberg AG Zürich,* Auktion X, 1989, no. 784; Paolucci 1991, p. 114, no. 150; Zwierlein Diehl 1991, nos 2231-2239; *Frank Sternberg,* Aukt. XXVII, 1994, p. 110, no. 793, pl. XL; *Christie's* New York, 4 June 1999, pp. 52-53, no. 112 and *Christie's* New York, 8 December 1999, p. 40, no. 78; Michel 2001, pp. 115-148, nos 181-242; Michel 2001a, pp. 59-63, nos 55-61, pls 9-10, p. 111, no. 124, pl. 20; *Christie's,* 13 December 2002, p. 59, no. 641.
3. M.d.M. González González, M.L. Prieto Prieto, *Ein Abrasax-Ring aus La Olmeda (Spanien),* in *ZPE* 97, 1993, p. 130.
4. Bevilacqua 1999, pp. 27-30; G. Bevilacqua, in *Pietro e Paolo* 2000, pp. 105, 198, no. 26.
5. J. Cherry, *Medieval Rings,* in AA.VV., *The Ring from Antiquity to the Twentieth Century,* London 1981, p. 61, no. 116.

161. Ring with incised bezel: Victory

Gold. Diameter 2.0; width 1.0

The ridged hoop widens progressively toward the top, bearing a raised elliptical bezel with an incision of the winged Victory, with crown and palm, facing right.

The ring is comparable to typologies documented in the Roman Imperial era beginning in the second half of the second century through the entire third century AD.[1] Also dated between the second half of the second and the first half of the third centuries AD is a similar specimen, for the characteristic of the ridged hoop, which was part of a group of gold artifacts found in Artena.[2]
The same period introduced engraved gems bearing the subject of the Victory, typologically and stylistically akin to that pictured here.[3]

Second half second - third century AD.

1. Marshall 1907, p. 107, no. 637, pl. XVII; Henkel 1913, pp. 30, 53, no. 386, pl. XIX; Battke 1938, p. 61, no. 24, pl. II; C. Beckmann, *Metallfingerringe der römischen Kaiserzeit im freien Germanien,* in *Saalburg Jahrbuch* 26, 1969, p. 38, 21st form, no. 631, pl. I,21a, from Dronrijp; Guiraud 1989, pp. 185-187, Fig. 21g, Fig. 24g, second half second century AD - third quarter third century AD.
2. Scarpignato 1978-79, p. 234, no. 3, pl. III,1-3.
3. *AGDS* I,3, nos 2632-2635, around the third century AD.

162. Ring with polygonal hoop

Copper and silver. Diameter 2.2; bezel 0.7.

Consists of a polygonal copper D-section wire hoop with a raised globular bezel in silver, bearing an incision of a standing human figure, dressed in a short tunic, with a raised (viewer's)

right arm, while the other is slightly detached from the body and holds an elliptical object.

Polygonal-section rings of undocumented provenance are commonly dated to the third-fourth centuries AD.[1] A more accurate placement, between the second half of the second century and the third century AD, is derived from studies conducted on findings from Roman Gaul.[2] Polygonal-section rings from the Snettisham treasure may be dated around the mid-second century AD.[3] Further chronological indications are supplied by iconographic elements, such as in the case of a polygonal-section ring with an incised bezel picturing the portrait of Iulia Domna or Iulia Cornelia Paula, datable around 218-220 AD.[4]
The incision on this ring's bezel also finds parallels in gems from the second-third centuries AD, which present a similar layout.[5]

Second half second - third centuries AD.

1. Cf.: Henkel 1913, nos 652-675, pl. XXVII, in bronze; *ibid.*, nos 390, in silver, 1811, in gold; Marshall 1907, no. 1439, pl. XXXIII, in bronze, purchased in Palermo; *ibid.*, nos 1199-1200, pl. XXIX, in silver.
2. Guiraud 1989, pp. 196-198, Fig. 47a, type 9a.
3. Johns 1997, pp. 41, 109, nos 301-302.
4. Vollenweider 1984, no. 315.
5. *AGDS* I,3, nos 2571-2572.

163. Raised-bezel ring with gem

Gold and worked gem. Diameter 1.8; max. height 2.2

Composed of a D-section ring terminating in a raised square bezel separated by a pair of hollows and containing a green faceted gem.

A similar ring, in the British Museum, is probably datable to the third century AD.[1] The chronology may be clarified by findings in Roman Gaul that indicate a period beginning in the second century AD, with a greater concentration in the third century AD.[2] Further comparisons may be found among examples known from the market.[3]

Second-third century AD.

1. Marshall 1907, p. 129, no. 789, Fig. 107.
2. Guiraud 1989, pp. 185-186, Figs 21a-22a.
3. *Galerie Günter Puhze* 5, Freiburg 1983, no. 59.

164. Ring with incised bezel: gradient human figure

Gold. Diameter 2.2; width 0.55

The ring is composed of a hoop with a central ridge, with symmetrical edges on top, terminating in a raised elliptical bezel with the incision of a human figure facing left.

The ring, with its concave and ridged shoulders, recalls late-Roman types dated mainly to the third century AD, but possibly as late as the fifth century AD.[1] Polygonal rings with concave shoulders, but without ridges, were found in the Snettisham treasure and are datable to around the middle of the second century AD.[2] More generally, it is comparable to Guiraud's type 3b-d, dated to the first half of the second to the third centuries AD, with a greater concentration in the third century AD.[3]

Second half second - third century AD.

1. Marshall 1907, no. 526, pl. XV, no. 1196, pl. XXIX, no. 1420, pl. XXXIII.
2. Johns 1997, p. 41, p. 109, nos 303-304.
3. Guiraud 1989, pp. 185-186, Figs 21-22.

165. Ring with embossed bezel: two confronting figures

Gold. Diameter 1.8; bezel 1.4 x 1.2

Consists of a wide sheet gold hoop with lobed edges, and a bezel in repoussé sheet gold picturing two standing confronting figures.

A comparison may be made with a similar ring from Ponza in the Museo Archeologico in Naples, similarly equipped with a repoussé sheet bezel in which two figures are pictured enacting the *dextrarum iunctio* gesture, dated to the third-fourth centuries AD.[1] A second specimen appears in the British Museum collection.[2]

Third - fourth centuries AD.

Fig. 32.. Fragment of a sarcophagus relief picturing the *dextrarum iunctio*. 160-170 AD. Vatican City, Vatican Museums, inv. 1477. Marble. Height 0.54 cm. Length 0.71 cm.

1. Breglia 1941, pp. 94-95, no. 994, pl. XXXIX,4-5, with previous bibliography; Siviero 1954, p. 115, no. 517, pls 240-241.
2. Marshall 1907, p. 48, no. 272, pl. VII.

166. Ring with gem

Gold and gem (blue corundum?). Diameter 1.8; bezel 0.9 x 0.7

The ring is composed of a carinate-section hoop, flattened and shaped into a pair of volutes at the attachment to the elliptical bezel with a smooth, raised border, in which a blue cabochon-cut gem is set.

A ring comparable to this, but with a square bezel, from Rome and in the former Pollak Collection, is dated to the third-fourth centuries AD.[1] Specimens of a similar typology are unanimously dated to the third century AD.[2] More generally, the ring is comparable with Guiraud's type 3f for Roman Gaul, dated between the first half of the second and the first half of the fourth centuries BC, but with a peak in appearances during the third century AD.[3]

Third century AD.

1. Greifenhagen 1975, pl. 60, nos 29-30.
2. Marshall 1907, p. 33, no. 202, pl. V, from Beirut, variant for its bezel in engraved gold; Henkel 1913, p. 269, no. 81, pl. IV; pp. 244-252, pl. XII; R. Laser, A. Siebrecht, *Ein silberner römischer Fingerring mit Merkur-Gemme von Langenstein, Kreis Halberstadt*, in *Ausgrabungen und Funde* 26, 1981, pp. 188-193, pl. 29; *Trésor d'orfèvrerie* 1989, p. 207, no. 159, from Saint-Genis - Pouilly (Ain), in silver and carnelian; *ibid.*, p. 251, no. 214, from Talmont-Saint-Hilaire (Vendée), in gold and glass paste.
3. Guiraud 1989, p. 185, Fig. 21f, p. 187, Fig. 25f.

167. Ring with incised raised bezel: running animal

Silver. Diameter 2.3; width 1.0

The ring consists of a hoop with lobed edges, centrally incised with a stylized palmette on either side adjacent to the bezel. The raised octagonal bezel bears the incision of a running animal facing left.

This is comparable to a Roman specimen from Sabratha, in Libya, dated to the second half of the

third century AD.[1] A variant form is known with a raised round bezel, dated to the third-fourth centuries AD[2].

Third - fourth centuries AD.

1. Hoffmann, von Claer 1968, p. 185, no. 126.
2. Ruxer, Kubczak 1976, p. 124, no. 48, Fig. 13, unknown provenance, with further comparisons.

168. Ring with incised bezel: mid-late Severian female portrait

Gold. Diameter 2.4; bezel 1.8 x 1.4

The circular-section hoop terminates in an engraved elliptical bezel with rounded edges: pictured is a female bust in profile facing left with a "helmet"-type hairstyle, featuring the characteristic curved locks on the nape of the neck.

The bust pictured on the bezel is consistent with portrait typologies from the mid- and late-Severian periods (particularly Elagabalus and Severus Alexander) from which various examples are known from glyptic production,[1] coinage[2] and statuary.[3] The hairstyle is exemplified in the portrait of Plautilla, wife of Caracalla, who died in 212 AD, that may be observed on a gem in the Cabinet des Médailles in Paris[4] and on another in Vienna, dated to 203-205 AD.[5] Privately commissioned portraits on cameos are also modelled on these.[6]

Fig. 33.. Late-Severian female portrait: Iulia cornelia Paula, Faustina, Orbiana. Circa 220-235 AD. The bust is modern. Vatican City, Vatican Museums, inv. 1822. Marble. Height 59 cm.

As in the following case (cf. no. **169**), these late-Imperial rings intentionally recall, for reasons of propaganda, Hellenistic-dynast typologies, both in their iconography as well as in the typology itself.[7] Rings of the same typology, with incised oval bezels, persist until the late sixth century AD, the period to which a specimen found in Syria is dated.[8]

The ring may most likely be placed within the third decade of the third century AD.

1. *AGDS* II, no. 546 and *infra*.
2. J.J. Bernoulli, *Römische Ikonographie*, II,3, Hildesheim 1969, Münztaf. III,4-5 (Orbiana), 6-7 (Iulia Mamaea); R.A.G. Carson, *Coins of the Roman Empire in the British Museum*, V, London 1975, *passim*, pls 91-97; *ibid.*, vol. VI, London 1976, *passim*, pls 10 (Orbiana), 5-6, 15, 17-18, 24, 26, 30 (Iulia Mamaea); Kent, Overbeck, Stylow 1973, pls 98-101, nos 420 (Iulia Soemia, 218/222 AD), 421-423 (Iulia Cornelia Paula, 219/220 AD), 424 (Iulia Aquilia Severa, 220/222 AD), 425 (Annia Faustina, 221 AD), 430-431 (Orbiana, 225 AD), 432 (Iulia Mamaea, 226 AD).
3. Fittschen, Zanker 1983, no. 149, pl. 178, Iulia Maesa and Iulia Soemia, ca. 220 AD; *ibid.*, nos 33-34, pls 41-43, Iulia Mamaea, 222-235 AD; cf. also *ibid.*, nos 154, 158-161, pls 181-182, 185-188.
4. Richter 1971, no. 584.
5. Zwierlein - Diehl 1991, no. 1729.
6. Dimitrova Milceva 1980, pp. 104-105, nos 296-298; Megow 1987, pl. 50,6-21; M. Henig, *The Content Family Collection of Ancient Cameos*, Oxford 1990, nos 45, 77-78.
7. Cf. for example the portrait of Berenice I, wife of Ptolemy I (323-285 BC) and mother of Ptolemy II: G.M.A. Richter, *The Portraits of the Greeks*, London 1965, III, p. 261, Figs 1776-1780; Richter 1968, no. 627; for the ring type: Guzzo 1993, p. 165, type IIB, no. 3, from Mottola, dated to the fourth century BC; cf. also: Hoffmann, von Claer 1968, p. 178, no. 116; Boardman 1970, pp. 361-362, type XVII.
8. Ross 1965, pp. 137-138, no. 179 N, pl. XCVIII, possibly made in Costantinople.

169. Ring with incised bezel: male portrait

Gold. Diameter 2.2; bezel 1.7 x 1.4

Composed of a circular-section hoop terminating in a pseudo-elliptical bezel bordered by a double twisted wire, bearing the incised portrait of a male figure, with his face in profile and his bust facing forward. The hair is adorned with a *taenia* fastened at the nape. The figure wears a *lorica* covered by a *chlamys* fastened on the left shoulder.

The elliptical-bezel ring, edged with beaded wire, is a typology affirmed in the late Roman Imperial age, beginning at least in the third century AD and continuing into the fourth century,[1] of which a version is also known with an engraved gem.[2] The form subsequently evolved during the late-Roman and Byzantine ages, between the fifth and seventh centuries AD, with the additional development of two pairs of granules at the top of the hoop at the attachment to the bezel.[3]
The bust pictured on the bezel is of particular interest, in that it corresponds to monetary portraits of Constantine II (337-340 AD, Caesar from 324 AD) (**Fig. 35**), Constans (337-350 AD, Caesar from 333 AD) (**Fig. 36**) or Constantius II (337-361 AD, Caesar from 323/324 AD) (**Fig. 34**).[4] Worth noting is the intentional emulation of iconographic models of the most ancient Hellenistic dynasts, particularly the Ptolemies.[5]

Second quarter fourth century AD.

Fig.34. Medallion of Constantius II. From the Calenzio Collection (1916). Circa 337-340 AD. Vatican City, Vatican Apostolic Library, Medagliere. Bronze. Diameter 3.44 cm.

Fig.35. Medallion of Constantine II. Uncertain provenance. 337 AD. Vatican City, Vatican Apostolic Library, Medagliere. Bronze. Diameter 3.47 cm.

Fig.36. Medallion of Constans I. Uncertain provenance. 337-347 AD. Vatican City, Vatican Apostolic Library, Medagliere. Bronze. Diameter 3.08 cm.

1. Marshall 1907, nos 511, 513; Henckel 1913, nos 288-289, pl. XV; Vollenweider 1984, no. 330.
2. *Sotheby & Co.*, 9th-12th Nov. 1937, p. 64, no. 302, pl. XI.
3. Ross 1965, p. 11, no. 6,F, pl. XIV, Constantinople or Syria, seventh century AD; ibid., p. 138, 179,Q, pl. XCIX, Costantinople (?), late sixth century AD; Rudolph, Rudolph 1973, p. 198, no. 159c.
4. R. Delbrück, *Die spätantike Kaiserporträts von Constantinus Magnus bis zum Ende des Westreichs*, Berlin-Leipzig 1933, pp. 78-82, pl. 7,1-6, pl. 8,1-9; Richter 1971, nos 602a, 603a; Kent, Overbeck, Stylow 1973, pls 141-142; H.J. Schulzki, *Ein spätrömischer Goldschatzfund aus Bonn (1930), in Die Münze, Bild-Botschaft-Bedeutung. Festschrift für Maria R. Alföldi*, Frankfurt am Main 1991, p. 366, pl. 26, no. 8.
5. G.M.A. Richter, *Engraved Gems of the Greeks and the Etruscans*, London-New York 1968, no. 620, Ptolemy II Philadelphus, 285-246 BC, or Ptolemy III Euergetes, 246-221 BC; Ead., *The Portraits of the Greeks*, London 1965, Fig. 1832, Ptolemy V, 210-180 BC; cf., in this regard, J. Charbonneaux, in *Bulletin de la Société Nationale des Antiquaires de France* 1958, pp. 79-80.

170. Ring with seal: head of Herakles in profile

Gold and stone. Diameter 2.2; bezel 1.4 x 1.1

The twisted wire hoop terminates in a cylindrical bezel, whose outer extremities are decorated with

two rows of braids, each formed from a pair of spiral-beaded wires placed side by side. The bezel contains an engraved stone picturing a bearded and crowned head in profile (Hercules).

Fig. 37. Fragment of a relief picturing a crowned Herakles. Mid-first century AD. Vatican City, Vatican Museums, inv. 1533. Marble. Height 34 cm.

The ring finds a parallel in specimens dated to the fourth century AD.[1] The subject reproduced on the gem counts precedents beginning in early Hellenism, appearing on gems dated to the late fourth - first half of the third century BC, and inspired by the typology of Lysippos' Farnese Herakles.[2] Various specimens are dated beginning in the first century BC and persist throughout the entire Roman Imperial age.[3]
This gem finds a parallel, consistently with the ring's typology, in late-Roman specimens.[4]

1. Henkel 1913, p. 43, no. 289, pl. XV; Deppert Lippitz 1985, no. 151, pl. 53.
2. G.M.A. Richter, *The Engraved Gems of the Greeks and the Etruscans*, New York 1968, no. 572.
3. Fossing 1929, nos 1121-1126, pl. XIV; Richter 1956, nos 415-416, pl. LIII; *AGDS* II, no. 472 (last quarter first century BC); *AGDS* III, pp. 116-117, nos 282, 286, p. 137, no. 426 (first-second centuries AD); Richter 1971, nos 263-268; Zwierlein Diehl 1973, no. 486 (late first century BC - early first century AD); *AGDS* IV, no. 190 (first half first century BC), nos 576-587 (mid-first century BC - first half first century AD), no. 1593 (second century AD); Boardman, Scarisbrick 1977, no. 67 (first century BC); Zwierlein Diehl 1991, no. 1620 (third quarter first century BC); *Christie's London, Fine Antiquities. The Properties of the Brooklyn Museum, New York, Sir Sidney Nolan O.M. A.C., C.B.E., The Late G. Wyndham Esq., sold by order of the Trustees and from various sources*, 9 December 1992, pp. 24-25, no. 39; *Frank Sternberg AG Zürich*, Auktion XXVII. *Antike Münzen, Renaissancemedaillen, Geschnittene Steine und Schmuck der Antike, Antike Kleinkunst*, Zürich 1994, p. 104, no. 756; Spier 1992, p. 99, no. 234 (first century AD).
4. Fossing 1929, no. 1778, pl. XX.

171. Ring

Silver. Diameter 1.5; bezel 0.8; width 1.0

The ring is composed of a filigree openwork hoop, made with a double plain wire repeated four times, alternating with a pair of helicoid wires. The circular bezel is composed of a fine strip of silver sheet edged with a row of granules and four triangles disposed orthogonally, also made up of granules.

In the absence of detailed comparisons, a general analogy may be indicated with rings in filigree that were highly recurrent in the late-Roman and Byzantine periods.[1]

1 Marshall 1907, no. 558, pl. XVI; Ruxer Kubczak 1976, pp. 125-126, no. 53, Fig. 16, third-fourth centuries AD; Ross 1965, no. 72, pl. XLV, from Costantinople, seventh century AD.

172. Ring

Silver. Max. height 2.3

Composed of a flattened hoop, with ridges and strigils in relief. The raised circular bezel is missing its gem.

The ring is comparable to a specimen in Berlin, also in silver, different for its square bezel but decorated with analogous raised grooves, dated to the fourteenth century AD.[1]

1. Battke 1938, no. 57, pl. V.

VARIOUS

173 – 188. Sixteen bracteates with embossed decoration: butterfly with spread wings

Gold. Max. diameter 1.4

Sixteen bracteates, each with three attachment holes, picturing a die-formed design of a butterfly with spread wings.

An analogous subject appears on several of the gold bracteates at the Athens Museum found in tomb III in Mycenae, from the second half of the sixteenth century BC, also circular but larger in diameter: 5.4-6.6 cm.[1] In comparison with these, however, there are certain stylistic differences that do not allow for a more definitive classification.

1. Becatti 1955, nos 53, 55, pl. XVII.

189. Embossed plaque – fragment

Gold. Length 3.8

Sheet gold fragment picturing a hippocamp (?).

A similar fragment figures among Etruscan material in the British Museum.[1]

Sixth – fifth centuries BC.

1. Marshall 1969, no. 1280,c, pl. XVI

190. Embossed plaque: bearded figure

Gold. Height 8.5; width 2.8

Die-formed and cut-out plaque picturing a seminude, bearded figure in profile, his hair fastened at the forehead with a *taenia* and braids falling on his shoulders.

191. Embossed plaque: female figure

Gold. Height 9.5; width 2.9

Die-formed and cut-out plaque picturing a female figure in profile, with a parallelepipedal sheet gold base decorated with a meander pattern. Her hair, with braids falling on her shoulders, is adorned with a diadem. She wears a long *chiton* and *himation*, the hem of which she holds with her right hand lowered along her hip. Her left arm is missing.

192. Embossed plaque: female figure

Gold. Height 10.0; width 3.8

Die-formed and cut-out plaque picturing a frontal female figure with the head seen in profile. She has a rich hairstyle, adorned with a diadem, and her braids fall on her chest and shoulders. She wears a long, pleated *chiton* and a *himation* whose hem she lifts with her raised right hand, while with her left, lowered along her hip, she holds a fold of her *chiton*. Attached to the lower portion is a strip of sheet gold, which is most likely pertinent to the base, as in the previous case.

193. Embossed plaque: frontal male figure

Gold. Height 9.5; width 3.0

Die-formed and cut-out plaque picturing a frontal, semi-draped male figure holding a garland (?) in his lowered right hand; his left arm is missing.

194. Embossed plaque: base fragment

Gold. Height 8.4

Fragment with a base in the form of a truncated pyramid, decorated with a frieze of confronting palmettes and volutes.

195. Embossed plaque: fragment with frieze of palmettes

Gold. Length 9.4

Fragment of die-formed sheet gold decorated with a frieze of confronting palmettes and volutes, framed above by a double row of bosses.

196. Embossed plaque: fragment with frieze of volutes

Gold. Length 3.1

Fragment of die-formed sheet gold with a frieze of confronting volutes.

(Nos **191-196**) Die-formed plaques of gilt silver with human figures are documented in the Archaic period in the Tarantine area, where they recur in funerary[1] or votive contexts,[2] datable on the whole between the second half of the sixth and the fifth centuries BC.

In Metaponto, a tomb in Casa Ricotta, datable to the second half of the sixth century BC, contained

male and female figurines in die-formed gilt silver sheet, including in some cases a parallelepipedal base analogous to those on these specimens.[3] Further findings are reported in Metaponto.[4]
Similar objects, specifically three die-formed heads of female divinities, are also known from the art market.[5]
Cut-out sheets, in some cases diadems or belts, with stamped phytomorphic decorations (palmettes, racemes, rows of dots), from a cult-related context, the Sanctuary of Apollo Aleus in Cirò, are approximately dated between the end of the fifth and fourth centuries BC.[6] According to a hypothesis initially formulated by P. Orsi and later shared by Guzzo, these sheets, which were found in apparently unrelated scraps, may have been cut out in ancient times from an integral and defined object by an artisan-merchant who worked near a sanctuary, carrying out the operation according to his customers' requests. A die-formed decoration with palmettes and confronting volutes recurs on a silver belt from the Lucanian sanctuary of Rossano di Vaglio, dated to the second half of the fourth century BC.[7]
More generally, the decorative motifs of palmettes, racemes, and confronting volutes may also be found on the diadem from tomb ß in Derveni, dated by its context to within 330 BC, but whose typology dates back to the fifth century BC,[8] in the funerary diadem from Athens at the Louvre Museum[9] or in collection material.[10] A comparison for the figurines on bases, in this case anonymous, may furthermore be made with a wreath from Armento, from a Lucanian tomb dated to the second half of the fourth century BC, which features several analogous elements.[11] In this, as in other cited cases, the Archaic taste could thus simply denote a stylistic delay.
These insufficiencies in comparisons do not allow for a definitive statement on the cultural area of pertinence for these items, which are, however, traceable to a Greek or Greco-colonial origin.

Fifth – fourth century BC.

1. *Ori e argenti* 1961, p. 96, no. 264, from Taranto, fifth century BC.
2. P.G. Guzzo, in F. D'Andria (ed.), *Archeologia dei Messapi*, exhibition catalogue, Lecce, Bari 1990, pp. 274-281, nos 134-140, Oria - Mount Papolucio, votive deposit, second half sixth – first quarter fifth century BC.
3. A.L. Tempesta, in *Bellezza e lusso* 1992, pp. 43-45, with bibliography; P.G. Guzzo, in *L'oro dei Greci*, Novara 1992, p. 256, no. 105, dated to the early sixth century BC.
4. Crucinia, tomb 238: *ibid.*, p. 45, notes 1,4; on the classification, cf. Guzzo 1993, pp. 266-267, type IV.A, pp. 106-108.
5. *Classical Art from a New York Collection*, 27/9-16/11/1977, André Emmerich Gallery Inc., New York 1977, no. 130.
6. P. Orsi, *Templum Apollinis Alaei ad Crimisa Promontorium*, Roma 1933, pp. 88-96; Guzzo 1993, pp. 268-269, type V.A.
7. P.G. Guzzo, in *Tesori dell'Italia del Sud* 1998, pp. 93-94, Fig. 28.
8. G. Calcani, in *L'Oro dei Greci*, Novara 1992, p. 276, no. 149.3.
9. Metzger 1976, pp. 5, 7, no. 5.
10. Rudolph, Rudolph 1973, p. 64, no. 49d.
11. *L'Oro dei Greci*, Novara 1992, no. 119, pp. 151, 260.

197. Cockleshell bracteate

Gold. Height 2.3; width 2.1

Stamped and repoussé plaque in the form of a cockleshell.

This is generically comparable to analogous Hellenistic objects, such as a specimen in the Merle de Massoneau collection from southern Russia.[1] Another jewelry element in the form of a cockleshell is known from the market.[2] An analogous amulet in the form of a shell, but in rock crystal, was found in a Roman tomb in Piraeus

from the first century AD.[3] Shell-shaped pendants may also be seen on a Roman necklace from Aquileia.[4]

Hellenistic or Roman Imperial (third century BC - first/second centuries AD).

1. Greifenhagen 1970, p. 50, no. 24, pl. 26.
2. *Frank Sternberg*, Auct. XXVII, 1994, no. 892, pl. XLVII.
3. *Gold of Greece* 1990, p. 64, pl. 45; A. Oliver Jr., in *Greek Jewellery from the Benaki Museum Collections*, Athens 1999, pp. 254-255, no. 34, Fig. 182.
4. Pavesi, Gagetti 2001, pp. 137-138, no. 48, pl. XIV.

198. Band with illustrated oval

Gold. Bezel 2.3 x 1.1; total length 6.8

Illustrated oval equipped with a thin sheet gold ribbon with perforated extremities joined by a

cord of double twisted wire. It pictures a naked figure, running toward the right in the direction of a bird with a long neck. It is probably the representation of a pygmy armed with a club (?) and hunting a crane.

This type of jewel does not have specific parallels. From an iconographic point of view, despite uncertainties, generic parallels may be made with representations of battles between pygmies and cranes on engraved gems[1] or glass pastes[2] dated to the Roman-Hellenistic period, in which, however, pygmies are represented as warriors, armed with shields, helmets and spears.[3] Naked pygmies armed with clubs and hunting cranes are pictured in relief on an Etruscan cinerary urn from Chiusi, dated to the end of the fourth - early third centuries BC.[4]

Third - first centuries BC.

1. Walters 1926, pl. XV, nos 1037-1038; *AGDS* IV, no. 183, first century BC; Zwierlein Diehl 1979, no. 1123, first century BC.
2. *AGDS* I,2, pl. 169, no. 1882, third-first centuries BC.
3. For the iconography: V. Dasen, *Pygmaioi*, in *LIMC* VII, 1994, pp. 594-601.
4. M. Sannibale, *Le urne cinerarie di età ellenistica*, Roma 1994, pp. 95-99, no. 13.

199-221. Twenty-two scaraboid elements

Gold. Pendants: length 1.1/0.9; width 0.7/0.8

The scarabs are made from a stamped gold sheet, closed at the base by a flat sheet.

222. Beetle-shaped element

Gold. Length 1.3; width 0.9

Beetle-shaped element equipped with a loop of

twisted wire on the base, in which is inserted a rod of double twisted wire with annular terminals.

A beetle-shaped element, wholly analogous to this, figures in the Ferdinando Cafiero Collection in the Barletta Museum and is dubiously dated to the Roman period.[1] Further comparisons are given by a specimen in the British Museum[2] and by seven scarab-shaped amulets in die-formed gold in the Gutman Collection.[3] In this same collection, a similar scarab is part of a Roman necklace (*see infra* no. **73**).

First - second centuries AD.

1. van den Driessche 1975, p. 15, no. 19, Fig. 18.
2. Marshall 1969, no. 2122, pl. XLI.
3. Parkhurst 1961, p. 230, no. 146g.

223. Truncated-cone element

Gold. Height 3.3; width 1.1
Fragmented in upper portion.

The hollow sheet gold pendant is closed on the underside and cracked on top; the decoration is articulated on two superimposed tiers, separated by stippled ridges, and is composed of gridlike designs and strigils.

Decorated conical elements and pendants are known from the Hellenistic age, as in the case of the necklace terminals from Iasos, tomb y, in the Smyrna Museum, early third century BC,[1] a specimen from the Kocakizlar Tumulus in Turkey, first century BC-first century AD,[2] and a reassembled necklace from Asia Minor or southern Russia, in the Gutman Collection.[3] In the Roman world, club-shaped pendants were widespread, intended as references to the cult of Hercules.[4]

Probably second - fourth century AD.

1. Levi 1964, p. 206, Fig. 11.
2. Atasoy 1974, p. 262, no. 23, pl. 52, Fig. 7.
3. Parkhurst 1961, pp. 54-55, no. 5.
4. *Galerie Günter Puhze, Kat. 8*, Freiburg 1989, no. 44; L. Ruseva Slokoska, *Roman jewellery. A Collection of the National Archaeological Museum, Sofia*, London, 1991, p. 151, no. 133, from Serdica, second-third centuries AD; Johns 1996, p. 142, pl. 2, from the Thetford treasure, late fourth century AD; Allason-Jones 1989, pp. 11-12, no. 5, no. 12, pl. 14, type 15, from the mid-first century to the fourth century AD; *Christie's*, 8 December 1999, p. 23, no. 41, p. 49, no. 105.

224. Garniture

Gold. Length 3.7; width 2.3, thickness 0.4

Sheet gold garniture decorated in repoussé and openwork and picturing a running feline, framed by raised ridges. The rear face is closed by a smooth plate.

This may be compared to Byzantine-era belt buckles or garnitures.[1] Each of these examples present abstract or stylized phytomorphic decorative elements; for the animalistic repertoire, compare a finial with a running feline from the Florence market.[2]

Sixth - seventh centuries AD.

1. B. Filow, in *Archäologischer Anzeiger* 29, 1914, p. 418, Fig. 1, from Bulgaria, in a context dated by monetary remains to 613-641; W.A. von Jenny, W.F. Volbach, *Germanischer Schmuck*, Berlin 1933, pl. 24,1,3, from Italy; Ross 1965, no. 6H, pl. XIV, from Costantinople; *ibid.*, no. 4F, pl. X; K. Weitzmann, *Age of Spirituality: Late Antique and Early Christian Art, Third to Seventh Century*, New York 1979, p. 326, no. 304; M. Kazanski, J.P. Sodini, *Byzance et l'art "nomade": remarques à propos de l'essai de J. Werner su le dépôt de Malaja Pereščepina (Pereščepino)*, in *Revue Archéologique* 1987, p. 80, Fig. 11, in the Istanbul Museum; Rudolph 1995, p. 293, no. 86, from the southern Balkans or western Anatolia.

2. J. Werner, *Byzantinische Gürtelschnallen des 6. und 7. Jahrhunderts*, in *Kölner Jahrbuch für Vor und Frühgeschichte* 1, 1955, p. 37, Fig. 1; cf. *ibid.*, pl. 4,5-8, in general for the shape.

225. Decorative element (?)

Gold and stone. Width 1.7/1.9

Composed of three perforated stone spheres, tied together by gold pins with heads in the shape of four-petalled flowers.

MATERIALS, TECHNIQUES AND CULTURE

By Maurizio Sannibale

In antiquity gold was undoubtedly rarer and more valuable than it appears to us today, misled as we are by the boundless capacities of the modern-day mining industry and world trade. In the ancient world, a long chain of commerce distributed precious metals, painstakingly researched and mined from the rare gold deposits found mainly in the Orient: India, Armenia, Asia Minor, Arabia, Egypt and Nubia, and even as far as the Urals and Siberia. Continental Greece relied not only on the gold supply from two Aegean islands, Siphnos and Thasos, but also on gold deposits in Thrace and Macedonia which later proved to be the fortune of the Macedon Kings beginning in the fourth century BC.

The distant origins of this precious material were cloaked in mythology. Such was the case of the griffins guarding the gold deposits in their endless confrontation with the Arimasps, legendary inhabitants of Scythia, in the area between the Danube and the Don, a reference to the peoples of the Eurasian steppes and the Scythian-Siberian culture that in fact produced many very precious artifacts in gold and electrum. Another popular myth was Jason's expedition for Colchis, a land where streams glistened with gold particles, in search of the Golden Fleece. At the same time an aura of splendor was evoked by the tradition of the legendary reign of Midas, king of Phrygia, from the memory of the gifts to Delphi by Gyges, king of Lydia in the first half of the seventh century BC, and the celebrated riches of Croesus, last King of Lydia (circa 560-547/546 BC). All of this fits in with the contemporary image of Asia Minor, overflowing with gold in the ancient imagination, land of the mythical city of Troy, rich with extraordinary goldwork as early as the end of the third millennium BC.

The art of the goldsmith reached the West a thousand years later compared to the great civilizations of the ancient Orient and Egypt: Greece was taken with it as early as the Bronze Age, while Etruria only learned of the precious metal in the late Iron Age and Orientalizing period, during the colonial movements and the Phoenician and Greek expansion toward the western Mediterranean. The birth of the urban phenomenon in Etruria represents an essential prerequisite for the development of goldwork that took place between the eighth and seventh centuries BC. Urban development created stable environments, well-equipped and protected, thus suitable for time-consuming and delicate work on the precious material. The rising aristocracies ensured, on their part, commissions and protection for those immigrant craftsmen who brought, in addition to the precious materials, their equally precious cultural and technological know-how.

During the course of the Orientalizing period in Etruria, goldsmiths relied on technologies and formal techniques that were also common to other types of production, such as silver, bronze, amber, wood, and even pottery. In the bucchero, a typical Etruscan pottery type developed around 675 BC, punches and engraving instruments entirely similar to those used in bronzeware and toreutics were used to execute the minute decorations for which it is known. These early cities of ancient Italy thus differed very little from the cities of the Renaissance that featured, nearly two millennia later, craftsmen and artists side by side, expressing their individual genius by means of the most diverse materials and artistic disciplines.

The Etruscans, according to ancient sources, held somewhat of a record for luxury and privileged living. This is reflected in Etruscan goldwork, which has left behind unmistakable and absolute masterpieces. Diodorus Siculus (*Bibliotheca,* VIII, 18,1: "Erant Sybaritae ventri ac deliciis addicti, tantaque apud eos aemulatio luxuriae erat, ut inter exteros populos, maxime Iones et Tuscos diligerent, quod hi quidem Graecorum, illi Barbarorum omnium luxuriosissimi ac mollissimi essent."), a Greek historian from the first century BC, made a telling parallel between the Etruscans, the inhabitants of Ionia and those of Sybaris, referring to a historic period that preceded the destruction of that rich Greek city of southern Italy in 510 BC. Many ancient historians have since written on the theme of decadence driven by luxury: the basic truth of historical fact, however, conceals an *a posteriori* moralistic judgment on the part of those, like Diodorus, who observed, during the first century BC, the politico-military decline of the Etruscans, a once rich and powerful people, rendered unwarlike by a privileged life. Specific laws in Archaic Greece and Rome gradually limited the use of gold in the private sphere, transferring it to the public sphere and to sanctuary treasures.

In the mid-fifth century BC, Roman law limited public ostentation of gold to dental prostheses and wreaths. The latter, being an honorific emblem of high symbolic value worn in times of victory, was stripped of its former aura of frivolity, though it was of known Etruscan origin (cf. no. **5**). Also of Etruscan provenance was the use of the gold *bulla* (cf. no. **108**), part of the ceremonial and symbolic apparatus of political and religious power transmitted to Rome by the Etruscans. In 215 BC, in the austere climate imposed by the dangerous wars against Hannibal, the Oppian laws limited the legal amount of personal gold to half an ounce, forbidding elegant dress and the use of chariots outside of religious ceremonies. The growth of Roman power eventually led to the abandonment of this rigor, which imperial citizens – powerful and not – viewed more with nostalgia than with disciplined observance. The Roman Empire collected riches not only from every corner of its territory but also from the furthest limits of the known world. It is thanks to this chapter in history that today we may admire precious and artistically remarkable artifacts such as those present in this collection.

TECHNIQUE

In order to better understand the descriptive sections of the catalogue, following is an outline of the most recurrent techniques in ancient goldwork[1], many of which have remained essentially unchanged in the modern goldsmiths' craft.

Technological aspects should not be considered unrelated to the cultural and artistic context of an artwork or artifact. Technology must thus be viewed as a substantial and fundamental element of the history of the ancient world that links science, art, and economics. An iconography may be copied; a technique is usually learned. This common thread that connects craftsmen, artists and different peoples of the ancient world that crossed paths, occasionally crosses history and survives in the unconscious and unvaried gestures of modern-day artists, guardians of an ancient knowledge. Other times, this thread was severed and resurfaced in the re-inventions and rediscoveries of certain techniques, each with its peculiarities defined by variations in time and space.

As will be possible to see below, the best goldsmiths from ancient times relied on elaborate and detailed techniques, to the point that today it is possible to better appreciate them with the help of a microscope, an instrument certainly unknown to the ancients. The complex creation of precious objects and jewels, composed of tens, sometimes hundreds or thousands of small parts, was undoubtedly one of the most appreciated elements of luxury, and offset the generally parsimonious use of the precious material, used at very high levels of purity, practically pure gold.

1. I would like to thank the restorer, Fabiana Francescangeli, for her precious help. With the observations that she made during the restoration of the Cini-Alliata collection, she helped me to select the most relevant technical details and to verify certain specifications to which I previously only had access in a preliminary form.

CHAINS

In ancient times, chains were rarely made from a series of links the way they normally are today. The procedure involved the creation of a series of closed wire links. These links were bent in the shape of a bow and slightly flattened in order to be hooked onto one another in a series (**Fig.1**). The method, known as *loop-in-loop*, could be modified by hooking each link to the previous two or more. The result was a double or triple chain that, slightly flattened, had the effect of a long braid of woven wire, rather than a series of links (**Fig. 2**). Chains made by soldering, mechanically flattened and welded at their extremities (**Fig. 3**), are documented from the Roman era, as are those simply made with twisted wire (**Fig. 4**).

Fig. 1. Gold earrings, fourth – early third century BC (no. **22**). Detail of *loop-in-loop* chain technique.

Fig. 2. Gold earring, late fourth – third century BC (no. **23**). Double chain.

Fig. 3. Gold necklace, first century AD (no. **72**). Chain with flattened figure-of-eight links.

Fig. 4. Gold, carnelian and rock crystal necklace, first-third centuries AD (no. **73**). Chain of double links twisted closed.

DECORATION WITH CHISELS OR PUNCHES

A chisel is a metal instrument composed of a rod with a variously shaped tip, tempered or hardened, that leaves behind its design when struck with a hammer. It was used both on solid metal and on sheets. In the latter case, it was necessary to place the sheet over a semi-rigid support in leather, pitch or lead, which would absorb the blows of the chisel and prevent the sheet from being excessively damaged or deformed.

The chisel was also used as a punch to repeat decorations and designs or to combine simple elements such as half-moons, studs, and hatches (**Fig. 5**), to produce more complex decorative designs (**Fig. 6**). To create continuous grooves, the tracing or profiling chisel was used, with its tip in the shape of a boat's keel, that "walks" along with continuous percussions.

Rounded-tip chisels were also used to press a sheet into a die, or for embossing (also known as the repoussé technique). To create embossed figures, the outlines were marked on the sheet and the decoration was carried out from the rear in negative, hollowing out the areas intended to be raised. The work then proceeded from the positive, redefining the volume of the raised parts and tracing the details. Naturally, every time the work surface was changed, the temporary support in pitch or other material had to be renewed (**Fig. 7**).

Fig. 5. Die-formed sheet gold *bulla*, first half fourth century BC (no. **74**). Hatched background with punched dots.

Fig. 6. Sheet gold disc over die-formed bronze, 750-725 BC (no. **80**). Punched geometric decoration.

Fig. 7. Gold *bulla*, early or first half fourth century BC (no. **96**). Details of repoussé decoration: figures in relief, punched circles in the background; spooled wire along the border.

GILDING

Ever since the onset of the goldsmith's art in ancient Italy, during the Orientalizing period, it was common practice to overlay an object made of bronze or silver with a thin layer of gold in such a sophisticated manner as to make it look like solid gold. The Etruscans were probably not familiar with the technique of gilding with mercury amalgam. For silver objects, a very thin gold sheet was applied and heated, forming a gold-silver alloy (**Fig. 8**).

Fig. 8. Silver ring with sheet gilding, early fifth century BC (no. **134**). Gilding detail.

WIRES

Wires, despite their apparent simplicity, are one of the most complex elements of ancient goldwork. Conceptually simple techniques contributed to the creation of an essential component of ancient jewelry that varied widely in structure.

Modern custom favors the wire drawing technique for the creation of wire. In this process, a hammered rod of wire with a fairy large diameter is pulled through a series of successively smaller holes in a steel draw-plate. This system, while not unknown in antiquity, was not used exclusively by the Etruscans and Romans. The most common method involved twisting a narrow, flat strip along its length; this resulted in very thin wires, even two-tenths of a millimeter in diameter, with a typical spiral seam visible under a microscope but appreciable even to the naked eye (**Fig. 9**). It has been observed that wires made in this way could be further regularized by being pulled through a draw-plate (**Figs 10-11**). Instead of a strip, it was also possible to use a twisted square-section wire, either single (**Figs 12-13**) or double (**Fig. 14**). These wires were the building blocks for more complex structures that often used a single or double pair of twisted wires. Furthermore, a thin wire could be spirally wound around a thicker wire (**Fig. 15**), or it could form a hollow solenoid cylinder: in this case, the central wire was removed after the thin core was completely wound (**Fig. 16**).

Fig. 9. Silver openwork bracelet, first quarter seventh century BC (no. **130**). Detail of openwork wires with soldered attachments.

Fig. 10. Gold earrings, second-third centuries AD (no. 59). Detail of the eyes, rendered in hollow, twisted and drawn wire.

Fig. 11. Gold hair spiral, second half seventh – first half sixth century BC (no. **3**). Detail of hollow, twisted and drawn wire decoration.

Fig. 12. Gold earring, second-third centuries AD (no. **41**). Body made of twisted square-section wire.

Fig. 13. Gold earring, second half third century BC (no. **24**). Detail of twisted and drawn square-section wire decoration.

Fig. 14. Gold earring, second-third centuries AD (no. **59**). Detail of the hook formed from a pair of twisted square-section wires.

Fig. 15. Gold leech-shaped earring (no. **19**). Detail of a wire wound in a solenoid cylinder around a central wire.

Fig. 16. Gold earring with frontal face, third-fourth centuries AD (no. **56**). Detail of a wire wound into a free solenoid cylinder.

FILIGREE

Wires of various thicknesses and shapes were placed side by side in linear sequences or shaped according to predetermined designs and soldered to one another (*see* Soldering and Granulation) to create so-called filigree decoration. The wires were either applied onto a plain background (**Figs 17-18**) of metal sheet, even in elaborate designs (**Figs 19-20**), or they became a freestanding "openwork" structure (**Figs 9, 21**).

Fig. 17. Gold *bulla*, early or first half fourth century BC (no. **96**). Suspension tube with filigree decoration of a pair of twisted wires. 9210).

Fig. 18. Gold necklace, fifth-fourth centuries BC (no. **71**). Detail of beads with filigree and openwork decoration.

Fig. 19. Silver fibula, third century BC (no. **127**). Filigree decoration with fishbone design, rendered by two pairs of confronting braided wires. The wires are made of twisted strips of sheet.

Fig. 20. Gold pendant, probably second century AD (no. **115**). Detail of the braided decoration on the sides, consisting of three wires made from twisted strips of sheet.

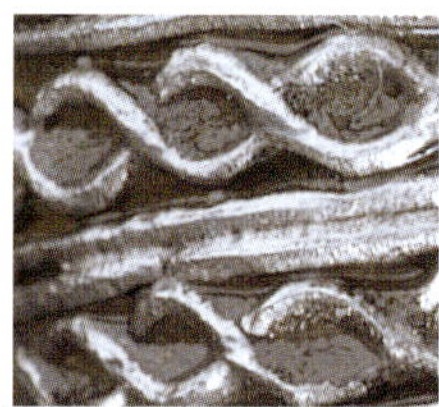

Fig. 21. Silver ring, late Roman or Byzantine (no. **171**). Filigree detail of wide two-string braid.

KNURLING

Once the plain wire was formed, various techniques were used to create different decorative effects. The most common types of decorative wire were beaded (**Figs 22-24**), spooled (**Fig. 25**), funnel-beaded (**Fig. 26**) and spiral-beaded or oblique spooled (**Fig. 27**). These were probably made by diagonally rolling an instrument equipped with a thick series of grooves over the wire, reproducing the shape of the groove in the negative on the wire. The instrument, of hypothetical reconstruction as it is neither documented in findings nor iconographic documents, was used in a sequence of oblique movements that produced a groove spiralling along the wire.

Fig. 22. Gold earring, second half fourth – third century BC (no. **21**). Detail of the disc with beaded wire decoration along the edge.

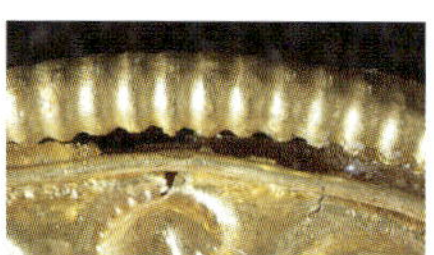

Fig. 23. Gold *bulla*, first half fourth century BC (no. **74**). Border detail with *trottola* or "pirouette" type beaded wire.

Fig. 24. Gold earring, second century BC (no. **29**). Disc with border decoration of grooved beaded wire.

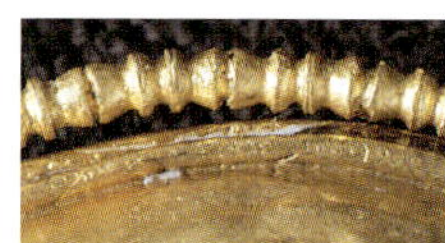

Fig. 25. Gold *bulla*, early or first half fourth century BC (no. **96**). Edge decorated with spooled wire.

Fig. 26. Gold *bauletto* earring, third quarter sixth century BC (no. **8**). Funnel-beaded wire detail.

Fig. 27. Gold *bulla*, first century AD (no. **108**). Oblique spooled wire detail

GRANULATION

A typical and refined decorative technique of very ancient origins, granulation had a remarkable aesthetic impact and was particularly developed in Etruria during the Orientalizing period (**Figs 28-30**). The tradition may be traced to the eastern Mediterranean: Mesopotamia, Egypt, Syria, Palestine, Asia Minor, Crete, Cyprus and Greece. The earliest objects decorated with this technique date back to the third millennium BC and were found in the royal necropolis at Ur. Technological precedents closer to the Etruscan tradition, however, were made in Syria between the eighteenth and fifteenth centuries BC, thus preceding it by about a millennium.

When the granules are particularly small (around 0.14 mm), the technique is known as *pulviscolo* (**Fig. 31**). In order to fully appreciate this elaborate process, one must consider that it would take about seventy of these minute grains in a row to reach a single centimeter in length. It has been calculated that a vase from Palestrina in London's Victoria and Albert Museum contains as many as 147,000 gold granules.

The technique, which fell into disuse with the end of the ancient world, was imitated only beginning in the nineteenth century –as in the case of the Castellani, the famous family of Roman goldsmiths and collectors - and not until the twentieth century was it rediscovered in its essential lines, without of course reaching the degree of complexity and refinement documented by certain ancient masterpieces.

The granules, according to the latest experiments and supported by direct observation and analyses of ancient materials, were made by heating to beyond 1100°C (2012°F) tiny gold fragments, obtained from wires or sheets, mixed with wood charcoal pow-

Fig. 28. Biconical gold bead, first half seventh century BC (no. **69**). Meander pattern executed in granulation.

Fig. 29. Pomegranate pendant, fourth-third centuries BC (no. **106**). Decoration with granules disposed in a triangle.

Fig. 30. Gold hair spiral, late seventh – first half sixth century BC (no. **4**). Decoration of granules disposed in a rosette and a tightly twisted square-section wire.

Fig. 31. Gold *bauletto* earring, last quarter sixth century BC (no. **9**). *Pulviscolo* decoration and S-shaped wire with a granule in each volute.

der and placed in an open crucible.

The soldering process most likely involved the use of copper salt or colloid hard-soldering.The granules were arranged beforehand, using pulverized copper salts mixed with vegetable glue. When heated to controlled high temperatures, so as to avoid melting the object (a bed of charcoal created the ideal reducing environment), a gold-copper alloy with a lower melting point was formed that fused the point of contact. The phenomenon would occur wherever the copper salt was located, and was used not only to solder granules but also wires to gold sheet, wires to other wires, and the individual parts of jewels composed of several pieces. Analyses of original samples with microprobes in electronic microscopy have confirmed a growing concentration of copper right in the point of contact between the granules and the metal support. It is worth noting that the ancient name for malachite (a basic copper carbonate), one of the copper salts most widely used in antiquity, used also as a pigment and as a cosmetic, was *chrysokolla*, from the Greek *chrysos* (gold) and *kolla* (glue), or "gold glue."

SHEETS

To enhance and embellish the surface of an object made of baser metals (*see* Gilding), thin sheets of gold or silver were often used, made in ancient times by specialized artisans. A remarkable iconographic and epigraphic document from the Roman period is a relief that illustrates an *aurifex brattiarius* (gold-beater) at work (**Fig. 32**). The process of hammering resulted in the production of sheets less than 25 thousandths of a millimeter in thickness. Pliny (*Naturalis Historia* XXX,61) sustained that with an ounce of gold one could produce more than 750 sheets about 16 cm^2 in size. The technique, which was simple but demanded extreme skill in manipulating and cutting out the fine gold sheets, consisted in placing very small gold fragments between layers of calf leather and hammering them with a special wide and flat-headed hammer. The operation, repeated several times, further cutting the increasingly thin sheets, allowed the artisan to reach thicknesses that approached one ten-thousandth of a millimeter.

Fig. 32. Relief of *aurifex brattiarius*. Vatican Museums, Statue Gallery, inv. 753 (= CIL VI, 9210).

SOLDERING

The need to join the various elements - often tiny components - that made up ancient jewels in their captivating and appreciated complexity, required the use of highly developed soldering techniques that proved invisible to the naked eye and perfect under a microscope (**Figs 9, 21**).

In addition to the copper salt system, described in relation to granulation, the ancients also used a method that involved the application of an alloy solder at the lowest melting point, in which a thin sheet, shaving, or chip of this solder was placed alongside or between the parts to be joined. An alternate mixed technique involved the simultaneous use of copper salts and alloy solder.

BIBLIOGRAPHY

M. CRISTOFANI, in CRISTOFANI, MARTELLI 1983, pp. 8-16.

C. ELUÈRE, ed., *Outils et ateliers d'orfèvres des temps anciens*, Antiquités nationales, mémoire 2, Société des Amis du Musée des Antiquités Nationales et du château de Saint -Germain-en-Laye 1993.

E. FORMIGLI, *Appendice tecnica*, in CRISTOFANI, MARTELLI 1983, pp. 321-333.

E. FORMIGLI, *Tecniche dell'oreficeria etrusca e romana. Originali e falsificazioni,* Firenze 1985.

E. FORMIGLI, ed., *Preziosi in Oro, Avorio, Osso e Corno. Arte e tecniche degli artigiani etruschi*, notes from the study seminar and experiments (Murlo 1992), Siena 1995.

E. FORMIGLI, ed., *Fibulae. Dall'età del bronzo all'altro Medioevo. Tecnica e tipologia*, Siena 2003.

J.F. HEALY, *Mining and Metallurgy in the Greek and Roman World*, London 1978.

G. MORTEANI, J.P. NORTHOVER, eds., *Prehistoric Gold in Europe. Mines, Metallurgy and Manufacture,* NATO ASI Series, Kluwer Academic Publishers, Dordrecht, Boston, London 1995.

G. NESTLER, E. FORMIGLI, *Granulazione etrusca. Un'antica arte orafa*, Siena 1994.

G. NICOLINI, *Techniques des ors antiques. La bijouterie ibérique du VIIe au IVe siècle*, Paris 1990.

J. RAMIN, La technique minière et métallurgique des anciens, Bruxelles 1977.

PAVESI, GAGETTI 2001

RESTORATION REPORT

The jewels in the Cini-Alliata collection are made for the most part of gold and silver and decorated with pearls, semi-precious stones, amber and gold paste.

The collection was already restored once around the early 1980s. The gold's state of preservation is excellent. A number of pieces still reveal traces of earth on their surface.

All of the silver artifacts present some superficial oxidation (Argentite (AgS) and more rarely Chlorargyrite (AgCl)) that has rendered the object's surface decoration more or less unclear. In some artifacts, corrosion of the copper alloy in the form of Cuprite (Cu_2O) and Malachite ($Cu_2(OH)_2CO_3$) may be noted due to the deforming alterations it has caused.

The cleaning process for the gold artifacts began with the use of a solvent (acetone) to eliminate the protective coatings applied in the previous restoration, while the epoxy resin could not be removed from the surfaces. The process continued with the use of a soft-bristle brush and demineralized water, and the subsequent drying and dehydration process was carried out with solvents. It was not deemed necessary to use protective coatings on the gold artifacts given their excellent state of preservation; however, a thin coat of acrylic resin – Paraloid B44 ® (methyl-methacrylate) – was applied to the portions of surfaces that come into contact with the methacrylate supports as a precautionary layer.

The cleaning process for the silver artifacts was carried out with complexing solutions that chemically bond (stabilize) the copper products of corrosion in the silver alloy. They were subsequently immersed in EDTA (ethylene-diamene-tetra-acetic acid trisodium salt) with a neutral pH. The immersion was repeated until the layers of Cuprite and Malachite were completely eliminated. The artifacts were then rinsed several times with demineralized water and finally dried and dehydrated with solvents.

A light polish of the silver surfaces was carried out in order to eliminate the brownish-black areas due to sulphurization: to this end the so-called "English red" was used (a very fine powder of mixed metal oxides, made into a paste with the addition of thickening agents) on small cotton swabs.

A final protection of the silver surfaces was necessary to prevent further sulphurization due to the presence of sulphur in the atmosphere: the surface was protected with a 10% solution of Paraloid B44 ® in acetone, and after thorough drying, a cellulose-based nitrocellulose lacquer was applied.

The semi-precious stones, pearls, mother-of-pearl and glass pastes did not require restoration due to their good state of preservation.

Fabiana Francescangeli

BIBLIOGRAPHIC ABBREVIATIONS

AGDS I,1
E. BRANDT, *Antike Gemmen in Deutschen Sammlungen, I,1. Staatliche Münzsammlung München. Griechische Gemmen von minoischer Zeit bis zum späten Hellenismus,* München 1968.

AGDS I,2
E. BRANDT, E. SCHMIDT, *Antike Gemmen in Deutschen Sammlungen, I,2. Staatliche Münzsammlung München. Italische Gemmen etruskisch bis römisch.republikanische, Italische Glaspasten vorkaiserzeitlich,* München 1970.

AGDS I,3
E. BRANDT, A. KRUG, W. GERCKE, E. SCHMIDT, *Antike Gemmen in Deutschen Sammlungen, Staatliche Münzsammlung München I,3. Gemmen und Glaspasten der römischen Kaiserzeit sowie Nachträge,* München 1972.

AGDS II
E. ZWIERLEIN DIEHL, *Antike Gemmen in Deutschen Sammlungen, II. Staatliche Museen Preußischer Kulturbesitz Antikenabteilung Berlin,* München 1969.

AGDS III
P. ZAZOFF, V. SCHERF, P. GERCKE, *Antike Gemmen in Deutschen Sammlungen, III. Braunschweig, Göttingen, Kassel,* Wiesbaden 1970.

AGDS IV
M. SCHLÜTER, G. PLATZ-HORSTER, P. ZAZOFF, *Antike Gemmen in Deutschen Sammlungen, IV. Hannover, Kestner Museum / Hamburg, Museum für Kunst und Gewerbe,* Wiesbaden 1975.

AION ArchStAnt
Istituto Universitario Orientale (Napoli). Dipartimento di Studi del Mondo Classico e del Mediterraneo Antico. Annali di Archeologia e Storia Antica.

AJA
American Journal of Archaeology.

ALEXANDER 1928
C. ALEXANDER, *Jewelry. The Art of Goldsmith in Classical Times,* New York 1928.

ALLASON-JONES 1989
L. ALLASON-JONES, *Ear-Rings in Roman Britain,* BAR British Series 201, Oxford 1989.

AMANDRY 1953
P. AMANDRY, *Collection Hélène Stathatos. Les bijoux antiques,* Strasbourg 1953.

ANDRÉN 1940
A. ANDRÉN, *Architectural Terracottas from Etrusco-Italic Temples,* Lund 1940.

ANDRÉN 1948
A. ANDRÉN, *Oreficeria e plastica etrusche,* in *Opuscula Archaeologica 5,* 1948, pp. 91-112.

ARNETH 1850
J. ARNETH, *Die Antiken Gold und Silber-monumente des K.K. Münz- und Antiken- Cabinettes in Wien,* Wien 1850.

Art of Ancient Italy 1970
Art of Ancient Italy: Etruscan, Greeks and Romans, André Emmerich Gallery Inc., April 1970, New York 1970.

Arte e Artigianato 1996
E. LIPPOLIS *(ed.), Arte e artigianato in Magna Grecia,* exhibition catalogue (Taranto 1996), Napoli 1996.

Arte e cultura in Croazia 1993
Arte e cultura in Croazia, dalle collezioni del Museo Archeologico di Zagabria, exhibition catalogue (Torino 1993), Roma 1993.

ATASOY 1974
S. ATASOY, *The Kocakizlar Tumulus in Eskisehir, Turkey,* in *AJA 78,* 1974, pp. 255-263.

BACCI SPIGO 1984
G.M. BACCI SPIGO, *Coppa vitrea ed oreficerie da sepolture di età ellenistica e romana a Naxos,* in *BollArte 25,* 1984, pp. 59-68.

BALDINI, LIPPOLIS 1999
I. BALDINI LIPPOLIS, *L'oreficeria nell'impero di Costantinopoli tra IV e VII secolo,* Bari 1999.

BARINI 1958
C. BARINI, *Ornatus muliebris. I gioielli e le antiche romane,* Torino 1958.

BATTKE 1938
H. BATTKE, *Die Ringsammlung des Berliner Schlossmuseums,* Berlin 1938.

BCH
Bulletin de Correspondance Hellénique.

BECATTI 1955
G. BECATTI, *Le oreficerie antiche dalle minoiche alle barbariche,* Roma 1955.

BEAZLEY 1963
J.D. BEAZLEY, *Attic Red-Figure Vase-Painters,* 2nd edition, Oxford 1963.

Bellezza e lusso 1992
R. CAPPELLI (ed.), *Bellezza e lusso. Immagini e documenti di piaceri della vita,* exhibition catalogue, Roma 1992.

BEVILACQUA 1999
G. BEVILACQUA, *Magica varia dall'Antiquarium Comunale,* in *Bollettino dei Musei Comunali di Roma 13,* 1999, pp. 18-30.

BIANCHI 1995
C. BIANCHI, *Spilloni in osso di età romana,* Milano 1995.

BIETTI SESTIERI 1992
A.M. BIETTI SESTIERI (ed.), *La necropoli laziale di Osteria dell'Osa,* Roma 1992.

VON BISSING 1933
W.F. VON BISSING, *Materiali archeologici orientali ed egiziani scoperti nelle necropoli dell'antico territorio etrusco, quinta serie, III. Museo Archeologico Etrusco di Firenze,* in *StEtr 7,* 1933, pp. 373-382.

VON BISSING 1938
W.F. VON BISSING, *Materiali archeologici orientali ed egiziani scoperti nelle necropoli dell'antico territorio etrusco, nona serie, III - Museo Archeologico di Firenze,* in *StEtr 12,* 1938, pp. 297-302.

BOARDMAN 1966
J. BOARDMAN, *Etruscan and South Italian Finger Rings in Oxford,* in *Papers of the British School at Rome 34,* 1966, pp. 1-17.

BOARDMAN 1967
J. BOARDMAN, *Archaic Finger Rings,* in *Antike Kunst 10,* 1967, pp. 3-31.

BOARDMAN 1970
J. BOARDMAN, *Greek Gems and Finger Rings. Early Bronze Age to Late Classical,* London 1970.

BOARDMAN 1975
J. BOARDMAN, *Intaglios and Rings, Greek, Etruscan and Eastern, from a Private Collection,* London 1975.

BOARDMAN, VOLLENWEIDER 1978
J. BOARDMAN, M.L. VOLLENWEIDER, *Ashmolean Museum, Oxford. Catalogue of the Engraved Gems and Finger Rings, I. Greek and Etruscan,* Oxford 1978.

BOARDMAN, SCARISBRICK 1977
J. BOARDMAN, D. SCARISBRICK, *The Ralph Harari Collection of Finger Rings,* London 1977.

BÖHME 1974
A. BÖHME, *Schmuck der römischen Frau,* in *Limes Museum Aalen 11,* 1974.

BONNER 1950
C. BONNER, *Studies in Magical Amulets chiefly Graeco-Egyptian,* Ann Arbor 1950.

BollArte
Bollettino d'Arte.

BollMusPont
Bollettino Monumenti, Musei e Gallerie Pontificie.

BORDENACHE, BATTAGLIA 1980
G. BORDENACHE BATTAGLIA, *Oreficerie,* in G. PROIETTI, *Il Museo Nazionale Etrusco di Villa Giulia,* Roma 1980.

BORDENACHE, BATTAGLIA 1983
G. BORDENACHE BATTAGLIA, *Corredi funerari di età imperiale e barbarica nel Museo Nazionale Romano,* Roma 1983.

BOSTICCO 1957
S. BOSTICCO, *Scarabei egiziani della Necropoli di Pithecusa nell'isola d'Ischia,* in *Parola del Passato 12,* 1957, pp. 215-229.

VON BOTHMER 1961
D. VON BOTHMER, *Ancient Art from New York Private Collections,* Catalogue of an Exhibition held at the Metropolitan Museum of Art, December 17, 1959 - February 28, 1960, New York 1961.

BREGLIA 1941
L. BREGLIA, *Catalogo delle oreficerie del Museo Nazionale di Napoli,* Roma 1941.

BROMBERG 1990
A.R. BROMBERG, *Gold of Greece. Jewelry and Ornaments from the Benaki Museum,* exhibition catalogue, Dallas 1990.

BURANELLI 1992
F. BURANELLI, *The Etruscans. Legacy of a lost civilization from the Vatican Museums,* exhibition catalogue, Memphis, Tenn., 1992.

CALINESCU 1996
A. CALINESCU, *Ancient Jewelry and Archaeology,* Bloomington-Indianapolis 1996.

CALIÒ 2000
L.M. CALIÒ, *La collezione Bonifacio Falcioni,* Monumenti Musei e Gallerie Pontificie, Catalogues 6/1-2, Città del Vaticano 2000.

CAMPOREALE 1969
G. CAMPOREALE, *I commerci di Vetulonia in età orientalizzante,* Firenze 1969.

CANTILENA 1989
R. CANTILENA, *Le oreficerie,* in AA.VV., *Le collezioni del Museo Nazionale di Napoli, I,2,* Roma 1989, pp. 75-85, 206-221.

CARNEGIE 1908
H. CARNEGIE, *Catalogue of the Collection of Antique Gems formed by James Ninth Earl of Southesk K.T.*, London 1908, vol. I.

CARUSO 1988
I. CARUSO, *Collezione Castellani. Le oreficerie,* Roma 1988.

CESNOLA 1903
L.P. DI CESNOLA, *A Descriptive Atlas of the Cesnola Collection of Cypriote Antiquities in the Metropolitan Museum of Art, New York, III,* New York 1903.

CHADOUR-SAMPSON 1997
B. CHADOUR-SAMPSON, *Antike Fingerringe/Ancient Finger Rings. Die Sammlung Alain Ollivier/The Alain Ollivier Collection,* Cambridge-London 1997.

Christie's, 16 July 1985
Christie's London, Fine Antiquities which will be sold at Christie's Great Rooms on Tuesday 16 July 1985. The Property of Lady Clark and from various sources, London 1985.

Christie's, 10 December 1985
Christie's London. Fine Antiquities. The Properties of the Marian Fathers and from various sources, 10 December 1985, London 1985.

Christie's, 6 July 1994
Christie's London. Fine antiquities. The properties of Canford School, sold by order of the governors, Mr. and Mrs. Eric Joyall, the late Sir Sidney Nolan, O.M., A.C., C.B.E., the Ian Woodner Family Collection, and from various sources, Wednesday, 6 July 1994, London 1994.

Christie's, 26 April 1995
Christie's London. Antiquities and Souvenirs of the Grand Tour, 26 April 1995, London 1995.

Christie's, 3 July 1996
Christie's London. Fine Antiquities, 3 July 1996, London 1996.

Christie's, 11 December 1996
Christie's London. Fine Antiquities, 11 December 1996, London 1996.

Christie's, 21 April 1999
Christie's London, Important Antiquities, 21 April 1999, London 1999.

Christie's, 4 June 1999
Christie's New York, Antiquities, 4 June 1999, New York 1999.

Christie's, 8 December 1999
Christie's New York, Ancient Jewelry, 8 December 1999, New York 1999.

Christie's, 6 December 2000
Christie's New York. Ancient Jewelry and Seals, 6 December 2000, New York 2000.

Christie's, 5 December 2001
Christie's New York. Ancient Jewelry, 5 December 2001, New York 2001.

Christie's, 14-15 May 2002
Christie's London. Antiquities, 14-15 May 2002, London 2002.

Christie's, 13 December 2002
Christie's New York. Ancient Jewelry, 13 December 2002, New York 2002.

Christie's, 11 December 2003
Christie's New York. Ancient Jewelry, 11 December 2003, New York 2003.

CIANFERONI 1992
G.C. CIANFERONI, *I reperti metallici, in Populonia in età ellenistica. I materiali dalle necropoli,* Atti del Seminario (Firenze 30 giugno 1986), Firenze 1992, pp. 13-41.

CIL
Corpus Inscriptionum Latinarum

Civiltà degli etruschi 1985
M. CRISTOFANI (ed.), *Civiltà degli etruschi,* exhibition catalogue *Firenze,* Milano 1985.

COCHE DE LA FERTÉ 1956
E. COCHE DE LA FERTÉ, *Les bijoux antiques,* Paris 1956.

COEN 1997
A. COEN, *Elmi di bronzo e corone d'oro: una rara associazione simbolica nelle sepolture etrusche di IV sec. a.C.,* in *Miscellanea Etrusco-Italica II* (Quaderni di Archeologia Etrusco-Italica 26), Roma 1997, pp. 89-107.

COEN 1998
A. COEN, *Bulle auree dal Piceno nel Museo Archeologico delle Marche,* in *Prospettiva 89-90,* 1998, pp. 85-97.

COEN 1999
A. COEN, *Corona etrusca,* Daidalos 1, Viterbo 1999.

CRISTOFANI, MARTELLI 1983
M. CRISTOFANI, M. MARTELLI (eds.), *L'oro degli Etruschi,* Novara 1983.

CULICAN 1973
W. CULICAN, *Phoenician Jewellery in New York and Copenhagen,* in *Berytus 22,* 1973.

D'AMBROSIO 2001
A. D'AMBROSIO, *I monili dallo scavo di Moregine,* in *MEFRA 113-2,* 2001, pp. 967-980.

D'AMBROSIO, DE CAROLIS 1997
A. D'AMBROSIO, E. DE CAROLIS, *I monili dall'area vesuviana,* Roma 1997.

D'ANGELA 1989
C. D'ANGELA, *Ori bizantini del Museo Nazionale di Taranto,* Taranto 1989.

DAVIDSON, OLIVER 1984
P.F. DAVIDSON, A. OLIVER Jr., *Ancient Greek and Roman Jewelry in the Brooklyn Museum,* New York 1984.

DENIS 1996
P. DENIS, *Recent Acquisitions of Ancient Jewelry by the Royal Ontario Museum,* in CALINESCU 1996, pp. 207-214.

DEPPERT LIPPITZ 1985
B. DEPPERT LIPPITZ, *Goldschmuck der Römerzeit im römisch-germanischen Zentralmuseum,* Bonn 1985.

DEPPERT LIPPITZ 1985b
B. DEPPERT LIPPITZ, *Griechischer Goldschmuck,* Mainz am Rhein 1985.

DIMITROVA MILCEVA 1980
A. DIMITROVA MILCEVA, *Antike Gemmen und Kameen aus dem archäologischen Nationalmuseum in Sofia,* Sofia 1980.

VAN DEN DRIESSCHE 1975
B. VAN DEN DRIESSCHE, *Les bijoux de la donation F. Cafiero au Musée communal de Barletta,* in *Bulletin de l'Institut historique belge de Rome 45,* 1975, pp. 5-17.

EAA
Enciclopedia dell'Arte Antica Classica e Orientale, Roma 1958-

ERGIL 1983
T. ERGIL, *Küpeler. Istambul Arkeoloji Müzeleri Küpeler Katalogu (Earrings. The Earring Catalogue of the Istambul Archaeological Museum),* Istambul 1983.

FITTSCHEN, ZANKER 1983
K. FITTSCHEN, P. ZANKER, *Katalog der römischen Porträts in den Capitolinischen Museen und den anderen kommunalen Sammlungen der Stadt Rom, III,* Mainz am Rhein 1983.

FOGOLARI 1958
G. FOGOLARI, *Adria. Tomba del III secolo av. Cr.,* in *NotSc* 1958, pp. 27-33.

FOSSING 1929
P. FOSSING, *The Thorvaldsen Museum. Catalogue of the Antique Engraved Gems and Cameos,* Copenhagen 1929.

FURTWÄNGLER 1900
A. FURTWÄNGLER, *Die antiken Gemmen, I-III,* Liepzig - Berlin 1900.

GABRICI 1910
E. GABRICI, *Necropoli di età ellenistica a Teano dei Sidicini,* in *MAL 20,* 1910, cols. 5-152.

GABRICI 1913
E. GABRICI, *Cuma,* in *MAL 22,* 1913.

Galerie Koller, 15 November 1982
Galerie Koller Zurich. Collection d'orfévrerie antique. Moyen-Orient, antiquité classique, époque byzantine, 15 November 1982, Zurich 1982.

GIULIANO 1957
A. GIULIANO, *Catalogo dei ritratti romani del Museo Profano Lateranense,* Città del Vaticano 1957.

GIUNTELLA 2000
A.M. GIUNTELLA, *Cornus I,2. L'area cimiteriale orientale. I materiali,* Oristano 2000.

GIVEON 1984
R. GIVEON, s.v. *Skarabäus,* in *Lexikon der Ägyptologie,* Band V, Wiesbaden 1984.

Gold of Greece 1990
Gold of Greece. Jewelry and ornaments from the Benaki Museum, exhibition catalogue (Dallas 1990), Dallas 1990.

GOODENOUGH 1953
E.R. GOODENOUGH, *Jewish Symbols in the Greco-Roman Period, II-III. The Archeological Evidence from the Diaspora,* New York 1953.

GORTON 1996
A. GORTON, *Egyptian and Egyptianizing Scarabs. A Typology of steatite, faience and past Scarabs from Punic and other Mediterranean Sites,* Oxford 1996.

GRAMATOPOL, CRACIUNESCU 1967
M. GRAMATOPOL, V. CRACIUNESCU, *Les bijoux antiques de la Collection Marie et Dr G. Severeanu du Musée d'histoire de la ville de Bucarest,* in *Revue roumaine d'historire de l'art 4,* 1967, pp. 137-158.

GREGORY WARDEN 1983
P. GREGORY WARDEN, *Bullae. Roman custom and italic tradition,* in *Opuscula Romana 14,* 1983, pp. 69-75.

GREIFENHAGEN 1967
A. GREIFENHAGEN, *Antiker Goldschmuck in Amerikanischem Privatbesitz,* in *Pantheon 25,* 1967, pp. 81-99.

GREIFENHAGEN 1970
A. GREIFENHAGEN, *Schmuckarbeiten in Edelmetall, I,* Berlin 1970.

GREIFENHAGEN 1975
A. GREIFENHAGEN, *Schmuckarbeiten in Edelmetall, II,* Berlin 1975.

GUIDOTTI 1994
M.C. GUIDOTTI - E. LEOSPO, *La collezione egizia del Civico Museo Archeologico di Como,* Como 1994.

GUIRAUD 1989
H. GUIRAUD, *Bagues et anneaux à l'époque romaine en Gaule,* in *Gallia 46,* 1989, pp. 173-211.

GUIRAUD 1996
H. GUIRAUD, *The Eauze Treasure,* in CALINESCU 1996, pp. 62-72.

GUZZO 1993
P.G.GUZZO, *Oreficerie dalla Magna Grecia. Ornamenti in oro e argento dall'Italia Meridionale tra l'VIII ed il I secolo,* Taranto 1993.

GUZZO 1998
P.G. GUZZO, *Ritrovamenti recenti di oreficerie dalla Lucania Antica,* in WILLIAMS 1998, pp. 55-65.

HACKENS 1976
T. HACKENS, *Catalogue of the Classical Collection, Museum of Art, Rhode Island School of Design. Classical Jewelry,* Providence 1976.

HADACZECK 1903
K. HADACZECK, *Der Ohrschmuck der Griechen und Etrusker,* in *Abhandlungen des arch. - epigraphischen Seminars der Universität 14,* Wien 1903.

HALL 1913
H.R. HALL, *Catalogue of Egyptian Scarabs in the British Museum,* London 1913.

VON HASE 1975
F.W. VON HASE, *Zur Problematik der frühesten Goldfunden in Mittelitalien,* in *Hamburger Beiträge zur Archäologie 5,* 1975, pp. 99-182.

HENIG 1978
M. HENIG, *A Corpus of Roman Engraved Gemstones from British Sites,* Oxford 1978.

HENKEL 1913,
F. HENKEL, *Die römischen Fingerringe der Rheinlande und benachbarten Gebiete,* Berlin 1913.

HIGGINS 1980
R.A. HIGGINS, *Greek and Roman Jewellery,* London 1980.

HOFFMANN 1970
H. HOFFMANN, *Ten centuries that shaped the west,* Mainz 1970.

HOFFMANN, VON CLAER 1968
H. HOFFMANN, V. VON CLAER, *Antiker Gold- und Silberschmuck,* Mainz am Rhein 1968.

HOFFMANN, DAVIDSON 1965
H. HOFFMANN, P.F. DAVIDSON, *Greek Gold Jewelry from the Age of Alexander,* Mainz/Rhein 1965.

HÖLBL 1979
G. HÖLBL, *Beziehungen der ägyptischen Kultur zu Altitalien* (EPRO 62), Leiden 1979.

HORNUNG 1976
E. HORNUNG – E. STAEHLIN, *Skarabäen und andere Siegelamulette aus Basler Sammlungen,* Mainz 1976.

JACKSON 1999
M. JACKSON, *New Evidence for Dating a Group of Ptolemaic Earrings,* in *Études et Travaux 18,* 1999, pp. 63-86.

JEHASSE 1973
J. JEHASSE, L. JEHASSE, *La nécropole préromaine d'Aléria,* Paris 1973.

VON JENNY, VOLBACH 1933
W.A. VON JENNY, W.F. VOLBACH, *Germanischer Schmuck,* Berlin 1933.

JHS
Journal of Hellenic Studies.

JOHANSEN 1994
F. JOHANSEN, *Catalogue Ny Carlsberg Glyptotek, Roman Portraits I,* Copenhagen 1994.

JOHNS 1996
C. JOHNS, *The Jewellery of Roman Britain,* London 1996.

JOHNS 1997
C. JOHNS, *The Snettisham Roman Jeweller's Hoard,* Cambridge 1997.

JOHNSTONE 1932
M.A. JOHNSTONE, *The Etruscan Collection in the Public Museum of Liverpool,* in *StEtr 6,* 1932, pp. 443-452.

JOVANOVIC 1978
A. JOVANOVIC, *Nakit u rimskoj Dardaniji / Jewelry in Roman Dardania,* Beograd 1978.

KARO 1899-1901
G. KARO, *Le oreficerie di Vetulonia, Parte prima,* in *Studi e Materiali di Archeologia e Numismatica 1,* 1899-1901, pp. 235-283.

KARO 1902
G. KARO, *Le oreficerie di Vetulonia, Parte seconda,* in *Studi e Materiali di Archeologia e Numismatica 2,* 1902, pp. 97-147.

KARO 1905
G. KARO, *Le oreficerie di Narce,* in *Studi e Materiali di Archeologia e Numismatica 3,* 1905, pp. 143-158.

KENT, OVERBECK, STYLOW 1973
J.P.C. KENT, B. OVERBECK, A.U. STYLOW, *Die Römische Münze,* München 1973.

LAFFINEUR 1980
R. LAFFINEUR, *Collection P. Canellopoulos, 15. Bijoux en or grecs et romains,* in *BCH 104,* 1980, pp. 345-457.

LEVI 1964
D. LEVI, *Le oreficerie di Iasos,* in *Bollettino d'Arte 49,* 1964, pp. 199-217.

LÉVY 1965
E. LÉVY, *Tresor hellenistique trouvé à Délos en 1964. Les Bijoux,* in *BCH 89,* 1965, pp. 535-566.

LIMC
Lexicon Iconographicum Mythologiae Classicae, Zürich-München 1981-.

LYMPEROPOULOS 1999
S. LYMPEROPOULOS, in *Greek Jewellery from the Benaki Museum Collections,* Athens 1999.

LIPPOLIS 1994
E. LIPPOLIS (ed.), *Catalogo del Museo nazionale archeologico di Taranto, 3, 1. Taranto. La necropoli. Aspetti e problemi della documentazione archeologica tra VII e I secolo a.C.,* Taranto 1994.

LISSI CARONNA 1980
E. LISSI CARONNA, *Oppido Lucano (Potenza). Rapporto preliminare sulla seconda campagna di scavo (1968),* in *NotSc* 1980, pp. 119-297.

LUSINGH SCHEURLEER 1996
R.A. LUSINGH SCHEURLEER, *From Statue to Pendant. Roman Harpokrates Pendants in Gold, Silver, and Bronze,* in CALINESCU 1996, pp. 152-171.

MAASKANT KLEIBRINK 1978
M. MAASKANT KLEIBRINK, *Catalogue of the Engraved Gems in the Royal Coin Cabinet The Hague. The Greek, Etruscan and Roman Collections,* The Hague 1978.

MAASKANT KLEIBRINK 1986
M. MAASKANT KLEIBRINK, *Description of the Collections in the Rijksmuseum G.M. Kam at Nijmegen. The Engraved Gems. Roman and non-Roman,* Nijmegen 1986.

Magie des Goldes 1996
Die Magie des Goldes. Antike Schätze aus Italien, exhibition catalogue (Wien 1996-1997), Milano1996.

Magna Graecia 2002
M. BENNET, A.J. PAUL, M. IOZZO (eds.), *Magna Graecia. Greek Art from South Italy and Sicily,* exhibition catalogue (The Cleveland Museum of Art 2002, Tampa Museum of Art 2003), New York-Manchester 2002.

MAL
Monumenti Antichi dei Lincei.

MARSHALL 1907
F.H. MARSHALL, *Catalogue of the Finger Rings Greek, Etruscan and Roman in the Departments of Antiquities, British Museum,* London 1907.

MARSHALL 1969
F.H. MARSHALL, *Catalogue of the Jewellery Greek, Etruscan and Roman in the Departments of Antiquities, British Museum,* London 1911 (reprinted1969).

MASSNER 1982
A.K. MASSNER, *Das römische Herrscherbild 4, Bildnisangleichung. Untersuchungen zur Entstehungs-unda Wirkungsgeschichte der Augustusporträts (43 v Chr. – 68 n. Chr.),* Berlin 1982.

MEFRA
Mélanges de l'École Française de Rome, Antiquité.

MEGOW 1987
W.R. MEGOW, *Kameen von Augustus bis Alexander Severus,* Berlin 1987.

METZGER 1976
C. METZGER, *Bijoux grecs, étrusques et romains,* Musée du Louvre. Petits guides des grands musées, 31, Paris 1976.

MC IVER 1924
R. MC IVER, *Villanovans and early Etruscans,* Oxford 1924.

MICHEL 2001
S. MICHEL, *Die magischen Gemmen im Britischen Museum,* London 2001.

MICHEL 2001a
S. MICHEL, *Bunte Steine – dunkle Bilder: "Magische Gemmen",* exhibition catalogue *(Hamburg 2001),* München 2001.

MIHOVILIĆ 1979
K. MIHOVILIĆ Prstenje i Naušnice Rimskog Doba Slovenije, in Arheološki Vestnik 30, 1979, pp. 223-242.

MINTO 1921
A. MINTO, *1921, Marsiliana d'Albegna,* Firenze 1921.

MINTO 1943
A. MINTO, *Populonia,* Firenze 1943.

Mistero di una fanciulla 1995
A. BEDINI (ed.), *Mistero di una fanciulla. Ori e gioielli della Roma di Marco Aurelio da una nuova scoperta archeologica,* exhibition catalogue (Roma 17 dicembre 1995 - 18 febbraio 1996), Milano 1995.

MONTELIUS 1895-1910
O. MONTELIUS, *La civilisation primitive en Italie,* Stockholm 1895-1910.

Monumenti del Museo Etrusco... 1842
Monumenti del Museo Etrusco Vaticano acquistati dalla munificenza di Gregorio XVI, Pontefice Massimo e per di lui ordine disegnati e pubblicati, edition B, Roma 1842.

MORATELLO 1999
C. MORATELLO, *Oreficerie antiche nelle civiche raccolte archeologiche di Milano,* in *Notizie dal Chiostro del Monastero Maggiore* 63-64, 1999, pp. 261-297.

Musei Etrusci...monimenta 1842
Musei Etrusci quod Gregorius XVI Pon. Max. in aedibus Vaticanis constituit monimenta linearis picturae exemplis expressa et in utilitatem studiosorum antiquitatum et bonarum artium publici iuris facta, edition A, Roma 1842.

Museo Chiaramonti 1
B. ANDREAE, K. ANGER, M.A. DE ANGELIS, W. GEOMINY, M.G. GRANINO, J. KÖHLER, M. KREEB, P. LIVERANI, M. MATHEA-FÖRTSCH, M. STADLER, A. UNCINI, *Bildkatalog der Skulpturen des Vatikanischen Museums I, Museo Chiaramonti 1,* Berlin – New York 1995.

NEWBERRY 1906
E. NEWBERRY PERCY, *Scarabs,* London 1906.

Not Sc
Notizie degli scavi di antichità.

OLIVER 1965-66
A. OLIVER Jr., *Greek, Roman and Etruscan Jewelry,* in *The Metropolitan Museum of Art Bulletin* 24, 1965-66, pp. 269-284.

OLIVER 1996
A. OLIVER Jr., *Roman Jewelry. A Stylistic Survey of Pieces from Excavated Contexts,* in A. CALINESCU, *Ancient Jewelry and Archaeology,* Bloomington-Indianapolis 1996, pp. 130-151.

ONDREJOVÁ 1976
I. ONDREJOVÁ, *Les bijoux antiques du Pont Euxin septentrional,* Praha 1976.

Ori Emilia 1958
N. ALFIERI, P.E. ARIAS, G. BERMOND MONTANARI, M. DEGANI, G.A. MANSUELLI, R. PINCELLI (eds.),*Ori e argenti dell'Emilia antica,* Bologna 1958.

Ori e argenti 1961
Ori e argenti dell'Italia antica, exhibition catalogue, Torino 1961.

Ori e argenti 1990
Ori e argenti nelle collezioni del Museo archeologico di Firenze, Firenze 1990.

Ori degli Elvezi 1991
Gli ori degli Elvezi. Tesori celtici dalla Svizzera, exhibition catalogue (Zurigo, Lugano, Basilea, Berna, Ginevra), Zurigo 1991.

Ori di Taranto 1985
AA.VV., *Gli ori di Taranto in età ellenistica,* Milano 1985.

PAOLUCCI 1991
G. PAOLUCCI (ed.), *La Collezione Terrosi nel Museo civico di Chianciano Terme,* Chianciano Terme 1991.

PARETI 1947
L. PARETI, *La tomba Regolini Galassi nel Museo Gregoriano Etrusco e la civiltà dell'Italia centrale nel VII sec. a.C.,* Città del Vaticano 1947.

PARKHURST 1961
C. PARKHURST, *Melvin Gutman Collection of Ancient Gold. Catalogue,* in *Allen Memorial Art Museum Bulletin* 18, 1961, pp. 39-298.

PAVESI, GAGETTI 2001
G. PAVESI, E. GAGETTI, *Arte e materia. Studi su oggetti di ornamento di età romana,* Milano 2001.

PFEILER 1970
B. PFEILER, *Römischer Goldschmuck der ersten und zweiten Jahrhunderts n. Chr. nach datierten Funden,* Mainz 1970.

PFROMMER 1990
M. PFROMMER, *Untersuchungen zur Chronologie früh- und hochhellenistischen Goldschmucks,* Tübingen, 1990 *(Istanbuler Forschungen 37).*

PFROMMER 1998
M. PFROMMER, *Unprovenanced Greek Jewellery: The Question of Distribution,* in WILLIAMS 1998, pp. 79-84.

PIERIDES 1971
A. PIERIDES, *Jewellery in the Cyprus Museum,* Nicosia 1971.

Pietro e Paolo 2000
Pietro e Paolo. La storia, il culto, la memoria nei primi secoli, exhibition catalogue (Roma, Palazzo della Cancelleria 2000), Milano 2000.

PIRZIO BIROLI STEFANELLI 1992
L. PIRZIO BIROLI STEFANELLI, *L'oro dei romani,* Roma 1992.

PLATZ HORSTER 1987
G. PLATZ-HORSTER, *Die antiken Gemmen aus Xanten,* Bonn 1987.

PLATZ-HORSTER 2001
G. PLATZ-HORSTER, *Antiker Goldschmuck. Antikensammlung Staatliche Museen zu Berlin,* Mainz am Rhein 2001.

POLLAK 1903
L. POLLAK, *Klassisch-antike Goldschmiedearbeiten im Besitze sr. Excellenz A.J. von Nelidow,* Leipzig 1903.

POLLINI 1987
J. POLLINI, *The portraiture of Gaius and Lucius Caesar,* New York 1987.

RAC
Rivista di Archeologia Cristiana.

REIBLICH 1996
E.L. REIBLICH, *Ringe und Ohrringe, in Asia Minor Studien 21 – Ausgrabungen in Assos 1992,* Bonn 1996, pp. 127-137.

RICHTER 1956
G.M.A. RICHTER, *Catalogue of Engraved Gems, Greek, Etruscan and Roman. Metropolitan Museum of Art New York,* Roma 1956.

RICHTER 1968
G.M.A. RICHTER, *Engraved Gems of the Greeks and the Etruscans,* London 1968.

RICHTER 1971
G.M.A. RICHTER, *Engraved Gems of the Romans,* London - New York 1971.

DE RIDDER 1911
A. DE RIDDER, *Collection de Clercq, Les bijoux et les pierres gravées,* VII,1, Paris 1911.

DE RIDDER 1924
A. DE RIDDER, *Catalogue sommaire des bijoux antiques,* Paris 1924.

ROCCO 2001
G. ROCCO, *Un cammeo in calcedonio con il ritratto di Augusto,* in *Xenia Antiqua* 10, 2001, pp. 27-34.

ROSE 1997
C.B. ROSE, *Dynastic commemoration and imperial portraiture in the Julio-Claudian period,* Cambridge 1997.

ROSS 1965
M.C. ROSS, *Catalogue of the Byzantine and Early Mediaeval Antiquities in the Dumbarton Oaks Collection, II. Jewelry, Enamels, and Art of the Migration Period,* Washington D.C. 1965.

ROWE 1936
A. ROWE, *A Catalogue of Egyptian Scarabs, Scaraboids, Seals and Amulets in the Palestine Archaeological Museum,* Le Caire 1936.

RUDOLPH, RUDOLPH 1973
W. RUDOLPH, E. RUDOLPH, *Ancient Jewelry from The Collection of Burton Y. Berry,* Bloomington 1973.

RUDOLPH 1995
W. RUDOLPH, *A Golden Legacy. Ancient Jewelry from the Burton Y. Berry Collection at the Indiana University Art Museum,* Bloomington 1995.

RUSEVA SLOKOSKA 1991
L. RUSEVA SLOKOSKA, *Roman jewellery. A collection of the National Archaeological Museum, Sofia* - London 1991.

RUXER, KUBCZAK 1975
M. RUXER, J. KUBCZAK, *Bijouterie antique de l'ancienne Collection Czartoryski à Cracovie, II, Parures du cou et du buste, in Archeologia* 26, 1975, pp. 95 ff.

RUXER, KUBCZAK 1976
M. RUXER, J. KUBCZAK, *Bijouterie antique de l'ancienne Collection Czartoryski à Cracovie. III. Parures de mains et des bras, in*

Archeologia 27, 1976, pp. 107-132.

Sammlung Naue 1908
Sammlung Professor Dr. Jul. Naue München. Keramik, figürliche Terrakotten, Marmorbildwerke, Bronze-und Edelmetallarbeiten, München 1908.

SCANDONE MATTHIAE 1975
G. SCANDONE MATTHIAE, *Scarabei e scaraboidi egiziani ed egittizanti del Museo Nazionale di Cagliari,* Roma 1975.

SCARPIGNATO 1978-79
M. SCARPIGNATO, *Un corredo di oreficerie romane nel Museo gregoriano etrusco, in Annali della Facoltà di Lettere e Filosofia, Università di Perugia* 16-17, 1978-79, pp. 223-237.

SCARPIGNATO 1981
M. SCARPIGNATO, *Corredo di oreficerie da una tomba vulcente nel Museo Gregoriano Etrusco, in BollMusPont* 2, 1981, pp. 5-19.

SCARPIGNATO 1985
M. SCARPIGNATO, *Oreficerie etrusche arcaiche, Monumenti Musei e Gallerie Pontificie, Museo Gregoriano Etrusco,* Cataloghi 1, Roma 1985.

SCATOZZA HÖRICHT 1989
L.A. SCATOZZA HÖRICHT, *I monili di Ercolano,* Roma 1989.

Schätze der Etrusker 1986
Schätze der Etrusker, exhibition catalogue (Saarbrücken), Firenze 1986.

Schmuck der Antike 1981
Schmuck der Antike. Gefässe und Geräte aus Bronze. Sonderliste T. Münzen und Medaillen AG, Basel, 15 Oktober - November 1981, Basel 1981.

SEGALL 1938
B. SEGALL, *Museum Benaki Athen. Katalog der Goldschmiede-Arbeiten,* Athen 1938.

SENA CHIESA 1978
G. SENA CHIESA, *Gemme di Luni,* Roma 1978.

SIVIERO 1954
R. SIVIERO, *Gli ori e le ambre del Museo Nazionale di Napoli,* Firenze 1954.

SMITH 1988
R. R. R. SMITH, *Hellenistic Royal Portraits,* Oxford 1988.

St Etr
Studi Etruschi.

Sotheby's, 9th November 1931
Sotheby's London. Catalogue of ancient gold jewellery etc the property of the Hermitage Museum Leningrad, 9th November 1931.

Sotheby & Co., 9th-12th Nov. 1937
Sotheby & Co., Catalogue of the Superb Collection of Rings, formed by the late Monsieur G. Guilhou of Paris, 9th-12th Nov. 1937.

Sotheby's, 10th July 1990
Sotheby's London. Ancient Jewelry, Middle Eastern, Greek, Etruscan, Roman and Egyptian Antiquities, South Italian Greek Pottery Vases, Ancient Glass and Art Reference Books, 10th July 1990, London 1990.

Sotheby's, 13th-14th Dec. 1990
Sotheby's London. Ancient glass, Egyptian and Middle Eastern antiquities, Irish bronze age gold ornaments, ancient jewellery, Greek, Etruscan and Roman antiquities, South Italian Greek pottery vases and Roman mosaics. Days of sale Thursday 13th and Friday 14th December 1990, London 1990.

Sotheby's, December 9, 2003
Sotheby's Antiquities, New York. Egyptian, Classical & Western Asiatic Antiquities, December 9, 2003, New York 2003.

SPIER 1992
J. SPIER, *Ancient gems and finger rings. Catalogue of the Collection. The J. Paul Getty Museum,* Malibu 1992.

Frank Sternberg, Aukt. XXVII, 1994
Frank Sternberg AG Zürich, Auktion XXVII, 7. und 8. November 1994. *Antike Münzen, Renaissancemedaillen, Geschnittene Steine und Schmuck der Antike, Antike Kleinkunst,* Zürich 1994.

STRØM 1971
I. STRØM, *Problems Concerning the Origin and Early Development of the Etruscan Orientalizing Style,* Odense 1971.

SUNDWALL 1943
J. SUNDWALL, *Die älteren italischen Fibeln,* Berlin 1943.

Sw Cyp Ex II
E. GJERSTAD, J. LINDROS, E. SJÖQVIST, A. WESTHOLM, *The Swedish Cyprus Expedition,* II, Stockholm 1935.

Sw Cyp Ex IV,3
O. VESSBERG, A. WESTHOLM, *The Swedish Cyprus Expedition, IV,3. The Hellenistic and Roman Periods in Cyprus,* Lund 1956.

Tesori dell'Italia del Sud 1998
Tesori dell'Italia del Sud. Greci e indigeni in Basilicata, exhibition catalogue (Strasbourg 1998), Milano 1998.

Tharros 1987
R.D. BARNETT, C. MENDLESON, *Tharros. A Catalogue of Material in the British Museum from Phoenician and other Tombs at Tharros, Sardinia,* London 1987.

TOMS 1986
J. TOMS, *The relative chronology of the villanovian cemetery of Quattro Fontanili at Veii,* in *AION ArchStAnt 8,* 1986, pp. 41-97.

TRENDALL 1967
A.D. TRENDALL, *The red-figured vases of Lucania Campania and Sicily,* Oxford 1967.

Tresor d'orfevrerie 1989
Tresor d'orfevrerie Gallo-Romains, exhibition catalogue (Paris-Lyon 1989), Paris 1989.

I trucchi e le essenze 2002
M. SCARPIGNATO (ed.), *I trucchi e le essenze. Cosmesi e bellezza nell'Umbria antica,* exhibition catalogue (Aix en Provence 2002), Perugia 2002.

VERNIER 1927
E. VERNIER, *Catalogue Général des Antiquités Égyptiennes du Musée du Caire. Bijoux et Orfèvreries,* Le Caire 1927.

Voghenza 1984
AA.VV., *Voghenza. Una necropoli di età romana nel territorio ferrarese,* Ferrara 1984.

VOLLENWEIDER 1966
M.L. VOLLENWEIDER, *Die Steinschneidekunst un ihre Künstler in Spätrepublikanischer und Augusteischer Zeit,* Baden-Baden 1966.

VOLLENWEIDER 1972-1974
M.L. VOLLENWEIDER, *Die Porträtgemmen der römischen Republik,* Mainz am Rhein 1972 (Katalog und Tafeln) - 1974 (Text).

VOLLENWEIDER 1984
M.L. VOLLENWEIDER, *Deliciae Leonis. Antike geschnittene Steine und Ringe aus einer Privatsammlung,* Mainz 1984.

WALTERS 1926
P.B. WALTERS, *Catalogue of Engraved Gems in the British Museum,* London 1926.

Werke 1970
Werke antiker Goldschmiedekunst, Sonderliste M, Münzen und Medaillen AG (September 1970), Basel 1970.

WILLIAMS 1924
C.R. WILLIAMS, *Gold and Silver Jewelry and Related Objects,* Catalogue of Egyptian Antiquities, The New York Historical Society, New York 1924.

WILLIAMS 1998
D. WILLIAMS, *The Art of the Greek Goldsmith,* London 1998.

WILLIAMS, TATTON-BROWN, WALKER 1991
D. WILLIAMS, V. TATTON-BROWN, S. WALKER, *A Lady from Miletopolis, in Classical Gold Jewellery and the Classical Tradition, Papers in honour of R.A. Higgins, in Jewellery Studies 5,* 1991, pp. 77-83.

WREDE 1981
H. WREDE, *Consecratio in formam Deorum, Vergöttlichte Privatpersonen in der römischen Kaiserzeit,* Mainz 1981.

ZAHLHAAS 1985
G. ZAHLHAAS, *Fingerringe und Gemmen. Sammlung Dr. E. Pressmar. Einführung und Katalog,* München 1985.

ZAHN 1929
R. ZAHN, *Sammlung Baurat Schiller. Werke Antiker Kleinkunst,* Berlin 1929.

ZOUHDI 1971
B. ZOUHDI, *Les influences réciproques entre l'Orient et l'Occident, d'après les bijoux du Musée national de Damas, in Annales Archeologiques Arabes Syriennes 21,* 1971, pp. 95-103.

ZOUHDI 1989
B. ZOUHDI, *Les bijoux antiques du Musée national de Damas,* in *Archéologie et histoire de la Syrie 2,* Saarbrücken 1989, pp. 557-565.

ZPE
Zeitschrift für Papyrologie und Epigraphik.

ZWIERLEIN DIEHL 1973
E. ZWIERLEIN DIEHL, *Die antiken Gemmen des kunsthistorischen Museums in Wien,* I, München 1973.

ZWIERLEIN DIEHL 1979
E. ZWIERLEIN DIEHL, *Die antiken Gemmen des kunsthistorischen Museums in Wien,* II, München 1979.

ZWIERLEIN DIEHL 1991
E. ZWIERLEIN DIEHL, *Die antiken Gemmen des kunsthistorischen Museums in Wien,* III, München 1991.

APPENDIX

HISTORIC-ARCHAEOLOGICAL NOTE: ITALY BEFORE THE ROMANS

By Maurizio Sannibale

TO READERS FROM THE AMERICAS

Jewels are undoubtedly the most captivating, rare and often enigmatic of ancient relics. Those that have reached Museums and rare private collections represent the few surviving objects, considered precious even in antiquity, that remained intact through wars and lootings, and escaped the greed of ancient and modern-day treasure-hunters. It is not surprising in fact that jewels make up an unusual category of archaeological artifacts, in comparison to less valuable but more recurrent materials that are better documented, studied and dated. Often they are no more than fortunate, isolated relics, usually found in tombs, or small "treasures," hidden in moments of crisis and danger, which human vicissitudes prevented from ever being recovered.

Many jewels have reached present collections without any information about their recovery or their provenance. The reconstruction of a history of ancient jewelry through indices and catalogues is therefore a demanding challenge that has been met with good results for over a century, integrating detailed typological classifications with chronological information supplied by better-documented material.

These precious relics, the fortunate survivors of a turbulent past, arise from an intricate succession of events, reconstructed through the study of ancient historic sources and the interpretation of archaeological data. For those who will have the patience to follow them, the following pages will cover Italy's major historic events and ethnic composition before the Romans. At the same time, for brevity's sake, I refer the reader to works undoubtedly better than mine in regards to the history and the art of the Romans, a period to which a representative part of this collection refers.

ITALY BEFORE THE ROMANS: NOT ONLY THE ETRUSCANS

During the reign of emperor Augustus, Italy, already politically and culturally unified under Rome, was subdivided into eleven regions whose denomination mainly reflected their traditional geographic and ethnic names, as if to honor an ancestral memory which was being erased by a world of expanding borders and increasing cultural homogeneity. Juridical and administrative cycles thus collected the sediment of a much more articulated and heterogeneous cultural reality, which, in its stratification throughout the course of the first millennium BC, characterized Italy before the Roman rule.

The physical configuration of the Italian peninsula, which connects the center of the Mediterranean to the heart of Europe, led to a remarkable susceptibility to external cultural influence. At the same time, however, its morphological variety (mountain ranges, hills, rivers) and diverse climates favored an extraordinary cultural stratification and an accentuated particularity in more or less limited areas. It is for this reason that from the earliest of times, languages of diverse origins, Indo-European and non, coexisted in nearby areas, as did people of different cultures, political and military organization, levels of technology and civilizations.

The major islands of the Mediterranean – which in ancient times were excluded from Italy's legal borders, extending from the Alps to the Strait of Messina – each presented peculiar characteristics while interacting with the mainland. Sardinia – populated by the Sardi, who as early as the second millennium BC had developed a peculiar civilization known as *Nuragic* (known for its *Nuraghi*, or characteristic stone fortresses with truncated-cone towers and false-vaulted domes) – was dominated by the Phoenician colonial movement until, around the sixth century AD, Carthage, not without resistance, ultimately affirmed its supremacy on the island. Nearby Corsica, which differentiated itself considerably from the civilization of the Sardi, while bearing undeniable influences, received strong Greek and Etruscan influences beginning in the sixth century BC. Sicily, in accordance with historic Greek tradition, was home to the *Sicani* (of Iberian origin or autochthonous) and the *Elymi* (from Anatolia or the Italian peninsula), both of whom settled in the western half of the island, while the *Siculi*, of Indo-European descent like the Latins, settled in the eastern-central part.

The ancient names of southern Italy's earliest indigenous peoples have survived, and may be correlated with archeological data. These were the *Oenotrii*, in the present Basilicata, and further south the *Chones* (possibly derived from the same *Oenotrii*), and the *Morgetes* and *Itali* in the present Calabria: from here, the name *Italia* extended progressively throughout the peninsula. What ultimately interfered with and marginalized these civilizations was Greek colonization, as well the expansionism of the Etruscans and particularly the Eastern Italics, namely the *Lucani* and *Bruttii.*

Campania represented a point of intersection and juxtaposition of different races: added to the earliest indigenous inhabitants (*Ausoni, Opikoi/Osci*) were Greeks, Etruscans, and Samnites. The latter descended from the inland mountainous regions beginning in the second half of the fifth century BC and conquered the most developed coastal cities, where they imposed their language and political organization without, however, challenging the cities' superior civilization, which ultimately seduced even them.

Located in the center of Tyrrhenian Italy was a small Italic nation, that of the Latins, whose name is inextricably linked to the destiny of one of their "frontier" cities, Rome, founded near a ford in the river Tiber: the opposite bank was Etruscan territory. The original territory of the Latins, namely the *Latium Vetus*, encompassed the Tyrrhenian strip immediately south of the Tiber, as far as Terracina, and the flat country between the Tiburtine and Prenestine hills, in the center of which rose the Alban hills. The Latins were organized in small communities (*populi*) associated by politico-religious ties, such as that of the thirty *Populi Albenses* that gathered on the summit of the Alban hill (the present Monte Cavo). Like nearby Campania, Lazio too was penetrated by Eastern Italic peoples of Osco-Umbrian language: Sabines, Aequi, Volsci.

The modern definition of Osco-Umbri, Umbro-Sabelli or Eastern Italics identifies one of the most important ethnic and linguistic groups of ancient Italy after the Etruscans and Latins. These populations were distributed throughout the central and southern parts of the peninsula, from Umbria to present-day Calabria, and created a momentary alliance only during the conflict with Rome, ultimately uniting Italy's other major ethnicities against the powerful city. In 295 BC, during the Third Samnite War, the Roman army defeated a coalition comprising Gauls, Etruscans, Umbri and Samnites, diverse peoples united in a supreme and desperate attempt at resistance. The Eastern Italics spoke an Indo-European language different from Latin, articulated into a variety of local parlances. This may be related to the ancient tradition that indicated the basins of Rieti and Amiterno as the primitive centers of dispersion of these groups. Among the earliest Eastern Italic peoples located in the center of the peninsula were the Sabines on the Abruzzian Apennines; in addition to being protagonists in Rome's primitive history, they are indicated as the original founders of many Italic peoples: the Umbri, Picenti, Sabelli or Samnites, which may also have given rise to the Lucani and the Bruzii. Following migratory movements at the end of the Archaic period, other groups of the same stock may be found in their definitive historic settings: Aequi (in Trevi, Carsoli, Alba Fucens), Marsi (Fucino basin, Marruvium) and Volsci. The latter expanded beginning in the early fifth century BC, encroaching on the Hernici and the Latins in the high Sacco valley (Fregellae, Ecetra) and in the Pontine plain (Terracina, Anzio, Satrico), and ultimately conquering the heart of *Latium Vetus* with the defeat of Velletri.

The Samnites (Caraceni, Pentri, Caudini, Hirpini and Lucani) originally inhabited the southern Apennines of Molise and Campania, from which they expanded throughout the south. The Frentani (Histonium/Vasto) and Larinates (Larino), on the other hand, were more peripheral, based along the Adriatic coast.

The Campani or Osci (Sidicini in Teano, Campani in Capua, Alfaterni in Nocera), whose name is perpetuated in the present Campania region, were of the same lineage as the Samnites, and encroached on the earlier Greek and Etruscan ethnicities present in the region, while the Lucani stepped in further south, home to the ancient Oenotrii, and defeated the Greek colonies of Posidonia – which later became Paestum – on the Tyrrhenian Sea, and Thurii and Heraclea on the Ionian. Finally, the Bruttii settled in present-day Calabria, founding their base in Cosenza.

The Umbri were the northern offshoots of the Eastern Italics, whose expansion beyond the Tiber basin reached the Adriatic coast and Romagna as far as Ravenna. Their major centers included: *Iguvium* (Gubbio), Tifernum, Sarsina, Sentino, Tadino, Plestia, Spello, Assisi, Spoleto, Otricoli and *Tuder* (Todi), the "border" city with Etruria (*tular* = "border" in Etruscan).

An Eastern Italic people, the Piceni, occupied the middle-Adriatic strip encompassing the present-day regions of the Marches and a large part of Abruzzo, with an undeniable influx from the Apulian area and the opposite shores of the Adriatic. The territorial extension of the Piceni, who flourished between the ninth and third centuries BC, crossed Augustus' *Regio V* territory (*Picenum*), extending from the Esino river in the north to the Saline or Pescara rivers in the south. The Augustan region actually defined the central nucleus of a much larger territory that extended from the Marecchia to the Punta Penna promontory on the Abruzzian coast, while internally it encompassed the Marches side of the Apennines and the back of the Aquilan plateaus, bordered in the West by the Aterno river.

The ethnic composition of the Piceni was anything but homogeneous, unlike that of the Etruscans and Latins on the opposite slope of the Apennines. Their name in itself does not correspond to that by which they were known in ancient times. The Greeks referred to them as the Peuceti (*Peuketieis*) of the Apulian region, while the Romans used the name *Picentes*. Only by the end of the Republic did the adjective *picenus* begin to designate the nation, known as the *Picenum*. Without entering into a close examination of the origins and composition of the middle Adriatic's ethnic mosaic, it is worth recalling Paul the Deacon's writings from the late eighth century AD, in which he attributes a Sabine origin to the Piceni following a *ver sacrum* or "holy springtime." This was a common ritual, practiced by the ancient Italics, that consecrated a group of youths – to whom the community could no longer guarantee support – to the search for new land. A woodpecker (*picus*), a totemic animal sacred to Mars from which the Piceni adopted their name, would guide the group toward their new homeland by perching on their banner. Peculiar objects belonging to this civilization have been found in the monumental tombs of the Picene princes, such as damascened weapons, sceptres, ornaments and jewels, prestigious objects imported from Etruria and Greece, tooled amber and ivory, as well as local toreutic, bronze and ceramic artifacts in highly original forms. Beginning in the fourth century BC the Piceno witnessed the arrival of the Celts, who settled north of the river Esino, as well as the founding of the Greek colony of Ancona. The Piceni, like the Etruscans, established relations with the people of central Europe also thanks to their position along the Adriatic, which stretched toward the Alpine ranges, meeting the end of the amber trade routes from the Baltic Sea. The Greeks considered the Po, which they called Eridanos, the amber river: it is in fact the setting for the myth of the Sun-sisters, who were transformed into poplar trees and whose tears for the tragic death of their brother Phaethon were transformed into the precious substance. Central Europe's main Transalpine trade routes not only revealed objects of Picene provenance or inspiration, which attest to the prestigious gifts exchanged between aristocrats, but further demonstrated clear influences in local statuary that provoke numerous questions on the circulation of artists and interesting currents of research.

Settled on the peninsula's southeastern extremity, in present-day Apulia, were ethnically and linguistically well-defined peoples, considered the last wave of Indo-Europeans from the East. Beginning in the south were the Messapii in the Salentine Peninsula, Peucetii and Dauni, respectively corresponding to the present-day provinces of Bari and Foggia. Also from

Messapic stock were the Salentini and the Calabri: curiously, the name Calabria, from the Middle Ages onward, denotes an entirely different region, namely the southwestern extremity of the Italian peninsula.

In the north, the Veneti comprised a defined and homogeneous ethnicity, established between the Adige and the eastern Alps, that spoke an Indo-European language different from the others, but which adopted an alphabet derived from the Etruscan. From an archaeological point of view, the culture known as "Atestina," whose burial grounds were found in Este, is referable to the Veneti.

More uncertain, also due to the scarcity of linguistic documentation, is the nature of the people generically termed Ligurians, who occupied northwestern Italy: present-day Liguria, part of northern Tuscany, Piedmont, Val D'Aosta and Lombardy, part of Trentino and Emilia. Their classification is complicated due to their Celtic influences and historic contacts with Greek (colonies of Monoikos/Monaco and Massalia/Marseille) and Etruscan civilizations, from which emerged such multi-ethnic port settlements as Genova and Luni.

COLONISTS AND INVADERS

The colonial movements of the Phoenicians and Greeks constitute one of the major dynamic elements in the development of western Mediterranean civilization, including that of Italy, from the beginning of the first millennium BC. Phoenician and subsequently Carthaginian colonization, documented at least as early as the ninth century BC, particularly concerned the African coasts west of Syrtis Major (Gulf of Sidra), southern Spain, western Sicily, Sardinia and the Balearic islands. The Italian peninsula, on the other hand, was only affected by commercial contacts that led local potentates to purchase luxury goods in the Orientalizing cultural phase, between the eighth and seventh centuries BC.

Ancient Italy's cultural history is strongly conditioned by the Greek element that overran the coast of southern Italy with colonial settlements, from the gulf of Taranto to the gulf of Naples and a large part of Sicily, excluding the western tip, in what later became Magna Graecia. Pithecussae, on the island of Ischia, and Cumae, on the Campanian coast, were the first settlements founded in the eighth century BC by the inhabitants of Eretria and Chalcis on the island of Euboea. Subsequent centers were those of Zancle (Messina), Naxos, Catania, and Leontini in Sicily; Rhegium was founded on the opposite shore of the Strait of Messina, at the extreme tip of the peninsula. All members of the Greek world participated, not without rivalry, in the race toward the West. In Sicily the Megaresi founded Megara Hyblaea, while the Corinthians established Syracuse. The Achaean cities of Metaponto, Sybaris, and Croton emerged on the Ionian coast, while the Spartans founded Taranto. Following the establishment of colonies seized from their mother country (Gela, by the inhabitants of Rhodes and Crete; Locri Epizefiri, by the Locresi; Siris by the Colophonians from Asian Ionia; Posidonia, by the Trezenii), secondary settlements were added as offshoots from the same colonies (Selinus, from Megara Hyblaea; Camarina, from Syracuse; Agrigentum, from Gela; Milazzo and Himera, from Zancle; Metauro, Medma and Hipponion, from Locri; Laos, from Sybaris…).

Ancient Italy's ethnic makeup is further complicated by the Celtic element which, deriving from historic Transalpine Gaul, led to the settlement in Italy of various peoples of that lineage beginning in the early sixth century BC: Insubri in Lombardy, Cenomani in the Brescia and Verona areas, Salluvii around the Ticino; Boii and Lingones thrived south of the Po, in Emilia and Romagna, at the expense of the Umbri and Etruscans: the Etruscan city of *Felsina* was definitively renamed *Bononia* (Bologna) by the Boii Gauls. Finally the Senones settled along the Adriatic coast, as far as the Esino, interacting with the local Picene culture. It is from these lands that the incursions to the Tyrrhenian area departed: in 390 BC the Gauls sacked Rome.

THE ETRUSCANS

The Etruscan civilization was one of ancient Italy's most important components, both for its territorial expansion and for its political and cultural prestige, largely relevant even in the more general context of the Mediterranean world. The Etruscans lived throughout the first millennium BC in a territory in central Italy, extending in the north to the river Arno, in the southeast to the river Tiber and in the West to the shores of the Tyrrhenian Sea: such was the region known in the Roman era as Etruria. Geographic and historic conditions have led to the current distinction of two areas, southern Etruria and northern-central Etruria, whose borders are roughly marked by the rivers Fiora and Paglia, which, not accidentally, nearly match the modern border between Latium and Tuscany. The population in more ancient times was distributed in small villages that soon became rich and powerful city-states, independent from one another and confederated in the famous Etruscan Dodecapolis: the federation's institutional seat was in the sanctuary of Voltumna, the *Fanum Voltumnae*, near Orvieto (*Volsinii*), where the city representatives would assemble annually to discuss and organize the policies shared by the entire Etruscan nation. Principal cities of southern Etruria were Veio (Latin *Veii*), Caere (*Chaisre, Cisra, Chaire*), Tarquinia (T*archuna, Tarchna*), Vulci (*Velch*), Volsinii (*Velsna, Velzna*); those in northern Etruria were Roselle (Latin *Rusellae*), Vetulonia (*Vetluna, Vatluna*), Populonia (*Pupluna, Fufluna*) and Volterra (*Velathri*), while inland cities included Chiusi (*Clevsin, Camars*), Perugia (Latin *Perusia*), Cortona (*Curtun*), Arezzo (Latin *Arretium*) and Fiesole (Latin *Faesulae*).
The Etruscans, who called themselves *Rasna* (the Romans called them *Etrusci*, the Greeks *Tyrrhenoi*), reached their maximum expansion during the sixth century BC, extending their political and cultural influence through a large part of ancient Italy. Etruscan cities in the south occupied part of present-day Campania, with their capital in Capua (*Volturnum*), followed by Suessola, Nola, Acerra, Nocera, Herculaneum, Pompeii, Sorrento and Marcina, the latter loca-

ted in the Salerno area according to ancient sources. In the north, with their main center in Bologna (*Felsina*), the Etruscans reached Mantua (*Manthva*) and the plain of the Po, also founding ports on the Adriatic coast as in the case of Spina.

The complex formative process of the Etruscan civilization, in its manifold and not entirely clear ethno-linguistic and cultural aspects, may be examined starting from the Bronze Age. Here it is possible to identify the beginning of the Etruscans' process of ethnogenesis, not only in terms of those economic and cultural characteristics defined by the territory (marine vocation, exploitation of mineral resources, craftsmanship, superior farming) but also in the long-range relationships that they established with the Mediterranean world and continental Europe. This caused Etruria to become, already in protohistory, a central entity, a bridge joining East and West in which a complex phenomenology contributed to the creation of an evolved urban civilization with peculiar traits. The Etruscans, acting as a hinge between East and West, disseminated not only goods, but also their alphabet (which later formed the foundations of the runic alphabet) into the heart of Europe. The Roman legions, curiously, continued to travel the same routes laid centuries earlier by Etruscan merchants.

The linguistic classification of Etruscan is still an open issue, as it is considerably distinct from the Indo-European family, despite certain similarities such as the inflection system and some desinences, in addition to consistent linguistic affinities, which in some cases could result from later borrowings. It is generally considered the relic of a more ancient linguistic Mediterranean or proto-Indo-European stock. Such a hypothesis is supported by a comparison with pre-Greek names that remained in the historic Greek but are of non-Indo-European origin. Suggestive affinities have been noted between Etruscan and the inscription on the Kaminia stele, written in the language spoken in Lemnos (and in nearby Imbros) before the Attic conquest at the end of the sixth century BC. This poses the question as to whether it is an ancient linguistic relic, evidence of a westward Tyrrhenian migration from Asia Minor during the second millennium BC, or the more recent result of an expansive Etruscan movement toward the Aegean.

Etruscan, while being a dead and "genealogically isolated" language, is paradoxically one of the most well-known and studied languages of ancient Italy, with more than 11,000 recorded texts. Unfortunately the few hundred or so known words, as well as the repetitive nature of the texts, for the most part onomastic ones but with significant exceptions in the religious and legal spheres, do not permit a real translation. The loss of Etruscan literature and the abandonment of the spoken language as early as the first century BC in favor of Latin have complicated the decipherability of the texts, to which little has been contributed by the "Etruscan Glosses," a group of sixty-odd words, handed down not always correctly by ancient authors, supplying translations in Greek or Latin. However, as the language's morphology and syntax are known, it is possible to distinguish the various elements in a text: gender and number, a verb from a noun, proper nouns, numerals, toponyms; furthermore, the rules of inflection are understood for nouns and appellatives, as is the identification of verbal forms and the definition of the

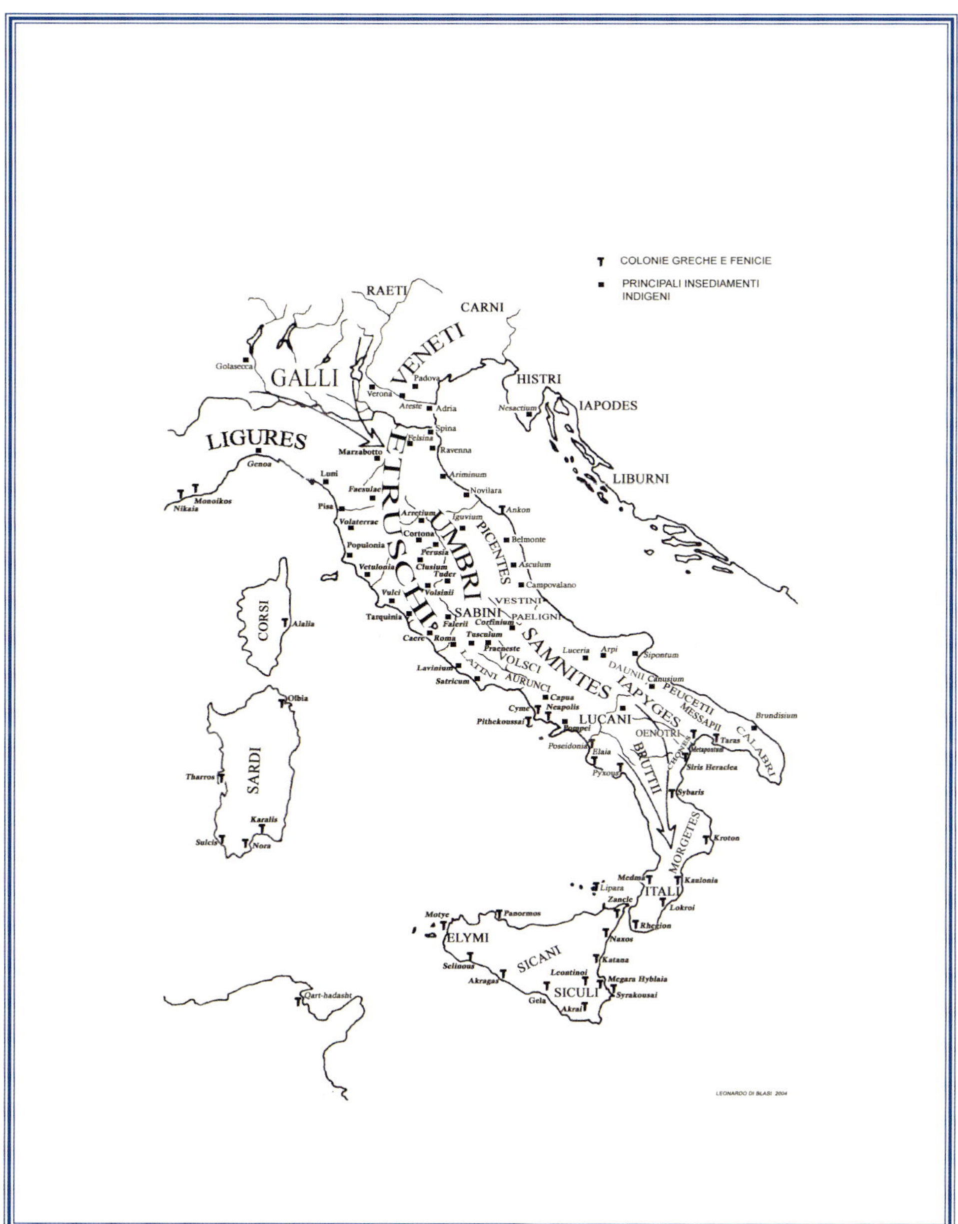

Pre-Roman ancient Italy.

semantic sphere for words of uncertain translation, thanks to the various methods available in linguistic research.

PROTOHISTORY

In the course of the Middle Bronze Age, from the sixteenth to the fourteenth centuries BC, Etruria was made up of stable settlements of limited size, in naturally defended areas; this system appears to have expanded during the Final Bronze or Protovillanovan periods, between the eleventh and tenth centuries BC, with centers equipped with artificial defenses.

The search for minerals, tied to metallurgic activity, led to the establishment of a precocious trade between the Tyrrhenian area and the eastern Mediterranean. The earliest exchanges with the Aegean area, in fact, date back to the Bronze Age, documented by findings of Mycenaean pottery and Cypriot bronze fragments. Throughout the Middle Bronze Age, ties to the Aegean world were strong, notably in the realm of metallurgy, characterized by a remarkable typological uniformity, particularly in terms of swords, daggers, knives, axes, and fibulae, which were often nearly identical. In the same period, contacts were made with Nuragic Sardinia that proved to be long lasting.

Starting in the Final Bronze Age the flow of Aegean imports slowed down, and as a result the typological uniformity eventually diminished, leading to the definition of typologies that were more restricted to localized areas.

Between the end of the tenth and the middle of the ninth centuries BC, in the early Iron Age and the beginning of the Villanovan culture – named after the Villanova necropolis near Bologna – the early Etruscans further established themselves. With the majority of their population living in densely inhabited areas, they began to form the cities that would later become historic capitals. Favoring one or more contiguous plateaus with natural borders, they also included free areas for farming. At the same time, a network of smaller settlements subsisted on sites occupied during the Final Bronze Age, while the coastal settlements were abandoned in what appears to have been a tendency toward defensive entrenchment. Houses were composed of oval or rectangular-plan huts with pole structures covered in woven foliage and clay; evidence for the appearance of these structures survives in the characteristic hut-shaped cinerary urns typical of Latium's Iron culture but also widespread in Etruria, particularly in Tarquinia, Vulci, Vetulonia and Bisenzio.

Archaeological documentation suggests the appearance of an emerging social class, with evidence of a warrior/aristocratic rank, and articulated into social classes with gentilicial structures possibly based on Greek cultural models. The system hinged on the institution of land as private property and on its hereditary transferability, which became the key to the wealth of the aristocrats, a wealth based not only on the production of primary goods through agriculture and animal breeding, but also on the management of mining activities, the monitoring of means of communication, and the institution of tolls.

From a visual arts perspective, the period between the Final Bronze Age and the early Iron Age was primarily marked by abstractism, with bronzeware featuring geometric decorations of angular designs, meanders, zigzags, swastikas, dots and studs, along with motifs such as the solar boat and stylized human figures. The deeper meaning of these symbols and images still remains unintelligible, even in the best of cases they do not lead us beyond the level of narration, as in the case of the schematic Villanovan hunting scenes.

The Iron Age saw a remarkable development in the technique of metallurgy and in the quantity of goods produced, both in bronze and in iron. Weapons, tools and ornamental objects registered a much larger diffusion and, with the growth of technological potential and the quality of life, the ground was laid for future developments.

THE ORIENTALIZING PERIOD

The Orientalizing period (circa 730-580 BC) was a vast cultural phenomenon which involved the entire Mediterranean basin, with technological trade and contacts, and the displacement of people and goods, that resulted in considerable economic growth and a real epochal "leap" for Etruria. A defining force in this phenomenon was the renewed Phoenician wave of expansion, due in part to pressure from the Assyrian empire between the reigns of Tiglat-Pileser III and Esarhaddon (744-669 BC), as well as to the westward colonial diaspora of the Greeks. It is in this cultural context, in fact, that the compilation of the Homeric poems was completed in Greece, narrating events much more ancient but inevitably conditioned by the current climate.

The Etruscan aristocracy, having established its leading role and consolidated its wealth, looked to the splendor of the Eastern courts for a role model. The practice of exchanging gifts among equals, around which revolved most commercial and diplomatic relations, resulted in a wide diffusion of goods, creating ties of reciprocity not only among men, but also between men and divinities, as in the Greek world, with offerings to sanctuaries. Along with the introduction of fine goods were also ideas, iconography and technology from the eastern Mediterranean (Egypt, Syria, Cyprus, Rhodes and Greece in general) and the Near East, as far as Urartu and Mesopotamia. The contacts made during the western colonization resulted in the acquisition not only of goods but also cultural models. A revealing case is that of symposium kitchenware, which simultaneously referred to the Greek and Near-Eastern worlds in its details: the metallic graters, associated with drinkware, recall the ancient Greek custom of mixing cheese with wine, while certain clay tripods traced back to northern Syria and the Phoenician colonies of the central Mediterranean, found in Etruria and Latium, were used as mortars for aromatic substances used to enhance the flavor of wine.

This period witnessed the peak in the development of an urban reality that particularly concerned the necropoles, as in the striking example of Cerveteri, where a sudden boom of the monumental tumulus was recorded, stretching as far as 60 meters in diameter, with its characteristic drum decorated with a complex sequence of smooth, round listels, possibly of direct Near-Eastern origin.

One of the most important innovations that took place in Etruria during the Orientalizing period was undoubtedly the acquisition of the alphabet and writing techniques, which probably occurred toward the end of the eighth century BC. The alphabet adopted by the Etruscans was essentially the Western Greek Chalcidian alphabet, probably acquired as a result of southern Etrurian contacts with the Euboeans that had settled in the Gulf of Naples. The earliest writing accessories were found in rich Orientalizing tombs as attributes of social rank, and present the didactic sequence of the twenty-six letters of the Euboean alphabet.

In Orientalizing Etruscan art, along with the preservation of local types and forms as well as the continuation of a geometric tradition, a new Phoenician style broke through that was predominantly animalistic, introducing new figurative themes. The new artifacts – including jewelry, ivory intaglios, amber, gems and probably wood, toreutics and pottery, either imported or produced locally by immigrant craftsmen – were characterized by a virtuosity and an eclecticism that experimented with all the potential of a given material.

THE ARCHAIC PERIOD

The Etruscan nation's prosperity and power in the Orientalizing period formed a precedent for the subsequent flourishing of the Archaic period, distinguished by further growth and expansion. In this period, Etruscan power in Italy was at its height, extending toward the plain of the Po and the Adriatic, consolidating its presence in Campania, monitoring the seas with piracy and commerce, and extending its control even on Rome (*Ruma* in Etruscan). It is in fact by the Etruscan dynasty of the Tarquinii, during the sixth century BC, that the future leader of the world was later transformed into a proper city.

In Tarquinia, tomb wall paintings, stemming from a tradition begun in the seventh century BC, reached their height. Archaic funerary themes seemed to reflect the optimism of an expanding society: the aura was joyous, and the afterlife was seen as a continuation of the activities and privileges of a comfortable life.

Around 540 BC a stylistic breakthrough occurred that resulted in the triumph of the Ionic style, defined by the arrival in Etruria of Greek artists from the shores of Asia Minor and the islands. Previously, the Persian advance of 545 BC had resulted in the exodus of the Ionic peoples toward the Phocaean colony of Alalia, in Corsica, founded in 565 BC. The combined reaction of the Etruscans and Carthaginians to this massive concentration, culminating in the battle of the Sea of Sardinia in 540 BC, had the effect of scattering the Phocaeans in the Etruscan cities, while others later founded Elea in the Cilento region. The presence of emporia in Etruria, as in the case of Gravisca, Tarquinia's port city, probably facilitated the accumulation of the Asian Greeks who had passed through and even left behind epigraphical evidence. It was in this period in Etruria that the substantial importation began of Attic, Laconic, Chalcidian and Greco-Oriental pottery, as well as the establishment of black-figure pottery workshops by immigrant Ionic craftsmen.

Southern Etruria's Attic pottery imports constitute a fundamental chapter in the history of Greek pottery and give a measure of the taste as well as the selective approach in terms of themes, style and quality exercised by the Etruscan clientele. Many late-Archaic Attic masters produced their work as a function of Etruscan exportation. Archaic bronzeware offers extraordinary examples that circulated widely in the ancient world well beyond the confines of Etruria, reaching as far as continental Europe and Greece: Archaic bronzes donated by the Etruscans may even be seen in Olympia.

Toward the end of the sixth century BC, perspective and foreshortening were introduced to the world of painting, which honored the latest accomplishments of the late-Archaic Attic masters. In the same period the Veio coroplastic school, confronted with temple architecture, which had become more monumental and had adopted decorative floral and geometric friezes, produced the larger-than-life acroterial statues of the Portonaccio Temple. The most famous surviving statue is that of Apollo, one of the most celebrated pieces in Etruscan art. Cerveteri workshops produced two clay sarcophagi with a bride and groom, also counted among the most famous and expressive pieces of archaic Etruscan coroplastics.

The initial decline of Etruscan power began toward the end of the sixth century BC, with the end of the rule of Tarquinius Superbus in Rome (509 BC) and the loss of road continuity with Campanian holdings. In Campania, in fact, the Etruscan defeat by Gerone of Syracuse in the naval battle of Cumae in 474 BC, which also annihilated their naval force, set off a period of crisis and complex reorganization.

THE CLASSICAL PERIOD

The first part of the fifth century BC coincided with a deep crisis that particularly affected the southern Etruscan cities after the battle of Cumae. Added to this crucial event were further destabilizing factors, such as the expansion of the Italic peoples of Sabellian stock, the displacement of Celtic peoples, and internal conflicts between aristocrats and plebeians. Maritime commerce from Vulci and Caere toward the Gauls came all but to a halt, a decline in commerce was recorded, and the number of tombs built for the emerging families of Tarquinia and Cerveteri decreased noticeably.

Greece, in contrast to crisis-ridden Etruria, had come out of the Persian wars victoriously, and enjoyed its Classical golden age around the middle of the fifth century BC with the art of Phidias and Polykleitos. Those same years, however, coincided with the stasis of public commissions, and as a result, no temples were erected in Rome and Etruria in the time of Phidias and the Parthenon.

The most dynamic and expanding centers were now the inland and northern cities and Po Valley Etruria. *Felsina*-Bologna became a metropolis, boasting massive imports of Attic pottery and bronzeware, mostly from Vulci. A similar commercial dynamic was recorded in Spina, which became a Hellenized emporium where Etruscans, Veneti and Umbri coexisted alongside the Greeks. This important maritime center near Comacchio even had a *thesauròs* in Delphi, as did Caere. Such centers as Marzabotto, Casalecchio sul Reno and Mantua were colonial cities founded for the purposes of expansionism and territorial control, also based on the trade routes that crossed Po Valley Etruria on their way to the Venetic and Illyrian areas and continued in the direction of central Europe's Celtic areas, where one could find the refined Etruscan bronzes and typical spouted *oinochoai*, known as *Schnabelkannen*.

In the course of the fourth century BC the southern coastal metropoles experienced a social and productive reorganization: intermediate classes resurfaced, although no longer to Archaic levels, as a result of a renewed demand following territorial repopulation. The fourth century also coincided with the first blows to the heart of Etruria proper, a prelude to its progressive absorption into the Roman state. 396 BC brought the fall of Veio, the first Etruscan city to be annihilated, followed in 384 BC by the Syracusan sack of Pyrgi. The conflict between Rome and Tarquinia lasted from 358 to 351 BC, followed by a forty-year truce. In 353 BC the Roman-friendly Caere, despite being briefly dragged into the war against Rome, became *municipium sine suffragio*. In the same period a widespread growth of mystery beliefs and practices, particularly Dionysiac, was recorded.

THE HELLENISTIC PERIOD

With the death of Alexander the Great there began a long period known as Hellenism, which ended with the Roman conquest of Egypt (31-30 BC), the last of the nations heir to Alexander's empire. Following the Macedonian conquests, an episodic phenomenon took place in which Greek art and culture was widely diffused, involving peoples from Macedonia to the Indian border, from the northern shores of the Black Sea to Egypt and Ethiopia. While the local schools varied greatly, Hellenistic art presented certain common characteristics that focused on the already existent trends from the fourth century BC: the humanization of religious themes and the preference for idyllic and anecdotal subjects. Objective naturalism was replaced by a search for every degree and nuance of the psychological and physical aspects of man, who was no longer at the center of the universe but one of nature's myriad subject matters. A serial, mass-produced art was born, with repetitions and re-elaborations of the same themes, subdivided by genre and marked by a sharp increase in the decorative arts.

Roman dominance in Etruria extended progressively throughout the third century BC, following interferences in such internal affairs as the support of the Arezzo aristocratic faction in 302 BC, and the defeat at Sentino of a coalition that included Etruscans, Gauls, Umbri and Samnites in 295 BC. The following half-century was characterized by a rapid sequence of events that led to Rome's rule over the southern Etruscan coastline: the victory of Roselle (292 BC), the fall of Vulci and Volsinii (280 BC) and the seizure of the Cosa colony (273 BC), the defeat of Volsinii (264 BC) and Falerii (241 BC). Southern Etruscan cities were penalized in their location and means of communication: roads built by the Romans between 240 and 170 BC marginalized the historic cities in that area. After the mid-second century BC the growing establishment of the agricultural estate (*latifundium*) caused a progressive depopulation of the region, which, with the colonization of the Gracchi, experienced a defining cultural hiatus.

Land seizures or colonial foundations did not affect northern Etruria. A relative social and political stability allowed for a lasting period of thriving artistic craftsmanship, also fostered by the appearance of a new emerging "middle" class. The existence of gentilicia originating from a first name (*praenomen*) is documented in the early second century BC in Chiusi and Perugia, evidence of unprecedented access to civil and political rights by the lower strata of society. The northern Etruscans appear to have been integrated into the Roman structure while preserving a strong sense of identity. Their demise arrived with the last century of the Republic: the civil wars, bringing bereavement and destruction, led to land seizures and colonial defeats at Chiusi, Arezzo and Fiesole. The final blow to the Etruscan nation was inflicted by the war of Perugia in 41-40 BC. Shortly thereafter the history of Etruria, inserted in the *Regio VII* of the Augustan division of Italy (27 BC), coincides with that of the Roman Empire.

TIMELINE

ETRURIA

Bronze Age, circa 2200/2000-900 BC
(Early: 2200/2000-1600 BC; Middle: 1600-1350 BC; Late: 1350-1150; Final (*Protovillanovan*): 1150-900 BC)

Iron Age (*Villanovan*), circa 900-730/720 BC
(Villanovan I: 900-770 BC; Villanovan II: 770-730/720 BC)
Orientalizing Period, 730/720-580 BC
(Early: 720-670 BC; Middle: 670-630 BC; Late: 630-580 BC)

Archaic Period, 580-480 BC

Classical Period, 480-323 BC

Hellenistic Period, 323-31 BC

ROME

Bronze Age, circa 2200/2000-900 BC
(Early: 2200/2000-1600 BC; Middle: 1600-1350 BC; Late: 1350-1150; Final: 1150-900 BC)

Latial Period I (Final Bronze), 1000-900 BC

Iron Age, circa 900-730/720 BC
- Latial Period IIA, 900-820 BC
- Latial Period IIB, 820-770 BC
- Latial Period III, 770-730/720 BC

Regal Period 753-509 BC
Foundation of Rome 753 BC

Orientalizing Period, 730/720-580 BC
- Latial Period IVA, 730/720-625 BC
- Latial Period IVB, 625-580 BC

The seven kings of Rome according to traditional chronology:
Romulus, 753-715 BC
Numa Pompilius, 715-672 BC
Tullus Hostilius, 672-640 BC
Ancus Martius, 640-616 BC
Tarquinius Priscus, 616-578 BC
Servius Tullius, 578-534 BC
Tarquinius Superbus, 534-509 BC

Early Republic, 509-367 BC

Middle Republic, 367-202 BC

367 BC: *Liciniae Sextiae* laws. Establishment of the plebeians and constitution of the *nobilitas*;
202BC: end of the Second Punic War

Late Republic, 202-31 BC

Roman empire,	31 BC - 476 AD	31 BC: Octavian's victory at Actium; death of Antony and Cleopatra. 27 BC: Octavian becomes Augustus. 476 AD: fall of the Roman Empire of the West; Odoacer, king of the Heruli, deposes the last emperor.

ROMAN EMPERORS

Julio-Claudians	
Augustus	31 BC – 14 AD
Tiberius	14 – 37 AD
Caligula	37 – 41 AD
Claudius	41 – 54 AD
Nero	54 – 68 AD
Flavians	
Vespasian	69-79 AD
Titus	79-81 AD
Domitian	81-96 AD
Nerva	96-98 AD
Trajan	98-117 AD
Antonines	
Hadrian	117-138 AD
Antoninus Pius	138-161 AD
Marcus Aurelius and Lucius Verus	161-169 AD
Marcus Aurelius	169-180 AD
Commodus	180-193 AD
Helvius Pertinax	193 AD
Didius Julianus	193 AD
Severans	
Septimius Severus	193-211 AD
Caracalla	211-217 AD
Macrinus	217-218 AD
Elagabalus	218-222 AD
Alexander Severus	222-235 AD
Maximinus Thrax	235-238 AD
Gordian I and II	238 AD
Pupienus and Balbinus	238 AD
Gordian III	238-244 AD
Philip the Arab	245-249 AD
Decius	249-251 AD
Trebonianus Gallus	251-253 AD
Aemilianus	253 AD
Valerian and Gallienus	253-260 AD
Gallienus	260-268 AD
Aurelius Claudius	268-270 AD

Aurelian	270-275 AD
Claudius Tacitus	275-276 AD
Florianus	276 AD
Aurelius Probus	276-282 AD
Carus	282-283 AD
Numerianus and Carinus	283-284 AD
Carinus	284-285 AD
Diocletian	284-305 AD
Maximian	286-310 AD
Constantius Clorus	292-306 AD
Galerius	292-311 AD
Maxentius	306-312 AD
Constantine	306-337 AD
Constantine II, Constans, Constantius	337-340 AD
Constans and Constantius	335-350 AD
Constantius	350-361 AD
Julian	361-363 AD
Jovian	363-364 AD
Valentinian, Valens and Gratian	364-375 AD
Valens and Gratian	375-378 AD
Gratian and Theodosius	379-383 AD
Theodosius and Valentinian II	383-392 AD
Theodosius	392-395 AD
Honorius	395-423 AD
Priscus Attalus	408-423 AD
Valentinian III	424-455 AD
Avitus	455-457 AD
Majorian	457-461 AD
Libius Severus	461-465 AD
Procopius Anthemius	467 AD
Alybrius	472 AD
Julius Nepos	475 AD
Romulus Augustulus	476 AD

SUGGESTIONS FOR FURTHER READING IN ENGLISH ON THE ETRUSCANS AND ANCIENT ITALY

Ancient Greeks West and East, Leiden 1999.

Ancient Italy in its Mediterranean Setting. Studies in Honour of Ellen Macnamara, London 2000.

G. BARKER, T. RASMUSSEN, *The Etruscans*, Oxford 1998.

J.D. BEAZLEY, *Etruscan Vase Painting*, Oxford 1947.

M. BENNETT, A.J. PAUL, in collaboration with M. IOZZO, *Magna Graecia. Greek Art from South Italy and Sicily*, Catalogue of an Exhibition organized by the Cleveland Museum of Art and the Tampa Museum of Art, New York – Manchester 2002.

A. BOETHIUS, *Etruscans and Early Roman Architecture*, Hamondsworth 1978.

L. BONFANTE, *Etruscan Dress*, Baltimore 1975.

L. BONFANTE (ed.), *Etruscan Life and Afterlife*, Detroit 1985.

G. BONFANTE, L. BONFANTE, *The Etruscan Language. An Introduction*. Second edition, Manchester 2002.

O. BRENDEL, *Etruscan Art*, Hamondsworth 1978.

F. BURANELLI, *The Etruscans. Legacy of a Lost Civilization. From the Vatican Museums*, with an Introduction and Translation by N.T. de Grummond, catalogue of an exhibition, Wonders, Memphis 1992.

N.T. DE GRUMMOND, *A Guide to Etruscan Mirrors*, Tallahassee 1982.

G. DENNIS, *Cities and Cemeteries of Etruria*, London 1907.

Mrs. HAMILTON GRAY, *Tour to the Sepulchres of Etruria*, London 1841.

D.G. HAMBLIN, *The Etruscans*, Time-Life Books, New York 1975.

S. HAYNES, *Etruscan Bronzes*, London 1986.

S. HAYNES, *Etruscan Civilization. A Cultural History*, Los Angeles 2000.

H. HENCKEN, *Tarquinia and Etruscan Origins*, London 1968.

D.H. LAWRENCE, *Etruscan Places*, New York 1932.

E. MACNAMARA, *Everyday Life of the Etruscans*, London 1973.

M. MORETTI, *New Monuments of Etruscan Painting,* University Park, 1970.

M. PALLOTTINO, *Etruscan Painting*, Geneva 1952.

M. PALLOTTINO, *The Etruscans*, ed. D. RIDGWAY, Hamondsworth 1978.

P. PERKINS, *Etruscan Settlements, Society and Material Culture in Central Coastal Etruria*, Oxford 1999.

E. H. RICHARDSON, *The Etruscans: Their Art and Civilization*, Chicago 1964.

E.H. RICHARDSON, *Etruscan Votive Bronzes: Geometric, Orientalizing and Archaic*, Mainz 1983.

D. RIDGWAY & F. SERRA RIDGWAY (eds), *Italy Before the Romans*, London 1979.

N.CHR. STAMPOLIDIS (ed.), *Sea Routes... From Sidon to Huelva. Interconnections in the Mediterranean 16th – 6th c. BC*, Museum of Cycladic Art, Athens 2003.

S. STEINGRÄBER, *Etruscan Painting*, New York 1986.

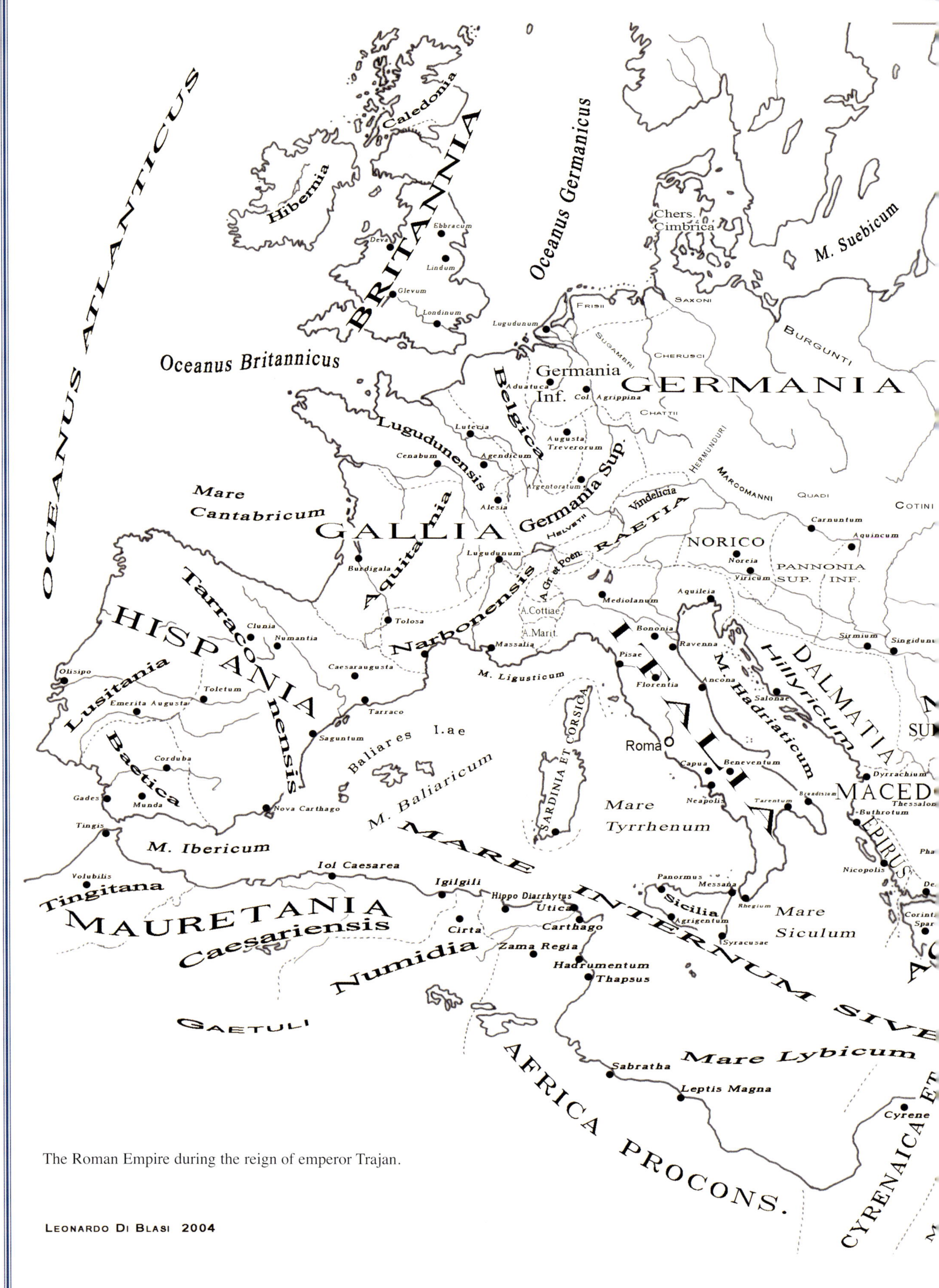

The Roman Empire during the reign of emperor Trajan.

LEONARDO DI BLASI 2004

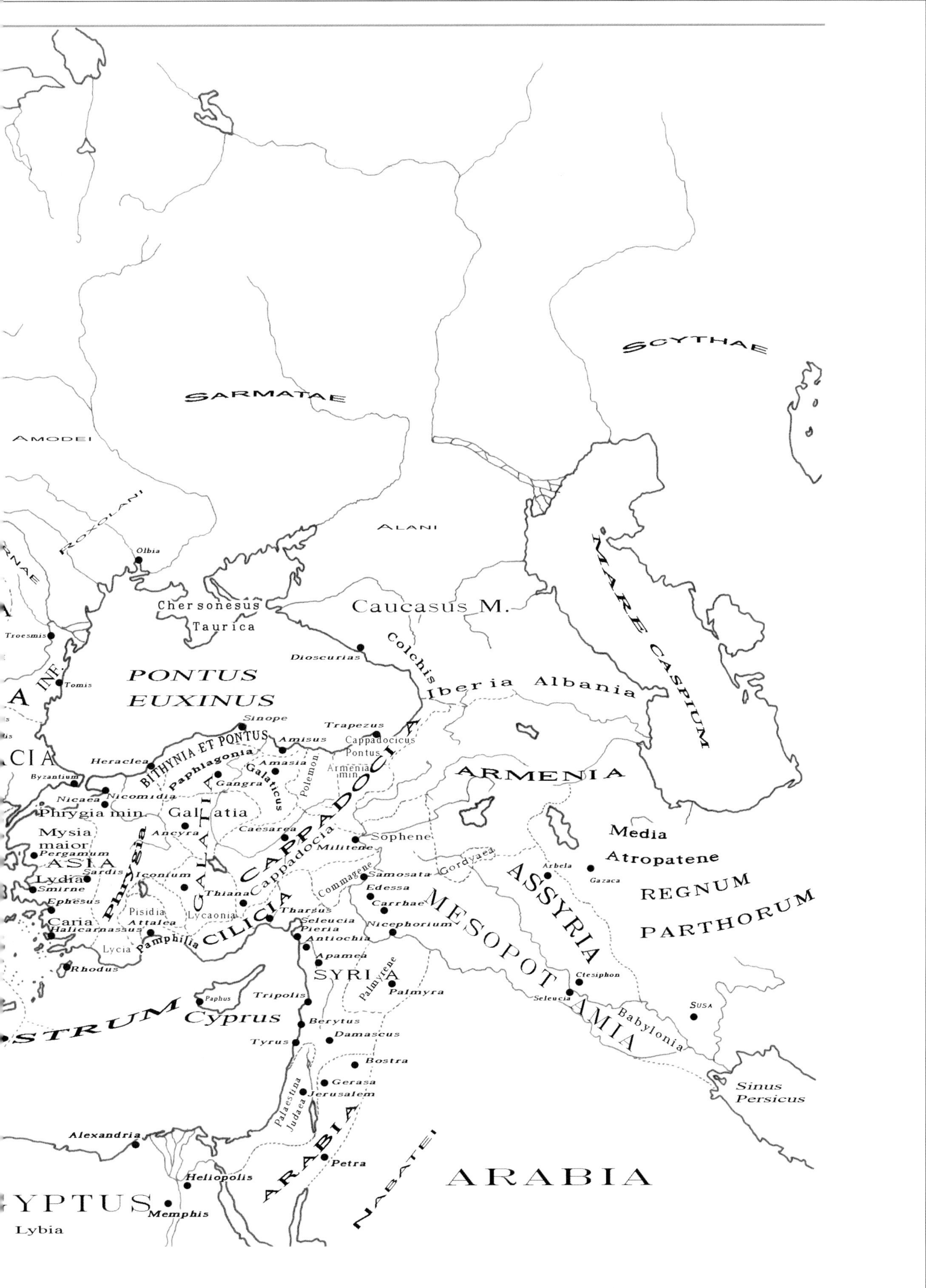
SCYTHAE
SARMATAE
AMODEI
ROXOLANI
ALANI
Olbia
Chersonesus
Taurica
Caucasus M.
MARE CASPIUM
Troesmis
Tomis
PONTUS
EUXINUS
Dioscurias
Colchis
Iberia
Albania
Sinope
Trapezus
Amisus
Cappadocicus
Pontus
Heraclea
BITHYNIA ET PONTUS
Paphlagonia
Amasia
Galaticus
Polemon
Armenia min.
ARMENIA
Byzantium
Nicomidia
Gangra
Nicaea
Phrygia min.
Galatia
GALATIA
CAPPADOCIA
Cappadocia
Mysia
maior
Pergamum
Ancyra
Caesarea
Sophene
Media
Atropatene
Militene
ASIA
Sardis
Phrygia
Iconium
Samosata
Gordyaea
Arbela
Gazaca
ASSYRIA
REGNUM
PARTHORUM
Lydia
Smirne
Commagene
Edessa
Ephesus
Thiana
Carrhae
MESOPOTAMIA
Pisidia
Lycaonia
Tharsus
Caria
Attalea
Seleucia
Pieria
Nicephorium
Halicarnassus
CILICIA
Antiochia
Lycia
Pamphilia
Apamea
Rhodus
SYRIA
Palmyrene
Palmyra
Ctesiphon
Seleucia
Babylonia
Susa
Paphus
Tripolis
Cyprus
Berytus
Tyrus
Damascus
Bostra
Gerasa
Jerusalem
Palaestina
Judaea
Sinus
Persicus
Alexandria
ARABIA
Petra
NABATEI
Heliopolis
Memphis
Lybia

GLOSSARY

Abrasax. *see* Abraxas.

Abraxas. Snake-footed giant with a cock's head, named after the magical word that accompanies its image on talismans, in which it represents a divine power. The magical value of the word *abraxas* lies in the parallel significance of the seven letters that form it: the sum of their numerical value is 365, which corresponds to the days of the solar year and the number of skies according to Gnostic speculation.

Achilles. Greek hero, son of Peleus and Thetis, celebrated for his strength and bravery, and nearly invulnerable with the exception of his famous heel: injured by Paris in that part of his body, he died during the Trojan War.

Aegis. Name of Zeus' shield with the thunderbolts, made by Hephaestus, upon which the father of the gods laid the skin of Amalthea, the goat that had nursed him as a baby, when she died. The same name identifies the breastplate worn by Athena that also bore the head of the gorgon Medusa.

Amon. Egyptian deity revered as the sun god beginning in the New Kingdom (1575-1080 BC). The god, represented with a ram's head, was identified with Zeus by the Greeks. At Oasis Siwa he was venerated as an oracular divinity (from the Libyan *aman*, meaning "water"). His oracle, widely celebrated in the ancient world, as much as the Greek ones of Delphi and Dodona, was invoked in 332 BC by Alexander the Great: he was proclaimed son of the god by his priests.

Amor. *see* Eros.

Annia Faustina. Great-granddaughter of Marcus Aurelius, wife by second marriage of the emperor Elagabalus, becoming his third wife and empress from 221 to 223 AD.

Antefix. Decorative element in terracotta, usually painted, that was placed at the eaves of the slope of a roof along its entire length, sometimes alternating subjects and colors of the single elements in a series. It was installed in correspondence with the last pan tile of the roof in order to conceal it.

Aphrodite. Greek goddess of beauty and love, of Oriental origin. Daughter of Zeus and Dione, born from the sea foam. Corresponds to Venus in the Roman world.

Apollo. Greek god of beauty and well-being that assumed the attributes of a more ancient sun cult. Son of Zeus and Leto and brother of Artemis. The various epithets by which he was known derive from the multiple roles for which he was recognized. As protector of music and poetry, he was also considered head of the Muses.

Arimasps. Legendary people of Scythia, according to the ancient Greeks. The one-eyed Arimasps were said to be fighting a constant battle against the griffins to sieze the treasures that they guarded.

Athena. Greek goddess of intellect and science. Metis (Intelligence) conceived her with Zeus who, afraid of being eventually overthrown by his offspring, swallowed the mother, still with the child in her womb. Athena, prodigiously assimilated into the body of the father of the gods, sprang out fully grown and armed for battle from the head of Zeus.

Athena Promachos. Literally "Athena Who Fights in the Foremost Ranks," this epithet underscores the warrior attributes of the goddess, pictured in arms and ready to charge. Her most famous representation from antiquity was the *Athena Promachos* by the sculptor Phidias, a colossal bronze statue, built on the Acropolis in Athens thanks to the revenue from Marathon and possibly later brought to Constantinople, whose appearance is known today only based on monetary incisions.

Barbula. Literally "small beard" in Latin. Constitutes a typifying element in Roman dynastic portraiture, indicating the youthful age of puberty, characterized by the appearance of soft down on a boy's face. The first shave, at age 17, marked the transition to adulthood. Sometimes the *barbula* was even worn in adulthood as a fashion and in an ideal subscription to the Hellenic philosophical world, as in the famous case of Nero's portraits.

Book of the Dead. The conventional name of an ancient Egyptian collection of funerary texts from different periods. In the belief that the souls of the deceased were prone to infinite dangers, all tombs contained a copy of the Book of the Dead that included magical formulas, hymns and prayers that would guide and protect the soul (Ka) in its journey through the underworld. After its arrival in the underworld, the *Ka* was judged by Osiris and the forty-two demons that assisted him.

Bracteate. Decorated sheet of precious metal.

Bucchero. Typical Etruscan pottery with characteristic black, refined clay, distinguished by its shiny black surface bearing decorations that could be incised, stamped or in relief. Developed around 675 BC, two varieties existed: the first, more ancient, thin-walled variety is known as *bucchero sottile*; the second, thick-walled and with serial decorations that were either stamped or impressed with a rotating cylinder on still-fresh clay, is termed *bucchero pesante*.

Bulla. Circular ornament worn by the Etruscans suspended from a necklace. It was introduced to Rome beginning in the Regal Period and worn exclusively as an amulet only by children, who wore it until their passage into adulthood. The use of the *bulla* persisted in Rome until the Imperial period.

Cabochon. The style of cutting the surface of precious and semiprecious stones in a convex and highly polished form without faceting.

Caduceus. The attribute of the god Hermes (*q.v.*), consisting of a winged wand with twisting serpents.

Canopic vase or urn. Derived from the Egyptian city with the same name, it was originally referred to by egyptologists to designate the four vases made to contain separately the viscera extracted from the deceased in the process of mummification. Later it was used also to designate a type of cinerary urn used to hold the cremated remains of the deceased by the Etruscans, particular in and around Chiusi. Etruscan canopic vases were characterized by the addition of anthropomorphic elements to the body of the vase, such as lids in the shape of a human head, with arms and hands, and wearing real or painted garments.

***Chiton*.** Garment of Greek origin, worn by women and men, consisting of a rectangle of fabric (wool or linen) that was wrapped and draped around the body and kept in place at the waist by a belt. The Ionic *chiton* was a lighter, feminine garment, sewn to form a sort of cylinder that was fastened at the arms and legs by buckles or stitches and also kept in place by a belt. The *chiton* was worn at knee-length or ankle-length.

***Chlamys*.** Men's cloak, originally from Thessaly or Macedonia, initially associated with military dress. Consisted of a piece of wool draped around the upper body and kept in place by a fibula (*q.v.*) on the right shoulder or at the neck. In Greece, the garment identified the army's commanding officer and symbolized young boys' transition to puberty. In Rome, the purple *chlamys* was worn by the military commander in chief.

***Circolo* tomb.** Tomb typology characteristic of the necropoles of the Etruscan city of Vetulonia beginning in the ancient Orientalizing period (late eighth century BC). The "interrupted circle" type dates back to this period: it is formed by rough stones driven into the ground that mark out circular spaces within which are arranged various *a pozzetto* tombs ("tomb in a well," where ash urns were placed in a sunken well) and *a fossa* tombs ("tomb in a trench," or sunken grave). "Continuous circles" appeared beginning in the seventh century BC, containing the richest tombs; these are composed of regular slabs, driven into the ground and slightly inclined toward the outside, that form circles 15-20 meters (50-65 feet) in diameter, but that may extend beyond 30 meters (100 feet), and enclose one or more *a fossa* tombs, often covered by slabs.

Cist. Elliptical-, circular- or rectangular-based bronze sheet vessel used to store ornamental and cosmetic objects. Well-known cists include those made in Praeneste (Palestrina) with incised drawings.

Coroplastics. The art of modelling shapes in terracotta.

***Dextrarum iunctio*.** In Latin means "union of the right hands," represented iconographically by the symbolic gesture of the joining of the right hands of bride and groom in a wedding celebration.

Dionysus. Greek god, son of Zeus and Semele. In addition to being associated with wine and orgiastic intoxication, he was also tied to the world of vegetation and of the dead. The Romans adopted his other Greek name, Bakchos, possibly of Lydian origin, turning him into *Bacchus* and assimilating him to the ancient Italic divinity *Liber Pater*.

Eros. Greek god of love, desire and amorous sentiments, son of Aphrodite and Ares, identified by the Romans as *Amor* or *Cupid*. Iconographically, the young Eros was often replicated in multiple forms and in various roles, always as a winged youth, also known as Erote or Amorino (cherub), that also appeared in idyllic and anecdotal contexts.

False rope. Type of relief decoration, in pottery and bronze, that reproduces the impression of a rope.

Farnese Herakles. Statuary type, known for the statue by the same name from the former Farnese collection, at the Museo Nazionale in Naples. Built by Glykon, it is a Roman copy of a sculpture by the Greek artist Lysippos (born in Sikyon around 370 BC). The statue represents the hero standing, at rest, naked and resting on his club, from which hangs his lion skin.

Faustina Maggiore. Annia Galeria Faustina (104-141 AD), known as Maggiore ("the elder"), daughter of the prefect Marcus Annius Verus and Rupilia Faustina. As a very young woman, around 117 AD, she wed the future emperor Antoninus Pius, and bore him two sons and two daughters. She was empress from 138 AD, the year of her husband's ascent to the imperial throne, until 141 AD, the year of her premature death. Games were celebrated and statues erected in her honor; furthermore, the emperor founded a charity institution for young women that were welcomed as *Puellae Faustinianae*.

Faustina Minore. Annia Galeria Faustina, known as Minore ("the younger"), born in Rome around 125 AD to Antoninus Pius and Faustina Maggiore. Already promised in marriage to Lucius Verus, in 139 she was engaged to her cousin Marcus Aurelius whom she wed in 145, bearing him 12 or 13 children. She was empress from 161, the year of her husband's ascent to the throne, until 175 AD, when she died at the age of about 50 in the Orient, at Halala, where a temple was later built in her honor, following her deification. Priestesses were established for her cult as well as a charity institution similar to that already dedicated to her mother.

Fibula. Accessory similar to the modern safety pin, composed of a pin, spring, bow and catch-plate for the insertion and blockage of the pin. Introduced in the Bronze Age, second millennium BC, it was used to fasten garments on the body. Other than bronze, used initially, specimens are known in precious materials, such as gold and silver, or in iron with bows overlaid in amber and other materials.

Filigree. Goldwork technique in which wire threads of different thicknesses and shapes were placed in linear sequences or shaped according to predefined designs and soldered to one another.

Fortnum Group. Conventional denomination of an Etruscan ring type, named after the collector and scholar who first studied them in 1873. The rings in the Fortnum Group, dated between the late fifth and fourth centuries BC, are made of sheet gold and are distinguished by a repoussé almond-shaped bezel, favoring themes tied to the heroic world.

Fortune. see Tyche.

Glass paste. Basic material for the creation of glass objects, processed by fusion and not by blowing. Ancient glass was made with a blend containing quartz (60-70%), soda (14-20%), lime (5-10%) and small percentages of metallic oxides, present either as impurities or intentionally added for color.

Gorgons. According to mythology they were three sisters, daughters of the marine divinities Phorcys and Ceto, named Stheno, Euryale and Medusa. Of these only Medusa, considered the principal Gorgon, was mortal. Their hair consisted of snakes, they had large, projecting teeth, bronze hands and golden wings. Medusa was killed in her sleep by Perseus, who used his shield as a mirror to avoid her direct glance, which had the power to petrify anyone that observed her directly. Medusa's head was placed by Athena on her shield or at the center of her aegis (*q.v.*).

Gorgoneion. Decorative motif reproducing Medusa's head. Reproduced in art and architecture of classical antiquity as an apotropaic motif, with the magical power to ward off dangerous people or things. The horrific features typical of Archaic Gorgons were replaced in the Classical and Hellenistic periods with humanized and pathetic features.

Granulation. Refined decorative goldwork technique with ancient origins, adopted and particularly developed in Etruria. It consists in the application of tiny gold granules on the surface of a jewel using a local micro-soldering process, in order to compose decorative motifs, fill in backgrounds and outline figures.

Hairpin. Large ivory or bone pin, used both in women's hairstyles and as an applicator for ointments and perfumes.

Harpokrates. The Greek name for Horus (*q.v.*) as a child, son of Isis and Osiris, pictured as a naked child with a finger held to his mouth. According to the myth, he was conceived after the death of his father Osiris and raised in secret by Isis to protect him from Seth, Osiris' brother. He was also thought to be a protector against poisonous animals, having been saved by his mother from the sting of a scorpion.

Hathor. Egyptian goddess, personification of the sky, whose name means "House of Horus" (Horus the sun god, *q.v.*). Initially pictured as a cow, she later assumed human features with bovine ears, or wore a crown formed by a sun disc held between two cow horns. Her characteristic hairstyle, known as *hathoric*, consists of a short wig that surrounds the face and terminates below with two curls on either side of the face. She was also identified as a funerary goddess that welcomed the dead at the edge of the desert. The motif of the head of the goddess Hathor, as well as its stylizations and re-elaborations, appears in Etruscan art beginning in the Orientalizing period.

Helios. Divinity that personifies the sun, born from the union of the Titan Hyperion and Theia (or Euryphaessa).

Hera. Highest female divinity on Mount Olympus, daughter of Cronus and Rhea, sister and wife of Zeus. In the Roman religion she was identified as Juno.

Herakles, Hercules. Greek hero, son of Zeus and Alcmene, famous for his mythical exploits. His constant opposition with Hera, due to her jealousy of Alcmene, caused a fit of madness in which he killed his wife Megara and their children. Upon orders of the oracle of Delphi, he became the servant of Eurystheus, who imposed upon him the famous Labors, through which he attained immortality. His cult was also widespread in ancient Italy, in Etruria (*Hercle*) and in Rome.

Hermes. Greek god, son of Zeus and Maia. Demonstrating particular cleverness since birth, Zeus appointed him messenger and also servant to Hades and Persephone. He was considered protector of tradesmen , thieves and travellers. As such, his image (*Herma*) was placed at intersections. His attributes include a broad-brimmed hat (*pethasos*), typical of travellers, winged boots and a caduceus, symbols of his role as messenger of the gods.

Hermes Psychopompos. The god Hermes in his role as conductor of the souls of the dead to Hades, god of the underworld.

***Himation*.** Wool or linen garment, usually white with colored edges. Composed of a large mantle that was draped on the body, it was worn by men and women over the *chiton* or *peplos*, without stitches or fasteners: starting on the shoulder, it wrapped around the body, back to front, covering it in large drapes. In the Classical and Hellenistic periods it was often the only garment worn by men, leaving the right arm and torso free.

Horus. Egyptian god of the skies and celestial bodies. Originally represented as a falcon, he was considered the highest celestial divinity. Later identified with the god Ra as Ra-Harakhte ("sun on the horizon"), he was represented with a human body and a falcon's head.

Impasto pottery. Protohistoric pottery made with unrefined clay with the addition of thinners such as straw, fiber, ground stone or ceramic, used to inhibit the formation of cracks on the surface of the artifact while firing. Vases were not made on a potter's wheel, but with the *cercine* or *colombina* method, that consisted in spirally winding long ropes of clay. The vase's internal and external walls were then smoothed by hand and finished with spatulas, and sometimes an additional fine layer of clay was added.

Isis. Egyptian goddess, wife of Osiris (*q.v.*) and mother of Horus (*q.v.*), protector of royalty. She was attributed with the power of giving life and death. Iconographically, her maternal aspect was particularly highlighted.

Iulia Aquilia Severa. Priestess of the temple of Vesta, sworn to virginity, she became wife to emperor Elagabalus in 220 AD, causing a scandal. The emperor, stating that the marriage held exclusively sacred value, initially rejected her and then remarried her the following year.

Iulia Cornelia Paula. Daughter of the prefect of the praetorium Julius Paulus, first wife to emperor Elagabalus, whom she married in 219 AD and by whom she was subsequently repudiated, so that he could marry Iulia Aquilia Severa the following year.

Iulia Domna. Originally from Syria, second wife to the future emperor Septimius Severus, whom she married around 185 AD, becoming empress in 193 AD. Mother of the future emperors Caracalla and Geta. After her death at Antioch in 217 AD, where she committed suicide, she was transported to Rome and laid to rest in the Mausoleum of Augustus. Elagabalus had her deified and her remains were transferred to the Mausoleum of Hadrian.

Iulia Maesa. Sister of Iulia Domna (wife of Septimius Severus) and mother of Iulia Soemia and Iulia Mamaea. Originally from Emesa (Homs), city on the Orontes in Syria. Key figure in court intrigues and power battles within the imperial court, she induced the election of her grandson Elagabalus as emperor. When he grew unpopular, she arranged for her second grandson, Alexander Severus (son of Iulia Mamaea), to inherit the throne. Between 218 and 226 AD, when she died at nearly seventy years of age, she held the reins of the imperial government in her hands.

Iulia Mamaea. Daughter of Iulius Avitus and Iulia Maesa, mother of the future emperor Alexander Severus (222-235 AD), whose education she personally supervised, protecting him from the evil influence of Elagabalus. She became empress in 222 AD, and continued to follow her son closely in the administration of the empire, sharing his fate in 235 AD, when, during a war against the Germans, she and her son were murdered by their own soldiers after they mutinied in favor of Maximinius, who succeeded Alexander Severus to the throne.

Iulia Soemia. Sister of Iulia Mamaea, married to Sextus Avitus Marcellus, with whom she had the future emperor Elagabalus (218-222 AD). An energetic and determined woman, she assisted her son in his government duties, even presiding in Senate meetings and visits to military encampments. She was killed along with Elagabalus in 222 AD.

Jason. Mythological character, descendant of Aeolus, and son of Aeson, king of Iolcos, and Alcimede. He was raised by the Centaur Chiron who taught him medicine. His name is tied to the myth of the Argonauts and the quest for the Golden Fleece, which was forced upon him by the usurper Pelias, his father's half-brother, in order to regain possession of his kingdom.

Knurling. Goldwork technique in which a continuous decoration was impressed on a plain wire thread. The most common types of knurled wire are **beaded, spooled, funnel-beaded** and **spiral-beaded**.

Lararium. In Roman times, the niche or small chapel that housed the images of the Lari, guardian divinities of the household (*Lares familiares*), to whom were offered fruit, figs and libations. It was situated in the *atrium*, the central hall of the Roman home, uncovered in the center, where domestic activities were carried out along with the family's public life and relations.

Lorica. A light cuirass used by Roman soldiers that protected the abdomen while allowing freedom of movement. It was molded to the shape of the body and composed of parallel metal strips applied to a leather support. The term also indicates a rigid cuirass used in parades and enriched with relief and ornaments in metal work.

Lunula. Literally "small moon" in Latin, a pendant in the form of a lunar crescent, used particularly in the Roman era as a symbol and amulet.

Lysippos. Greek sculptor born in Sikyon around 370 BC, he was one of Alexander the Great's favorite artists, and portrayed him in several famous works. His art developed the naturalistic and rational canon of Polykleitos, including impressionistic and illusionistic models. Lysippos' nude statues are distinguished by the elastic and slender form of the bodies, accentuated by the reduced portion of the heads.

Mercury. Roman divinity, corresponding with Hermes (*q.v.*).

Municipium. Community within a city that preserved a certain level of internal autonomy while being incorporated into Roman citizenship.

Municipium sine suffragio. A *municipium* with a charter that ensured a considerable administrative autonomy, but with limited rights compared to Roman citizens: their members had civil rights, *ius conubii* and *ius commercii*, or the right to contract marriage and trade with Roman citizens, but they were not given political rights, such as voting and participating in the public life of the Roman state.

Nike. Personification of Victory, pictured as a winged woman. Nike is foremost an epithet for Athena, whose iconographic popularity grew particularly after the Persian Wars and in the Hellenistic period.

Oenomaus. Mythical king of Pisa in Elis and father of Hippodamia. He had killed all of his daughter's previous suitors by challenging them to a chariot race in which he had the upper hand, as his divine horses were the gift of his father, the god Ares. Pelops, however, won the race,either by bribing Myrtilus, the king's charioteer, who sabotaged his lord's carriage, or by using his winged horses that were a gift from Poseidon.

Oinochoe. From the Greek *oînos* (wine) and *chéō* (pour). Jug for drawing and pouring wine, with a single handle and a circular or trefoil-shaped mouth.

Okeanos. Titan, son of Uranus and Gea, brother of Tethys. In the most ancient conception, he represents the personification of the primordial sea god, from whose fertile power all rivers are generated. His daughters, the Okeanides, were the personification of streams and springs. Before the progress of geographical studies – the doctrine of the earth's spherical shape dates back to the school of Pythagoras (*b.* Samos 570 – *d.* Metaponto ca. 490 BC) – Okeanos was thought to be an enormous river that surrounded the entire flat disc of the earth.

Olla. Rounded vase, often in unrefined clay, equipped with a lid, with or without a handle. It was used as a container to conserve or cook food. In the Roman Imperial period it was also used as a cinerary urn to hold the ashes of the deceased.

Orbiana. Roman empress between 225 and 229 AD, one of the three wives of Alexander Severus, she was rejected for partly unknown reasons. She is known in historiography with the name *Seia Sallustia Orbiana*, an abbreviation of the official *Cneia Seia Herennia Sallustia Orba Babbia Orbiana.*

Osiris. Egyptian divinity, husband of Isis (*q.v.*), initially associated with the fertility of the earth. Reborn after his death, he was worshipped as ruler of the dead and was very important in the funerary cult.

Patera. Flat, saucer-like, handleless vessel with a raised button in the center (defined by the Greek *omphalós* = navel, or in Latin *umbo* = button, cone), used in antiquity for libations and sacrifices.

Pelops. Greek hero, son of Tantalus, king of Sipylus in Lydia. As a child he was killed and cut up into pieces by his father, who served up a macabre banquet for the gods. None of them accepted except for Demeter, who devoured his shoulder. The gods recomposed the body of Pelops and gave him back his life, replacing his devoured shoulder with an ivory one. Zeus, outraged at the horrific event, damned Tantalus and his stock. Pelops was cupbearer to Poseidon, who gave him prodigious winged horses with which, according to one version of the myth, he won the chariot race against Oenomaus. He was considered the first mythical founder of the Olympic games.

Peplos. Garment worn by Greek women, composed of a long rectangle of fabric. Fastened at the shoulders by a fibula and left to hang vertically along the body, it produced a sequence of thick vertical folds.

Plautilla. Fulvia Plautilla, daughter of the prefect of the praetorium of Septimius Severus, Caius Fulvius Plautianus. She wed Caracalla in 202 AD and became empress. Due to her questionable morality, her husband had her exiled to the island of Lipari where, in an act of supreme hate, he then had her murdered.

Poseidon. Divinity in the Greek pantheon, son of Cronus and Rhea, brother of Zeus and husband of Amphitrite. As god of water, he was also associated with storms and earthquakes. Later his image consolidated into one of a benevolent sea god.

Prefect of the praetorium. Commanding Officer in the army of the imperial guard (praetorians) in ancient Rome. In the late Imperial period this powerful figure (a sort of Minister of the Interior) often acted as arbitrator in the elimination and succession of many emperors.

Pulviscolo. Decorative technique typical of the goldsmith's art. It is a variation of the granulation technique (*q.v.*), characterized by the use of tiny granules, measuring approximately 0.14

mm in diameter.

Pygmies. Mythical nation of people of small stature, mentioned by Homer in the Iliad, and located south of Egypt or in India according to another version. In mythology and iconography the Pygmies are represented in a constant battle against the cranes. Gerana, the mythical queen of this nation that bestowed divine honors upon her, was punished by Hera for her impiety toward the Olympian gods, and transformed into a crane (*géranos* in Greek). As the cranes were compelled, at Hera's orders, to wage a constant war against the Pygmies, Gerana could not return to her old home and embrace her son Mopsos. The story of the battle between Pygmies and cranes is also known as *geranomachia*.

Ra. Egyptian god of the sun. Associated with Amon (Amon-Ra), originally a divinity tied to air and water, he was worshipped as king of the gods.

Runic. Alphabetic writing system used by the Germanic peoples north of the Alps. Also called Futhark, after the sequence of its first six letters. Surviving documents are dated beginning in the second-third centuries AD and were found in areas peripheral or external to the Roman Empire, such as Romania and Scandinavia. It is thought that the runic alphabet was developed by the Germanic peoples before the Roman conquest, as it has many aspects in common with the alphabets from pre-Roman northern Italy: the north-Etruscan alphabet and the Venetic alphabet (derived in turn from the Etruscan).

Scarab. Sacred animal to the ancient Egyptians, symbolizing renewal and resurrection, reproduced in amulets intended particularly for funerary use. Widely circulated in the Mediterranean basin and the ancient Near East, these amulets were also included in the creations of the Etruscan goldsmiths, variously used in pendants, necklaces, rings and even as seals.

Sol. Roman divinity equivalent to Helios (*q.v.*).

Taenia. A cloth band or ribbon that was pictured in Greek iconography as a fastener for hair or other parts of the body. In the case of athletes, it symbolized a prize won in a competition, and as such, figures were sometimes shown wearing more than one *taeniae*.

Thesauròs. In ancient Greece, a small building in the form of a temple annexed to a sanctuary, used to preserve votive gifts and holy vessels.

Thoth. Egyptian divinity associated with the moon. He assisted the sun god Ra in carrying the world and judged the dead with Osiris. He was also held to be inventor of writing and calculation, and was worshipped as patron of the arts, sciences and scribes, and represented as an ibis or a baboon, considered his sacred animals. The Greeks identified him with Hermes.

Tinia. Etruscan divinity, identified with the Greek god Zeus (*q.v.*) and the Roman god Jupiter. The Etruscans also attributed a funerary aspect to the father of the gods, given his association with gods of the underworld such as *Calu/Calus*, as implied by the epithet *calusna* on an Etruscan inscription.

Troilus. Mythological figure, younger son of King Priam and Queen Hecuba of Troy. He was killed by Achilles, who ambushed him by the spring where he was watering his horses, permitting the subsequent fall of Troy, which, according to an oracle, would have been impossible if Troilus had reached the age of twenty. According to another version, Achilles fell in love with Troilus after seeing him at the spring, and killed him in the Temple of Apollo Timbreus, where the youth had tried to seek refuge from the hero's morbid interest.

Tumulus. Etruscan tomb of aristocratic attribution, developed in the Orientalizing period after eastern Mediterranean models. The chamber tomb, built and/or dug out of the bedrock, was covered by a mound of earth, extending up to 60 meters (200 feet) in diameter, contained within a circular wall (known as a drum) that was decorated with a complex sequence of friezes and mouldings, along which was located the access corridor (*dromos*). A tumulus could be used by different generations of the same gentilitial group and hold more than one chamber tomb. The vault could be accessed by a bridge or stepped podium.

Tyche. Greek goddess, daughter of Okeanos and Tethys, personification of Chance, identified with the Roman Fortuna. She was worshipped under various appearances and with a variety of attributes. Her importance grew in the Hellenistic and Imperial periods as an imponderable and sovereign force that changed the course of events and guided destinies according to an unknown plan.

Ureus. Female cobra, symbol of the goddess Uaget, patron of Lower Egypt, and the eye of Ra (*q.v.*). Used as a talisman against the god's enemies, the ureus was placed on the pharaoh's crown for protection and also as a symbol of divine and royal power. Because of the ability snakes have of shedding their skin, the ureus was also symbolic of rebirth and resurrection.

Venus. One of the most important divinities in Roman religion, originally an Italic divinity whose name is associated with the force of life, the luxuriance of plants, sexuality, love, and the favor of the gods. Around the fourth century BC the process of identification with the Greek goddess Aphrodite (*q.v.*) was complete.

Venus the Victorius, *Venus Victrix*. The warrior appearance of the goddess of love, paired with Mars. The Victrix epithet, meaning giver of victory, appeared in Rome around 215 BC, the same year in which a temple dedicated to Venus was erected on the Capitoline Hill. In the climate of the anti-Carthaginian propaganda, during the Second Punic War (218-202 BC), the myth of the Roman descendance of Aeneas, Aphrodite's son, was emphasized. She is often represented in statuary, applied arts and Roman coinage: the seminude goddess, leaning against a column or pillar, sometimes assisted by a cherub, bears a lance or spear, a helmet or the palm of victory, while her shield rests on the ground.

Vertumnus. Latin form of the Etruscan national god Voltumna (*q.v.*). A statue was dedicated to him in the Forum and he was celebrated with a feast day on August 13. He was attributed with the ability to transform himself and thus became associated with the changing seasons.

Victoria. Personification of Victory for the Romans, corresponding with Nike (*q.v.*). She was greatly worshipped in the Republican and Imperial periods. Iconographically, she appears both in reference to military victory and as an eschatological symbol in funerary scenes, in which she underlines the heroic conception of life: the deceased is seen as a winner in the race of life.

Voltumna. Etruscan national deity with ambivalent and contrasting features: malevolent monster, god of vegetation, of uncertain gender, great warrior god. Voltumna was worshipped at a sanctuary in Volsinii (Orvieto), political and religious headquarters of the twelve-city Etruscan league.

Zeus. Chief Greek deity, son of Cronus and Rhea, king of men and father of the gods. Inhabiting the summit of Mount Olympus, originally he was known as god of the bright heavens and atmospheric phenomena, from which derives his attribute of the thunderbolt. As a baby, he was hidden by Rhea in a cave on the island of Crete to keep him from being devoured by his father. With the help of his brothers and sisters he fought and defeated Cronus and the Titans, ensuring world domination for the Olympic divinities: Zeus ruled the heavens and the earth, Poseidon the sea, and Hades the underworld. As supreme deity, he was also defender of royal power and social hierarchy. He was also assimilated to the principal deities of other peoples, such as Amon and Jupiter.

Printed in May 2004 by
Nova Tiporom s.r.l.
Roma